THE LAST NIGHT
OF THE YANKEE DYNASTY

THE
LAST NIGHT
OF THE
YANKEE
DYNASTY

The Game, the Team,
and the Cost of Greatness

B U S T E R   O L N E Y

An Imprint of HarperCollinsPublishers

Frontispiece photographs: Jeter: J. Paul Burnett/*New York Times*; Clemens: Vincent Laforet *New York Times*; O'Neill: Barton Silverman/*New York Times*; Martinez: Chang W. Lee/*New York Times*; Torre: Chang W. Lee/*New York Times*; Hernandez: J. Paul Burnett/*New York Times*; Rivera: Vincent Laforet/*New York Times*; Pettitte: Barton Silverman/*New York Times*; Cone: Barton Silverman/*New York Times*; Williams: AP/Wide World Photos.

HarperCollins books may be purchased for educational, business, or sales promotional use. For information, please write: Special Markets Department, HarperCollins Publishers Inc., 10 East 53rd Street, New York, NY 10022.

FIRST EDITION

Designed by Lovedog Studio

Printed on acid-free paper

Library of Congress Cataloging-in-Publication Data is available upon request.

ISBN 0-06-051506-6

04 05 06 07 08   WBC/RRD   10 9 8 7 6 5 4 3 2

For Richard and Jane Leonard
and for Lisa

THE YANKEES still had time to come back. Eighth inning, Game 6, 2003 World Series, in Yankee Stadium, and they were down 2–0 to the Florida Marlins, seemingly at the mercy of 23-year-old Josh Beckett. The Marlins' pitcher had barely enough facial hair to form a goatee, but he had blown away the Yankees in the first seven innings, his fastball hissing, his curveball arcing through the strike zone. Beckett and his teammates needed only a handful of outs to become the first visiting team in 22 years to splash Champagne in the Yankees' home.

But the Yankees had often come back under dire circumstances during Joe Torre's tenure as manager. Twenty-five of their 56 postseason victories from 1996 to 2001 occurred after they had fallen behind; it was a trademark of those teams. And Beckett was working Game 6 on short rest, something he had never done before. A walk or a single and then perhaps the Yankees would start piecing something together. Maybe Beckett would start to tire.

But in the executive offices high above the field, George Steinbrenner had decided the game was over and had already begun laying out the early schedule for the Yankees' off-season reconstruction.

This was not unusual. Before the Yankees had come back to win the

1996 World Series, Steinbrenner had complained that the Yankees would be a national embarrassment, and yet even after they won that World Series and three of the next four, establishing baseball's first dynasty since the advent of free agency, Steinbrenner's pessimism intensified. The better the team did, it seemed, the more he had to lose and the more panicked he became, his hyperventilating beginning in the first innings of each postseason series and evolving into anger and hopelessness. When Steinbrenner had publicly praised his players for their resilience, his comments had amused many of his front-office employees; they thought that Steinbrenner, at heart, was a quitter.

Some of his executives believed Steinbrenner had tactical reasons for forecasting doom; by expressing his doubts early he would position himself to say "I told you so" and assign blame. After defeat, he was imperturbable, stepping back and reloading. But in the midst of the competition, he expected only failure. Five innings into Game 2 of the 2003 playoffs, after the Yankees had missed on scoring chances repeatedly, Steinbrenner had summoned general manager Brian Cashman and begun berating him. "You're horseshit, and you're overpaid," Steinbrenner snapped, reminding Cashman of his frequent warnings that the team was flawed. "No one will take your contract off my hands." Lou Lamoriello, the general manager of the New Jersey Devils, was in the room, along with Yankees president Randy Levine, and their presence only made the situation more tense. "Maybe the Mets will take you," Steinbrenner barked. "You have permission to talk to the Mets."

The Yankees had gone on to knock off Minnesota and then Boston in the American League playoffs, but in Steinbrenner's world, only the World Series mattered, and in the eighth inning of Game 6, Beckett was sticking it to the Yankees, and Steinbrenner was fuming. He cornered Cashman. "Meeting in Tampa Monday," he said. "And it's not going to be pleasant."

Alfonso Soriano singled to lead off the bottom of the eighth for the Yankees, but Beckett got out of that inning and cut down the Yankees in order in the ninth, tagging out Jorge Posada on a dribbler along the first-base line to end the game. The Marlins shouted and screamed like a Little League team as Torre and others watched from the Yankees' dugout.

. . .

IN PAST years, the Yankees had played with that kind of unrestrained joy, too. They had leaped and hollered and wept when they beat Atlanta in 1996; older Yankees would remember the home-stadium crowds from that postseason as the most passionate they had seen. They had been knocked out of the first round of the 1997 playoffs, then played 1998 with extraordinary focus, winning 125 games and the World Series. They had hung together through the hard year of 1999, through the diagnosis and treatment of Torre's cancer and the family deaths endured by several players, and then become the first team in more than a quarter century to win three consecutive World Series, when they beat the Mets in 2000. And in 2001, in the wake of September 11, they had played for a devastated city.

But by 2003, only eight Yankees remained from the championship years—Bernie Williams and Mariano Rivera, Derek Jeter and Jorge Posada, Jeff Nelson and Andy Pettitte, and David Wells and Roger Clemens. The others in the Yankees' clubhouse had inherited the legacy, and like second-generation scions, they found that everything they did was held up against the daunting standards of years before. The burden of those expectations weighed on the team, especially the newcomers: they could prepare thoroughly and play well throughout the regular season, win the American League East and a couple of playoff series, and none of that would matter unless they won the World Series. Pitcher Mike Mussina had glanced at the standings at the end of the 2003 regular season, which Steinbrenner had filled with harping about the supposed failures of the coaching staff, and was stunned to see that the Yankees actually had won 101 games—just the third time in the last 23 seasons that they had racked up 100 victories. It was the worst and hardest 101-win season imaginable, Mussina thought.

AFTER LOSING to the Marlins in Game 6, the Yankees filed into their clubhouse, more weary and disgusted than disappointed. Don Zimmer, the Yankees' bench coach since the championship run began in 1996, dressed quickly and met with a small group of reporters, sputtering angrily about Steinbrenner and announcing that he was fed up with the owner and intended to quit. That morning Zimmer had woken up with plans to blast Steinbrenner publicly, but his wife had talked him out of going too far. Zimmer's bitterness saturated his words anyway. "The only thing I can say is that for 25 years, Steinbrenner has called me 'Zimmer' and I've called him 'the Boss,'" Zimmer said. "He's no longer the Boss. He's just Steinbrenner."

Torre talked to friends in his office. He, too, had battled Steinbrenner all year, bickering with the owner in the newspaper, something he had never done in his first seven years as manager. There was one season remaining in Torre's contract, and within days he would say that he had no interest in managing the Yankees beyond 2004.

Clemens embraced teammates as he departed, thinking he had played his last game. Pettitte walked out the hallway leading past Torre's office and hugged coach Mel Stottlemyre, promising to call in the off-season. Within weeks, Pettitte would sign with the Houston Astros, publicly citing a desire to play in his hometown; privately, friends said, Pettitte was put off by the growing dysfunction in the Yankees' organization, and he was sure Steinbrenner had little regard for him. Clemens—who, like Pettitte, lived just outside of Houston—was immediately attracted by the idea of joining Pettitte, a close friend, and signed with the Astros as well. The departures of Pettitte and Clemens, pieces from the soul of the championship teams, felt like defections.

Stottlemyre wasn't sure he wanted to return in 2004, either. He was deeply loyal to Torre and the players, but he thought the atmosphere that had developed around the Yankees was absurd, and believed the team should be allowed to draw some satisfaction from playing all the way to Game 6 of the World Series. "Even though we got beat," he said, "we should feel better than we do." By winning so regularly since 1995, Stottlemyre thought, the team had created a monster with Steinbrenner and the fans.

Many of the players had answered a few questions from reporters and then quickly scattered, but Jeter remained at his locker, slumped in a chair, still in full uniform, answering questions about why the Yankees lost, his dull tone belying his frustration. Someone asked about the state of the Yankees' dynasty, and Jeter paused, trying to figure out a way to maneuver through that question.

The truth was that no matter how many stars Steinbrenner acquired, it would be impossible to re-create the greatness of those Yankees teams.

The truth was that the dynasty had ended two years before, on a warm autumn night in Arizona.

CHAPTER 1

MARIANO RIVERA sometimes paused to stand behind the crowd of teammates watching *The Jerry Springer Show* in the Yankees' clubhouse. As they laughed loudly and exhorted the on-screen combatants, Rivera remained silent, shaking his head. To him, the remedy for the many misbehaving teenagers on the program was clear: rigid discipline. Establish rules, and if the children don't adhere, then physical punishment—a paddling that would hurt and be remembered—must always follow. Growing up in Panama, he had been weaned on discipline. His father worked as a fisherman, collecting sardines to be processed for animal feed, a job that took him away from home a week at a time, and if little Mariano fell into trouble he would dwell in dread until his father returned, knowing that his mother would report his worst offenses. If he broke a window with a ball, he knew he would be spanked. There was no getting around this: mistakes are made, and consequences follow. His father insisted that Mariano be accountable for his behavior and show respect for others, and years later Mariano expected the same from his own children.

Rivera, the Yankees' closer, thought players should act properly, as well; he despised pitchers who were disrespectful to opponents—glaring insolently at hitters and stomping and swaggering around the mound like angry Neanderthals, pumping a fist to celebrate the smallest successes. You should act as though you've won before, Rivera believed; you should act as though you expect to win again. Some pitchers grew mustaches and beards and groomed them in arcane ways to make themselves look threatening, but this made Rivera more certain they were actually very much afraid. During a Yankees game in Toronto in 1999, Blue Jays closer Billy Koch stalked in from the bullpen, a spaghetti strand of beard descending from his lower lip to his chin, and after throwing his first fastball for a strike, he lingered at the apron of the mound to stare at the batter. Rivera watched from his own bullpen and seethed. What a tough guy, he smirked to himself. What a joke. Show some respect for the game. Show some respect for yourself.

There was inflexible structure to everything Rivera did. Some of the other Yankees adhered only grudgingly to the team's policy against long hair and beards, and a few holdouts always took the field with day-old facial growth. But Rivera shaved before every game and had his thinning hair cut close to his scalp, like stitches on a baseball. He wore his uniform precisely to code, with the cuffs of his uniform pants raised to the proper height above his heels, and he followed the same disciplined regimen before, during, and after games. When Rivera emerged from the Yankees' bullpen to pitch, he held his glove in his right hand and jogged steadily to the mound, running on the balls of his feet, his head always tilted downward—the coolest entrance of any closer, teammate Roger Clemens thought, because it was so understated. Rivera never looked angry or arrogant or intense. He had the demeanor of a customs agent, serious and polite. All eyes were on him whenever he stepped out of the bullpen, though, because Rivera was the most successful relief pitcher in postseason history. The Yankees had won four World Series in five years from 1996 to 2000, resurrecting the dormant franchise, and many opposing players thought Rivera was the linchpin of the team's success.

Other closers had blown leads in the World Series—Atlanta's Mark Wohlers in 1996, Cleveland's Jose Mesa in 1997, Trevor Hoffman of the Padres in 1998, the Mets' Armando Benitez in 2000. Rivera, on the other hand, had been flawless: the Yankees had won the last 16 games he had pitched in the World Series, a streak that began in 1996. Take Rivera away from the Yankees and give them any other closer, Indians slugger Jim Thome said, and they probably would have won one or two championships, instead of four. As the Yankees prepared to play Game 7 of the 2001 World Series against the Diamondbacks, it was 1,490 days since Rivera had last blown a lead in the postseason.

In 1997, the year in which he replaced John Wetteland as the Yankees' closer, Rivera allowed a home run to Indians catcher Sandy Alomar Jr. with the Yankees needing just a handful of outs to eliminate the Indians in the Division Series. The Indians had gone on to win that game and the series, and questions naturally followed about whether Rivera would rebound psychologically after a pivotal defeat; baseball history was littered with relievers who'd been wrecked by one terrible moment. Rivera assured everyone he was OK, that he hadn't really given much thought to the loss. This was a white lie.

Rivera had mulled over Alomar's home run and had decided—belying the facade of respect that masked his competitiveness—that Alomar was fortunate he had been on the mound that day. Alomar, a right-handed hitter, had hit a fastball for the home run, high and away, driving it over the right field wall. Any other pitcher, Rivera concluded, would have thrown the ball with less velocity, and instead of hitting a home run, Alomar probably would have mustered only a long fly ball. In other words, Rivera believed he was the reason Alomar hit a home run—that *he* controlled the situation, even in defeat. I made the home run, he decided, his extraordinary confidence not only intact through the failure, but steeled by it.

Rivera almost never talked in team meetings. But as the Yankees gathered in the visitors' clubhouse of Arizona's Bank One Ballpark on November 4, 2001, preparing for the decisive Game 7 of the World Series, he made up his mind to speak at the end of the meeting, after the others finished.

He expected he would throw the last pitch again that night; so did the rest of the Yankees' veterans, who had come to believe they could not be beaten in pivotal moments like this. They had once won 14 consecutive World Series games, a record-setting streak that began in Game 3 of the

1996 World Series and ended in Game 3 of the 2000 Subway Series against the Mets, and they had prevailed in 11 consecutive postseason series. But the Diamondbacks had outhit and outpitched the Yankees for six games, and crushed them in Game 6 the night before, thumping Andy Pettitte in a 15–2 victory. The dynasty was vulnerable, and yet the Yankees were sure they would win Game 7; they felt it was their destiny, all the more so at this exceptional and difficult time.

Fifty-five days before, Jorge Posada, the Yankees' catcher, had been at a hospital in downtown Manhattan, where his 21-month-old son was recovering from surgery. Posada had brought a videotape of children's shows, but as he turned on the television, he saw the image of the north tower of the World Trade Center, smoke billowing from a horizontal slash in its side. Posada phoned Derek Jeter, who was asleep in his Manhattan apartment, and Jeter flicked on his television. Tino Martinez, the team's first baseman, had been lying in bed when his wife called from Florida, and Martinez walked into his living room and opened the curtains to a full view of the tragedy. From his downtown apartment, Chuck Knoblauch could see the towers, and he and the others watched the world change.

As the gravity of the situation became apparent, reliever Mike Stanton rushed to retrieve his children from school. Clemens struggled to place a call to his Texas home through the jammed phone lines, and when he finally reached his sons, he heard the fear in their voices. He and his wife, Debbie—who was in New York to see her husband's first attempt to achieve his 20th victory of that season—decided to drive to Texas, taking turns at the wheel. Scott Brosius's three children had already gone home to Oregon to begin the school year, and Allison, nine years old, cried on the phone. "We need to be a family now," she told her father.

Four days after the attacks, most of the Yankees worked out together at Yankee Stadium, the smell of smoke thick in the air. General Manager Brian Cashman already understood that when baseball resumed, the Yankees would become a symbol of the city, and before the first workout, he led the players onto the infield, where they knelt and prayed. At first, the players were deeply uncomfortable with the notion that they might be viewed as representatives of New York; none of them had lost family members or close friends, as many New Yorkers had, and few of them resided in the city in the off-season. "This is just baseball," Brosius said.

The team sent a group of players to the Lexington Avenue armory, where relatives were bringing hairbrushes for DNA samples and dental records and photos. The players hesitated before they went inside, feeling like intruders. Bernie Williams, the Yankees' center fielder, saw a big wall filled with posters of the missing, hundreds of pictures. We're only ballplayers, he thought, and we couldn't possibly have anything to offer that might help the people inside. "Are you sure this is what they want?" one of the players asked Cashman.

Months later, the players would distinctly remember the wounded faces of the people they had seen. "There was a lot of sadness in that room, a lot of desperation," said Williams. "From adults to children to older people, just waiting. Not a lot of noise, but a lot of chaos." Williams was introduced to a wife looking for her husband, and was humbled by her sadness. "I'm not a doctor, I'm not a counselor, I don't know what to say," Williams said. "All I know is, I think you need a hug." And he embraced her.

After that, Williams remembered, "I saw it all clearly. I realized why we were there." There was a little girl waiting for word of her father, and when she saw Jeter, her face brightened; she was excited to meet him, to talk with him, for a few minutes. A boy paused in his grieving to ask right fielder Paul O'Neill about his foot injury. Players from the Yankees—and from the Mets and other New York area sports teams who made appearances and contributed money—of course did not have the power to change the past. But they realized that when they played, when they shook hands and signed autographs and gave hugs, they could provide some emotional relief, if for only a few minutes or hours. Players began contacting city representatives directly to ask where they might help. It reminded people that we were going to get back to normal, thought Rudy Giuliani, New York City's mayor. "You needed to be reminded of that with so much death," he said months later. "You needed to be reminded that life goes on, and baseball reminds you of that."

After six days, baseball games resumed. The Yankees played in Chicago September 18, some of them weeping during the pregame ceremonies; Torre, thinking of the children affected by the tragedy, was unable to hold back. Though White Sox fans were usually hostile, now they welcomed the New York team with cheers and banners; I LOVE NEW YORK, AND EVEN THE YANKEES, read one sign. The Yankees were hated for their dominance and their aura of arrogance, for the blustery reign of Steinbrenner. But in the aftermath of the September 11 attacks, they were cheered on the road as well as in their devastated home city. Giuliani heard clapping as he walked through Ground Zero on the night of September 19, and drawn by the enthusiasm, he found a dozen workers around a television at a trailer, cheering the last out of Clemens's 20th victory.

The Yankees returned to Yankee Stadium on September 25, and before the pregame ceremony, Clemens passed a long line of city servicemen and -women wishing him luck. The Yankees lost that game but clinched the division title when Boston was defeated the same night, and after the game, Torre lingered in his office with Giuliani. The circumstances, Torre told Giuliani, "make you feel very insignificant." The American League playoffs began, and some players from the Oakland Athletics—the Yankees' first-round opponent—arrived at a firehouse to share lunch with the firefighters. Slugger Jason Giambi was good-naturedly warned by firefighters that the food he ate had been tampered with; by game time, they assured him, he would be stricken with diarrhea. Giambi was offered a place to sleep at the firehouse, on the condition that he not leave until the playoffs were over.

But Oakland won the first two games at Yankee Stadium, leaving the Athletics only one victory shy of clinching the series; during Torre's time as manager, the Yankees had never been in this position—two games down and one defeat away from getting knocked out. Most of their lineup was beset with nagging injuries, and they were not hitting. Posada slammed a home run in the fifth inning of Game 3 in Oakland, and Mike Mussina assumed it would be the team's only run. There was no reason to expect more. In the bottom half of the seventh inning, the Athletics had two outs and a runner at first base, and left fielder Terrence

Long pulled a double into the right field corner. When Yankees right fielder Shane Spencer overthrew two cutoff men, Mussina's heart sank; Jeremy Giambi, the Oakland base-runner, was going to score the tying run, and the Yankees might be eliminated within the hour. But Jeter scrambled from his position at shortstop to back up the relay men, fielded Spencer's throw on a hop as he crossed the first-base line, and while in foul territory, flipped it sideways to Posada, who tagged out Giambi on the calf. Mussina raised a fist: the Yankees were still alive. They would win Game 4, and Clemens, pitching with a bad leg, helped win Game 5 in Yankee Stadium, stunning the Athletics. Gaining momentum, they thrashed Seattle in the American League Championship Series, crushing the Mariners 12–3 in the final game, as the fans in Yankee Stadium playfully and loudly taunted their opponents and their manager, former Yankee Lou Piniella. "The one thought that did come to my mind strangely enough is, 'Boy, this city suffered through a lot and tonight they let out a lot of emotions,'" said Piniella. "And I felt good for them in that way. And that's a strange thought to come from a manager who is getting his ass kicked."

As the Diamondbacks beat Atlanta for the National League championship, though, the veteran Arizona players—many of whom were playing in a World Series for the first time—quietly warned one another to ignore the public sentiment. "Obviously, we felt for New York, but we didn't feel for the Yankees," said Arizona catcher Damian Miller. "That was the talk in the clubhouse. We talked about it all the time. We looked at it as, 'This is a baseball game against the New York Yankees, and not the city of New York.' We wanted a World Series ring, too, and we were not going to let it affect us."

Asked about the oft-cited mystique and aura of the Yankees, Arizona pitcher Curt Schilling responded tersely, "Mystique and aura—those are dancers in a nightclub." The Diamondbacks won the first two games of the World Series, played in their home park, as Schilling and Randy Johnson allowed a total of six hits. But the Yankees' sense of destiny was intact. Tino Martinez and others made a point of projecting confidence in their postgame interviews, as if they were speaking directly to the Diamondbacks and reminding them of how many times the Yankees had won before. Posada and Jeter had gone to dinner with Martinez after they returned to New York from Arizona, and their conversation was equally assured. Clemens would pitch Game 3, and if they could win Game 3, the players agreed, they could not be stopped.

The playoffs and the World Series had been played amid heightened security, spurred by concerns that terrorists might attack during a game, particularly after it was announced that President George W. Bush would throw out the first pitch before Game 3. Minutes before he took the field, the president went to an indoor batting cage to warm up. Jeter tagged along, asking him whether he was going to throw from the pitching rubber or from the apron of the mound, where the president was less likely to bounce a throw to the catcher. Bush indicated he was going to attempt the shorter throw. "If you throw from the base of the mound," Jeter cajoled, "they are going to boo you. You really need to take the rubber."

Bush asked Jeter if the fans would actually boo. "Yeah, it's New York," Jeter said. Jeter had been teasing, but Bush jogged to the mound, his windbreaker filled out by a bulletproof vest, and climbed the rubber before pumping a strike. The crowd roared, and the next morning Bush told press secretary Ari Fleischer how he felt the emotion emanating from the stands. That moment, the president said, would stand as a highlight of his time in office.

The Yankees won Game 3, but they continued to struggle for runs. Schilling started Game 4 and pitched exceptionally on three days' rest, and Arizona carried a two-run lead into the ninth. Paul O'Neill singled with one out, but Diamondbacks closer Byung-Hyun Kim struck out Bernie Williams, bringing Martinez to the plate, seemingly the dynasty's last line of defense—and Martinez launched a ball into the stands in right-center field, the celebration shaking Yankee Stadium. Jeter won the game in the next inning with an opposite-field homer in the first minutes of November, tying the World Series at two games apiece. Scott Brosius, the Yankees' third baseman, had gone home that night saturated with adrenaline, and as dawn approached and he struggled to get to sleep, he phoned a friend, Brian Tebeau, back in his Oregon hometown. *Can you believe that?* Brosius asked. *You'll never see anything like that again in your lifetime.* Hours later, Brosius stood at home plate in precisely the same circumstances: bottom of the ninth, two outs, Yankees down by two runs, Kim on the mound, runner on base. Kim spun a slider, and the pitch drifted over the plate. Brosius swung and immediately raised his arms, knowing that the baseball he hit—incredibly, improbably—would land in the left-field stands and tie the score.

(Within days of the 1929 stock market crash, Mule Haas of the Philadelphia Athletics hit a game-tying two-run homer in the ninth inning of Game 5 of the World Series. But nobody had equaled that feat for 72 years—until Martinez and Brosius did so on back-to-back nights at Yankee Stadium.)

Alfonso Soriano singled in the 12th inning, and as Chuck Knoblauch slid across home plate and leaped to his feet, the ballpark erupted again; some players recalled feeling the ground shake underneath them. The Diamondbacks walked off the field, stunned. They had been beaten by the impossible, Schilling would remember later, and had seen things they had never seen before. But most of the Arizona players had been around long enough to understand how to deal with failure, and by the time they returned to the clubhouse, some of them were already barking how things would be different when they returned to Arizona for Games 6 and 7. Steve Finley, the Diamondbacks' center fielder, stepped through the clubhouse door and pierced the air with profanity. "These guys have their ghosts here," he shouted, "and we've got our ghosts in Arizona." Schilling, reminded by a reporter of his dismissive remark about the Yankees' mystique and aura, smiled slightly and said, "I didn't know they'd make an appearance at Yankee Stadium."

Andy Pettitte, a part of the Yankees' championship run from its outset, started Game 6, but the Diamondbacks' hitters had broken his code, picking up on a habit: As Pettitte moved into a set position with runners on base, he pulled his hands straight down, from his chest to his waist, whenever he intended to throw a fastball. But when he wanted to throw an off-speed pitch, Pettitte looped his hands in front of him, like a pregnant woman running her hands over her belly. Keying on this, Arizona scored 12 runs in the first three innings and routed the Yankees, 15–2, forcing a seventh and final game—the first time any of these Yankees had played a Game 7. They had always won with extreme efficiency in the past, but now many of their longtime stars were in decline, frayed by injuries. They were also keenly aware that many of the Yankees would be playing their final game with the team. Paul O'Neill had tucked away his home uniform after Game 5; after nine seasons with the Yankees and 17 seasons in the major leagues, he was retiring. There was already wide speculation that club executives wanted to replace Tino Martinez, the first baseman for six seasons, with Oakland slugger Jason Giambi. Chuck Knoblauch, the leadoff hitter for three championships, had finally been conquered by a bizarre inability to make simple throws; club officials had nearly traded him during the season and did not intend to retain him. Third baseman Scott Brosius, though only 35 years old, had begun to make plans for retirement, and Luis Sojo, whose hit in the 2000 World Series had finished off the Mets, would soon end his playing days, as well. Other players who had been part of the team's resolute core had departed in recent seasons: David Cone, Joe Girardi, Tim Raines, Chili Davis. The Yankees would always be competitive, powered by money and by Steinbrenner's intense desire to dominate those around him, and a handful of players who had been integral to the championships would remain for years to come—Jeter, Williams, Posada, and Rivera. But as they waited for Torre to open the team meeting, they all knew an era would end that night. "You didn't want to say it was the end of the book," Jeter said later, "but it was the end of a chapter."

Torre was an eloquent speaker, and the players found the tone of his meetings uniformly pitch-perfect. He was usually calm and direct in his postseason talks, knowing that the players would feel smothered by an intense lecture. On those occasions when the Yankees played without energy, he would be sharp and critical without being loud. Near the end of the 1998 season, during which the Yankees had won a record 125 games, they played terribly in Tampa Bay, and Torre called a meeting and berated them for taking the game for granted. Don't assume that you can just turn it off or turn it on anytime you want, he scolded. When Torre spoke like this, O'Neill said, you felt as if you had made your father mad, and you wanted to do anything you could to please him. Torre summoned the players together only when there was something serious to discuss, and invited others to talk, calling on veterans over the years, from Cone to Girardi, Jeter, or O'Neill. Torre closed some of his meetings with the ritual of asking Posada what the Yankees do. "We grind it," Posada would respond, grinning and turning his fist.

This time, Torre asked Gene Monahan, in his 29th year as the Yankees' trainer, to speak to the players. Hours before, as they walked into the ballpark, Torre had mentioned the pregame meeting. "I'm not sure how I'm going to get these guys going tonight," Torre mused. "I might throw you out there, Geno." Monahan didn't take the manager seriously; he talked to the players about procedural stuff each year, at the beginning of the first meeting in spring training, but he had never given them motivational speeches.

And yet, before Game 7 of the 2001 World Series, Torre turned to Monahan and said, "Geno, you started this off in spring training, so you might as well finish it."

Others in the room thought Monahan was an excellent choice. He was the keeper of the flame, with an acute sense of the team's history and a profound belief in the Yankees' tradition. If a player achieved an important milestone or a record, Monahan would retrieve the baseball involved in the play and carefully write the details across its face. When Torre asked him to speak, Monahan was overcome by anxiety, until he started talking.

He spoke about the team's pride, all the hard work they put in every season, all the hours spent pushing and driving and grinding through the summer. "And no matter what happens," Monahan said, "I know that everybody in this room will do their best. We're going to handle ourselves with as much dignity and professionalism as possible, and we're going to help each other out. I know that when we're done, in a few hours, you're going to walk off as champions."

Monahan mentioned the United States, implicitly referring to the recent tragedy, passion gathering in his voice, and tears began forming in his eyes and in the eyes around him. Monahan never specifically mentioned that a core group of Yankees would be departing, but that knowledge framed his words. Monahan finished, reaching a climax perfectly. "If you wanted to have the best Knute Rockne speech, Geno gave it," said one veteran player. "He out-Rockne'd Rockne. Everybody was fired up, everybody was ready to play." The players clapped, the meeting began to break up, and then Rivera stepped forward into the middle of the room. He had something to say.

His teammates were surprised. Rivera was genial and laughed easily and was respected by the other players, but he was thought of as a private person, generally quiet, particularly in group settings. Rivera rarely revealed much of what he thought or felt, but now he spoke, two hours before Game 7. "Just get the ball to me, and we will win," Rivera said, his voice rising. And then Rivera shifted his focus, other players recalled later, and began talking about faith and fate.

Rivera was deeply religious, had funded the construction of a church in Panama, and had vague plans to work as a minister when his playing career was over. Speaking to his teammates, he chose words that had comforted him in the past. "Whatever happens tonight," Rivera said aloud, "is in the hands of God."

The Yankees had a relatively large number of practicing Christians on the team, but Rivera's words confused many of the players in the room. "I wasn't sure what he was talking about," said one veteran, "but I wished he hadn't said it. I wished he had just let the meeting end with Geno's speech—that was the perfect way to end it."

Rivera finished, saying, "Let's kick some butt," and there was clapping, but some of his teammates walked away wondering about Rivera's choice of words. It didn't sound like him, one veteran said later, because above all else, Rivera was about confidence and control. He talked as if they were bystanders to history, some players thought, rather than the architects of their own destiny.

CHAPTER 2

GEORGE STEINBRENNER would never entrust his team to God. That would mean giving up too much control. Instead, the Yankees' owner audited the team from moment to moment, like a caffeinated rent-a-cop monitoring a Wal-Mart through security cameras. His involvement could be good fun if you happened to be a guest in his private box in Yankee Stadium. He could be a genial and gracious host, and if he criticized a player in your presence, you might feel as if he were confiding in you. He might even ask for your opinion and tell you how his executives had screwed up. But if you worked for Steinbrenner, the experience of watching a game with him could be overpowering.

About a dozen executives and subordinates were compelled by their responsibilities to be with Steinbrenner in the visitors' clubhouse in Arizona during the 2001 World Series. He watched the games on television monitors there, partly because of his own superstition—the Yankees seemed to play better, he thought, when he was in the clubhouse—and the owner's frantic intensity made the atmosphere stifling. If the Yankees were ahead, a colossal disaster was probably imminent, in Steinbrenner's mind. If they were behind, he voiced every complaint, every doubt, replayed every mistake, the color squeezed out of him as in a clenched fist.

"It would make you sick to your stomach," said one longtime employee, "like you had waded into a cesspool." He would rip the players or some- one on the Yankees' staff, and if you occupied the seat next to him, it did not take long to figure out that he probably ripped you, too, when you were out of sight.

Most of the Yankees' nonuniformed employees were truly petrified of Steinbrenner. The mood of the support staff and middle management changed dramatically, a Yankees player noticed, when Steinbrenner was around. "They were all afraid of being the one who did something to set him off," said the player. Even the bravest among them was leery, know- ing that any conflict with Steinbrenner could be intense and protracted. He would fume at employees who weren't in uniform—yelling at Brian Cashman, at vice president Mark Newman, calling his executives re- peatedly when he was unhappy, ordering secretaries to track them down at their offices and at their homes so he could berate them.

But Steinbrenner's style had evolved somewhat over his tenure as owner of the Yankees. He did not challenge players in the newspapers as often or as bluntly as he once had, and the players mostly regarded him with fondness and respect. And during the dynasty, Steinbrenner was no longer the classic micromanager he once had been. In the 1980s, Stein- brenner had bullied his general managers into making deals he wanted, or simply negotiated the deals himself, and driven the team to the bot- tom of the American League East standings, a decline for which he was widely mocked. But in the '90s, when the Yankees were rebuilt into a competitive and financial juggernaut that plowed through the league, Steinbrenner won back a measure of appreciation from the Yankees' fans, and he seemed reluctant to put himself at risk again.

His executives had made that success possible by holding on to prospects like Williams and Rivera and changing the competitive dynam- ics of the organization. So instead of pushing them aside and assuming full responsibility, Steinbrenner often deferred to their judgments—but only, it seemed, because this was a safer play for him, not necessarily be- cause he had faith in their choices. He rarely exercised his full authority during the championship run; he could have stepped in at any time and taken over and made the moves himself (and did so on smaller matters, with some success, such as the signings of Darryl Strawberry and Dwight Gooden and the '98 promotion of Orlando Hernandez). Instead, Steinbrenner positioned himself to publicly second-guess the officials. *My general manager and manager say this team is good enough to win,* he would say time and again, *and I hope they're right.*

Privately, Steinbrenner hammered at his executives to make big trades, trying to badger Gene Michael into dealing Williams in 1994, unsuccessfully pushing Cashman to deal an army of prospects for Randy Johnson in 1998, and then for Sammy Sosa in 2000. He was forever impetuous, his modus operandi changing from inning to inning, game to game, while Michael and Cashman and other executives tried to keep him tethered to a sane course of management.

But you could make an argument to Steinbrenner and he would listen, said Michael, the Yankees' general manager from 1990 to 1995, and if you presented the same argument twice—making a strong stand—he would often relent. Both Michael and Cashman seemed to understand that they held a stick of their own when fending off Steinbrenner's demands. If Steinbrenner ordered them to make a move they believed was unwise, Michael or Cashman could simply say, *Hey, no problem, but I'm going to tell the reporters that it was your fucking idea,* and then the Boss would back off, apparently wary of placing himself in the bull's-eye of public opinion again.

But if Michael or Cashman made strong arguments, reaching the point that they might be read as insubordinate, their asses were on the line. This could have been left unsaid, but the Boss would say it, anyway: *You fucking better be right.* When they made mistakes—as Cashman did in losing arbitration cases to Jeter and Rivera in the spring of 1999— Steinbrenner's verbal abuse could be withering. When their decisions were vindicated, they didn't necessarily earn any extra measure of respect or trust from Steinbrenner. In fact, he was just as likely to revise history and inform them that a particularly good decision had been his idea all along.

Some baseball officials who knew of the perpetual tug-of-war waged between club executives and Steinbrenner debated a philosophical question: was it more astounding that the Yankees, with all of the franchise's financial power and Steinbrenner's willingness to spend money, went 14 seasons between playoff appearances—1981 to 1995—or that the Yankees won four World Series in five years, in spite of Steinbrenner's attempts to make changes? That such a debate was raised did not reflect well on Steinbrenner, the head of a corporation worth hundreds of millions of dollars.

Casual cheerfulness did not really suit Steinbrenner. He might chat his way through the Yankees' offices, but these moments seemed to make his employees uneasy; they assumed that more complaints were imminent and would soon blow through them with Category Five intensity. The owner, many of his employees thought, was insatiable, and they were merely stepping-stones to his success, their own lives irrelevant. A few days before Christmas in 1995, Rob Butcher, the Yankees' director of media relations, went home for the holidays, telling Steinbrenner he would return to New York if news broke. "Don't bother," Steinbrenner told Butcher. "We don't really need you." Steinbrenner probably threatened to fire somebody in the organization at least once a day, Butcher said years later, but this time, he meant it.

Getting yelled at by Steinbrenner, one employee said, "is like being hit by a machine gun. Rapid fire, coming at you pretty hard. He's a loud talker, and it feels like he's screaming at you, even when he isn't. And he's demeaning." You IDIOT, how could you do something SO IDIOTIC? Everyone IN THE WORLD is going to see what an IDIOT you are. Steinbrenner knew precisely which emotional button to push with each employee, some club officials thought. "It's like he's got a mental catalogue of how to get under the skin of each person," said one executive.

Cashman, for example, argued against trading Soriano to Anaheim for center fielder Jim Edmonds in the spring of 2000, and after Edmonds was dealt to St. Louis and opened the season strongly for the Cardinals—instead of the Yankees—Steinbrenner forced Cashman to chronicle Edmonds's performance with daily faxed reports. *I'm trying to help make you better*, Steinbrenner told Cashman. Others in the organization thought the practice wasn't much different from housebreaking a dog, with Steinbrenner rubbing Cashman's nose in the mess to humiliate him.

Some employees often declined to speak about even trivial matters on or off the record, convinced Steinbrenner would follow through on his threats to administer lie-detector tests. A reporter's questions to a Yankees official would have to be in code: around the trade deadline, a question such as "Have you bought any new furniture?" might actually mean, "Have the Yankees completed the trade?" This way, if Steinbrenner forced an official to submit to a lie-detector test, he could state definitively, No, I never answered a question about whether we made a trade.

The competitive dynamic of the baseball seasons seemed to bring out the worst in Steinbrenner. There were 162 games in the regular season, and no single game could, in itself, have any lasting impact on the team. But Steinbrenner would watch each game as if it represented clear and incontrovertible evidence of the direction of the team—and that meant 162 opportunities for doubt and reevaluations. It was a mind-set that stemmed from his boyhood fondness for football—Big Ten football, in particular—in which even one defeat could wreck a season for Ohio State or Michigan. By his third decade as the Yankees' owner, Steinbrenner acknowledged that his football mentality could not be realistically applied during baseball's season. A ballplayer's psyche would be ground into dust if he thought this way, and instead, the players compartmentalized each day, each game, avoiding any broad view of their season. But while Steinbrenner recognized that logic, he usually ignored it.

If Tino Martinez popped out on a given at-bat, Steinbrenner was apt to declare that he had lost his bat speed. If Cone surrendered a home run, Steinbrenner might call Cashman or Newman and bark at him: *Why did we spend big money on an aging pitcher?* Steinbrenner was especially attuned to comments by television broadcasters, parroting their observations as gospel. He once summoned Cashman into his office and said a strong baseball authority had given him insight into why one of the Yankees' pitchers was struggling. Cashman, who realized at once that a sports anchor had just uttered the same words on television, said, "I just watched the pregame show, too."

Torre left the team in March 1999 after being diagnosed with prostate cancer and returned in May following weeks of treatment and rest. When the Yankees played poorly in the weeks that followed, Steinbrenner fretted about Torre's performance. He's lost the energy to do the job, he told others in the Yankees' front office. He's just not going to be the same. But Steinbrenner, in keeping with his new approach to running the Yankees, did not change managers. Instead, he just complained; his primary administrative function during the championship run, besides providing the cash necessary for success, was identifying the potential for failure—which was inherent, of course, in every decision by his employees.

Steinbrenner spent most of his time at his home in Tampa, but when he was around Yankee Stadium, his presence was reflected in the tense faces of the employees outside of the clubhouse. Dirt tracked onto the floor might set him off, and a loitering summer intern could prompt an immediate change in the front-office structure. On one occasion the Yankees' primary parking lot—where players, press, and executives left their cars—overflowed with unauthorized vehicles, and Steinbrenner stood outside with a pass list, jabbing a finger angrily as he instructed security on how to check credentials. Once, while a reporter was interviewing Steinbrenner in his office, he summoned two food-service employees and pushed a pretzel at them. "You call that fresh?" he said, challenging them. "Try it. It's baked, baked, baked. The salt's baked right off it."

Any piece of litter meant the organizational structure was fraying. Steinbrenner once saw some loose paper cups lying around the team's minor league complex in Tampa, and soon Newman held a serious meeting with the managers and coaches about the cups, telling them they had to do a better job of policing the area. "That day, everyone was on red alert for trash lying on the ground, because George Steinbrenner was expected to visit again," recalled Gary Denbo, a hitting instructor in the organization for 12 years. The next day, Brian Butterfield, a minor league coach, walked out of the clubhouse with garbage bags tied to his belt on both sides and forks tied to the end of his shoes, picking up trash, drawing laughs. Steinbrenner was not around, of course.

Steinbrenner was once asked about his treatment of his employees, and he cited a former Green Bay Packer's comment about Vince Lombardi. "'He treats us all the same, like dogs,'" Steinbrenner said, quoting. "Vince said, 'Winning is a habit, but unfortunately, so is losing.'"

When the Yankees won the World Series, Steinbrenner sobbed with joy as Commissioner Bud Selig handed him the championship trophy. But club executives knew from experience that within hours of sharing in Champagne, Steinbrenner would be back in their faces about the next season, pushing, badgering, accusing them of getting soft.

GEORGE STEINBRENNER was the oldest child and only son of Henry G. Steinbrenner, "a superachiever that I would never match," the Yankees' owner once said. Henry Steinbrenner graduated from the Massachusetts Institute of Technology and won the low hurdles at the Penn Relays. When he became the president of the family-owned shipping business, the Kinsman Marine Transit Company, Henry Steinbrenner was the sort of executive who knew precisely how much was being earned and how many paper clips the company owned, and he was the sort of parent who obsessed over how his son could improve his grades and standing among classmates. He pushed George, who would build his own set of hurdles in shop class and line them up in the backyard of the family's gentleman farm in Ohio. Henry cajoled his son to hurdle with the correct form, to dress in a jacket and tie daily, to answer him properly: yes, sir; no, sir. If George finished second, his father wanted to know why he had failed to finish first.

Henry started George in business when he was nine, buying him 200 baby chickens, ducks, and geese. The George Company, it was called, and the boy cleaned the roosts and gathered the eggs and sold them, carefully recording the details in a ledger: eggs laid, eggs sold, eggs broken, receipts and debts.

George went to Culver Military Academy in Indiana, and then to college in the East, like Henry. But he failed to gain entrance to MIT and attended Williams College, instead. Henry had been an NCAA champion in hurdles, and although George practiced and practiced, he was never as good as his father. "He wasn't the kind of guy who would come up and say, 'You did an outstanding job,'" George Steinbrenner once said. "But there were times I could tell he was really happy. One time, after I had a particularly good [football] game, he waited outside the locker room. He said: 'C'mon, let's go over to the canteen. Let's get something to eat.'"

Henry's criticism, however, could be direct and cruel. George Steinbrenner would finish at Williams and go on to work as a football assistant coach at Northwestern and Purdue, assume control of the family shipping business, and buy into the American Ship Building Company. Yet when George bought the Yankees in 1973, at age 42, Henry remarked that his son's purchase "was the first smart thing he's ever done." The Yankees were, in a sense, a bauble for George to present to his father, a baseball fan. When George was a boy, he had gone to the Hotel Cleveland to see the Yankees as they arrived in town to play the Indians. He never saw the players, but years later, he would vividly recall their bags aligned together, including that of Joe DiMaggio, adorned with a Yankees logo. After buying the Yankees, George Steinbrenner introduced DiMaggio and Bill Dickey to his father.

He made an extraordinary success of the Yankees, even by the standards of Henry Steinbrenner. He bought the team for $10 million in 1973, and 26 years later, 37.5 percent of the Yankees was reportedly sold for $225 million, as part of a merger with the New Jersey Nets and Devils. The value of the Yankees was thought to be close to a billion dollars, and that was before the establishment of the team's own television network, YES. Steinbrenner had recognized and exploited the financial potential of the Yankees, and by doing so he built the dominant superpower in a baseball universe increasingly inhabited by franchises with third-world finances. More important, under Steinbrenner, the club's tradition of achievement was reawakened. After losing the 1964 World Series to St. Louis, the Yankees had faded from contention, finishing out of first place for 11 consecutive seasons. More to the point, they all but disappeared from the spotlight; fans would refer to this era as the Horace Clarke years, in reference to the benign second baseman who held his job despite a succession of mediocre seasons. But when Steinbrenner arrived, the team began to dominate the news.

The Yankees won the American League pennant three years after Steinbrenner purchased the team, and in 1977 and 1978 they beat the

Los Angeles Dodgers in the World Series—their first back-to-back titles since 1961–62. Steinbrenner's philosophy was to invest in stars and create bold headlines. He signed free agents like Catfish Hunter, Reggie Jackson, and Goose Gossage, hired and fired managers repeatedly, filled the notebooks of reporters with incendiary quotes, and became a tabloid favorite. But it wasn't long before his impetuosity began to erode the very power he had built.

Steinbrenner traded no-name prospects for big-name players, strip-mining the Yankees' minor league system—a practice that ultimately inflicted serious damage on the organization, leaving the team without the needed influx of young and cheap talent. Some of the best free agents began shying away from Steinbrenner's money, reluctant to step into the Bronx Zoo dysfunction that was the organization's most discernible trait in the 1980s.

But in spite of the team's waning on-field performance, the Yankees' already staggering financial might continued to mount. In 1988, the Yankees agreed to a 12-year, $486 million television contract with the Madison Square Garden Network; their local broadcast revenue was estimated to be at least 50 percent more than every team's other than the Atlanta Braves and Chicago Cubs, and almost 20 times greater than the Montreal Expos'. The team arranged a groundbreaking 10-year, $95 million apparel deal with Adidas. And as they began winning again in the mid-'90s, attendance at Yankee Stadium climbed, eventually surpassing three million in 1999.

In 1991, the Yankees' payroll was just over $27 million, the ninth highest in baseball, according to figures compiled by the Major League Baseball Players Association—a budget well within range of most teams in the game: 11 other teams had budgets within 25 percent of what the Yankees spent, and eight teams spent more. But in 2001—by which time the major leagues had expanded to 30 teams—only six teams spent within 25 percent or more of the Yankees' $122 million budget. And the annual payroll figures didn't include the enormous sums the Yankees doled out in trades and their signings of international free agents.

Rival baseball executives acknowledged Steinbrenner's success and admired his willingness to pour his money back into the team. Many franchises were determined to lock down their budgets, either to increase profits or reduce losses, and this made them far less competitive. But Steinbrenner was dedicated to insuring the success of the Yankees in the standings, reinvesting his profits in the team's roster. Most teams strained to develop or acquire three reliable starting pitchers; in 2001, the Yankees had six. Every member of the starting lineup on the night of Game 7, other than second baseman Alfonso Soriano and left fielder Shane Spencer, had been an All-Star at least once, and the next year, Soriano would steal 41 bases and hit 39 home runs. And the already gaudy budgets that Steinbrenner set during the winter immediately became obsolete once the Yankees lost a few games; if there was a hole in the roster, he generally gave his executives the authority to expend the cash or prospects necessary to fill it. If Steinbrenner had to choose between making money and winning ball games, Gene Michael believed, he would always choose the latter.

"You play within the rules, and we have an economic system in baseball that creates the disparity we're talking about," said Jerry Colangelo, the chairman of the Arizona Diamondbacks. "Because of [Steinbrenner's] ability, and because the resources are there and his team is playing in the biggest market in the country, he's doing exactly what most people would like to do. I do think there's a lot of jealousy involved from some other people in the game, because they don't have the means to compete."

Baseball's financial structure contained no provision for budgetary equality among the teams. Although the teams shared national television revenue, each retained almost all of the money it earned in its own market; Steinbrenner was like a poker player with mountains of chips in a game without limits. He could play imperfectly but always raise his bet to overpower his competitors, forcing them to fold—and many did, choosing to play at the $50 million table rather than try to compete at Steinbrenner's level.

Steinbrenner was widely regarded as a bully, the owner who beat the others with the biggest and sharpest stick and taunted them to challenge him. He once questioned whether AL president Gene Budig had ever worn a jockstrap. He publicly needled the crosstown Mets and rival Red Sox when they played badly. He wondered aloud whether a fellow owner, John Henry, could match Steinbrenner's record of paying dividends to investors. "It's a matter of style," said Larry Lucchino, an executive who worked with Baltimore, San Diego, and Boston. "George is often highly critical of other clubs, and what they do or don't do."

He insinuated repeatedly that some of the struggling clubs were simply mismanaged, and rival executives resented him for it. It was just not possible, they thought, to expect teams like the Kansas City Royals, with their modest revenue streams, to consistently play on the level with the Yankees and other large-budget teams. You have to give credit where credit is due with the Yankees, said Colangelo, "but it's pretty hard with the 17th largest market, with our resources, to compete year in and year out."

Steinbrenner's peers—and some of his employees—thought at least part of his success was due to luck: he was born wealthy and had struck gold with his investment in the team, but he lorded over others as if he was the model businessman. Steinbrenner, former player Jim Bouton once remarked, was born on third base and thought he'd hit a triple.

His ambition and money had restored the Yankees and, at the same time, diminished them. The team would play remarkable baseball during their championship run, maintaining an intense devotion to excellence and to one another. But for many baseball fans, the Yankees' accomplishments were cheapened, and they viewed the team as a gauche, gold-plated franchise papered over with Steinbrenner's cash and depreciated by his pomposity.

MANY YANKEES employees came to despise the owner, but they also found him capable of mystifying benevolence. He would intermittently order the firing of dozens of low-paid employees during the championship run or cut their benefits; the cuts were supposed to help offset the rising salaries of the players, but this was like saving paper clips to pay for an aircraft carrier. Yet the team's payroll of many nonuniformed personnel included some who had once worked for Steinbrenner but no longer had any functional value. Bob Lemon, who had managed the Yankees to the World Series title in 1978, kept getting paychecks after retiring, and Steinbrenner also kept widows of former employees on his payroll. He seemed intent on keeping some of his aging friends busy. "He figures that if he sends them home, they are going home to die," said a Yankees official. "It's hard to explain, because he can be the nastiest motherfucker to them their whole lives, but he won't cast them out. I don't know why he does it that way, whether it's guilt or charity."

Ket Barber, a former classmate of Steinbrenner's at Culver Military Academy, held a job as special assignment scout for the Yankees. It was an honorary title; he did not file any scouting reports. He had once worked on Steinbrenner's horse farm in Florida. "If I wasn't quitting, I was getting fired on a very, very regular basis," said Barber. "George is loyal to his friends, but he and I went through a period of time where he felt I had been disloyal. We barely spoke for a period of six or seven years, and I don't really understand why. Either he forgot about it or he decided to move on."

Steinbrenner would angrily cast out players, managers, and coaches, and then bring them back and pay them more than they were probably worth; it was a common cycle. The first time Steinbrenner gave Darryl Strawberry a second chance, he warned the slugger that if he didn't follow through with his drug rehabilitation, he would have no greater enemy than Steinbrenner. But even when Strawberry failed repeatedly, Steinbrenner kept supporting him, giving him exorbitant contracts to help him cope with some of his financial trouble.

"He'll pull over on the side of the road and give money to somebody in trouble, and then a few hours later, he's apt to cut the benefits of his employees," said one executive. "It makes no sense."

But then, much of what Steinbrenner did as Yankees owner was odd, inexplicable. His employees, former and current, swapped stories about him like baseball trading cards. During a season opener in Milwaukee early in his tenure as owner, he pounded on the glass that lined the side of his private booth during the national anthem, screaming at Pat Gillick—one of the Yankees' executives—while jabbing a finger in the direction of the field, and then to his own head. Gillick was baffled. Steinbrenner kept gesturing the same way, over and over, pointing to the field, then to his head. Because Gillick couldn't hear Steinbrenner, he walked over to his box. "Call down there to have Munson take his hat off during the anthem!" Steinbrenner shouted. Another time when Steinbrenner was in Milwaukee, in the glass-enclosed box of Brewers owner Bud Selig, reporters watched him bark at Mickey Morabito, who was among the first of Steinbrenner's many media relations directors. In full view of reporters, Steinbrenner snapped, "Tell them I'm not here."

He tended to view any decision that went against the Yankees as part of a larger conspiracy, whether it was an umpire's call or some issue among the owners. For instance, some said he worried that the Mets monitored the Yankees' clubhouse whenever the two teams played at Shea Stadium. Even during Game 5 of the 2000 World Series, when the Yankees had control, Steinbrenner complained about the Mets' supposed espionage. David Cone saw a microphone underneath a table—placed there by television flacks preparing for the postgame celebration—and noticed a red light beaming next to it. "Boss, there's the microphone," Cone said, playing to the owner's delusions, and Steinbrenner barked repeatedly that he wanted the microphone wire cut. When a water pipe burst in the visitors' clubhouse in the midst of Game 4, as Steinbrenner bent to help clean up the mess, he told others that the Mets probably were responsible.

He negotiated contract extensions with Torre and Cashman, but perturbed by the cost of re-signing them, Steinbrenner wouldn't allow his media relations staff to issue press releases. And after Yankees president Randy Levine completed talks on a 10-year deal with Derek Jeter's agent, Casey Close, Steinbrenner waited a week before formally approving the contract. In the interim, he met with Jeter and reminded the shortstop of the responsibilities inherent in the longest deal in club history, a conversation that bordered on humiliating, in the minds of several executives in the Yankees' organization. Jeter had served the organization well, earned a contract that fell within market value, waited through negotiations, and then Steinbrenner treated him like a teenager who had asked for the keys to the family car. With the completion of the deal in sight, it seemed to others that Steinbrenner wanted to show off his own power to Jeter and give him a last lecture.

But during the championship run that began in 1996, Steinbrenner mostly catered to his players, joking with them, empathizing with them, and the players generally liked him, a marked contrast to the response of previous generations of Yankees. When Steinbrenner became owner in the '70s, some players thought him to be an amateur with no understanding of their sport. They assumed—correctly—that he dictated many of the team's lineup alterations, and these intrusions offended them. Steinbrenner held meetings to lecture the players, hectoring them like a Big Ten football coach, which accomplished little except to infuriate them. He charmed and wooed free agents, and in the process alienated players already on his team. But after hoarding All-Stars, sometimes two or three at the same position, Steinbrenner overreacted to the slumps that occur inevitably in every season and criticized the players to reporters. The fans at Yankee Stadium seemed to reflect George's mood: if Steinbrenner called attention to Graig Nettles's hitting problems in the morning's *New York Post,* fans would boo Nettles that night. Late in the 1982 season, the Yankees' players requested a meeting with Steinbrenner and complained about his public comments, asking him to restrain his remarks to reporters.

But Steinbrenner changed at the rate of tectonic drift, and slowly the attraction of playing for the storied franchise waned. The veterans who won the Yankees' championships in 1977 and 1978 dispersed. Sure, Steinbrenner would pay top dollar, but free agents began to understand that a multiyear contract with the Yankees meant multiple years of instability and insecurity, and increasingly, it meant failure; after losing the World Series in 1981, the Yankees would not make the playoffs for more than a decade. There was no fun in playing for the Yankees, and the players blamed Steinbrenner. One player told reporters, without allowing them to use his name, that Steinbrenner's increased schedule of business flights was good news because it meant there was a greater chance he would perish in a crash. In 1998, Steinbrenner recalled those days, saying, "I just don't think they understood my attitude toward discipline. My experience [with my father] was that the longer I went, the more I appreciated [the discipline]. . . . I don't want these guys to think of me as a father figure, but I love to be around these guys, to have fun with them, to joke with them, have a good personal relationship with them. If they're not the right kind of citizens, they won't stay around here long."

The Yankees' players of the '90s, aware of the increasing budget disparity among teams, appreciated Steinbrenner's willingness to spend. And by then, Steinbrenner was established in baseball, and the players were more receptive to his obtuse attempts to befriend them. "I don't know what it was like in the '70s or '80s, but I think for the first time, he had a team which understood him and liked him," said David Cone. "For the first time, there was a mutual respect between the owner and the players."

Some players viewed him as a wealthy eccentric. Most of the time Steinbrenner's outfits included a white turtleneck or tan slacks or both, and he spoke in a persistent staccato that was easily and widely imitated. He sometimes stopped to impart advice to slump-ridden players, spewing mantras and sounding like a Tony Robbins disciple. You've got to be tough, he would say, shaking his right fist emphatically before leaving a trail of bemused smiles in his wake. Some players referred to him as Boss, and some—like Cone and O'Neill—called him George, while Derek Jeter and Roger Clemens addressed him as Mr. Steinbrenner. This generation of players regarded him as the person who made the team's greatness possible, made their lives comfortable. If an extra batting-practice pitcher was required, one was supplied immediately. Some teams would scrape by with a handful of batboys, but the Yankees had a batboy army, Chuck Knoblauch noted. If the Yankees needed a middle reliever or a spare outfielder in midseason, the players understood Steinbrenner would want to get the best available. Brosius once cut himself shaving, bleeding on his white dress shirt, and Steinbrenner phoned to have a new shirt delivered immediately.

Steinbrenner occasionally complained about the players' performance in the newspapers, but usually did so without the nastiness of earlier years. Rather, he would just state the obvious: *Andy Pettitte is in a slump, and he needs to pitch better.* Most of his players believed Steinbrenner had the right to say these things. Steinbrenner owned the team, he paid the salaries, and the players knew when they came to New York that Steinbrenner would sometimes publicly point out a player's failing; it was a well-established part of the package of playing for the Yankees. If they played poorly they almost came to expect him to say something. The players who complained about Steinbrenner's public comments found their teammates generally unsympathetic. "If you don't want to be on George's radar, then you shouldn't have come here in the first place," Cone said. For the players, this was part of the cost of greatness.

Steinbrenner seemed to care more and more about how the players felt about him, and they were treated much differently from his other employees. Steinbrenner could shout at Cashman in the upstairs offices at Yankee Stadium before stalking through the freshly mopped halls, snapping at attendants, and then he might walk into the clubhouse and joke genially with Jeter about how their favorite Big Ten football teams— Jeter was partial to Michigan, Steinbrenner to Ohio State—were faring in the early weeks of the season. Jekyll and Hyde.

He needed the players; they validated him. Steinbrenner had been an unknown shipbuilder before buying the Yankees, and as he reached his 71st birthday, he was a celebrity, an acknowledged success in business. He loved being recognized, loved the attention. "Ego-wise, I'd be lying if I told you I didn't," he said. "You walk into a restaurant, you can usually get a table. You're standing on the corner with five other guys yelling for a cab, he'll usually come to you. Nobody remembered me when I was a shipowner or shipbuilder." Everybody has an ego, Steinbrenner said. "There's no owner who isn't in it because of his ego. I, at least, admit that."

After one of the Yankees' many playoff victories, Steinbrenner spoke with reporters in the middle of the clubhouse at Yankee Stadium, his blazer untouched by the Champagne being sprayed around him. Jeter approached from behind, holding a bottle in his right hand. The shortstop had a knack for drawing in those on the fringes of the clubhouse society, like Hideki Irabu and Ramiro Mendoza, and now, with Steinbrenner chattering away, Jeter announced that *someone* was much too dry. As he emptied the bottle over the owner's head and messed up his hair, Steinbrenner giggled like a child. He was clearly overjoyed at being included in the celebration, Champagne dripping from his chin. The boy who stood at the Hotel Cleveland and stared at the numbered bags of the Yankees' players would have loved to be noticed like this.

But before Game 7 of the 2001 World Series, Steinbrenner was nervous, saturated with anxiety. His need to prod and push made him especially miserable during the World Series, when the rosters were set, decisions were final, and yelling and screaming and ranting changed nothing. He could only sit back and watch, and the hours in the visitors' clubhouse during Game 7 were wrenching for Steinbrenner and those around him. He paced anxiously, moving from room to room, and bat-boys and clubhouse attendants avoided him, talking in low voices in case he careened unexpectedly around a corner. Two of the attendants stood at the bathroom urinals chortling about Steinbrenner, when they suddenly realized he was walking up behind them. "I finished [urinating], turned around, and he was standing right there," said an attendant. "I said, 'Hello,' he said nothing. We spent the rest of the game worrying about if he heard us."

The tension grew in Steinbrenner and throughout Bank One Ballpark and the players on both teams. As Roger Clemens and Curt Schilling prepared to warm up in the bullpens, the Diamondbacks fans already were standing, waving pom-poms. Schilling glanced over at Jeff Motuzas, the Arizona bullpen catcher, and Motuzas's face was ashen. "How awesome is this?" Schilling asked him.

"I thought you'd be scared to death," Motuzas replied.

"Oh, I am," Schilling assured him.

Schilling strolled to the mound to pitch the top of the first inning, and he warmed up easily, conserving energy. As catcher Damian Miller whipped the ball to second base at the conclusion of the warm-up pitches, Schilling stepped to the side of the mound and pulled the gold cross from underneath his jersey, holding it against his lips as he said a prayer. The cap he had worn superstitiously throughout the World Series was discolored, the bright purple faded by sweat. Schilling had guaranteed the Diamondbacks would win if he took the mound in Game 7, but this did not seem like an audacious prediction as much as a confident statement of fact. He had started five games in the postseason and allowed four runs, pitching three complete games.

Jeter, leading off for the Yankees, took a couple of practice swings outside the batter's box. The Yankees' shortstop glanced toward the mound and made eye contact with Schilling. The Arizona pitcher smiled, and Jeter smiled slightly and nodded, as well, an acknowledgment from 60 feet and 6 inches. They both understood, Schilling thought, that they would never play in another game like this. Jeter set his feet, turned his head so he could see Schilling with both eyes, and lifted his bat over his head.

CHAPTER 3

THE YANKEES were sure they would see a sliver of vulnerability in Curt Schilling. He was pitching for the third time in nine days, making his second consecutive start on short rest, and he had to be a little weary, the Yankees' hitters believed. Perhaps Schilling would try to conserve energy early, some of the Yankees thought, by relying on his off-speed pitches.

The fastball was Schilling's primary weapon, and in Game 1, he had surprised the Yankees by throwing a lot of splitters and sliders. Before he threw Game 4, with three days' rest instead of his normal four days, they assumed he would try this tack again. But instead, Schilling attacked them with fastballs, throwing strikes and getting ahead in the count.

By Game 7, the Yankees had mustered only six hits and two runs in 14 innings against Schilling, and by any standard, he had dominated them. But these Yankees had too much experience and success against great pitchers to be intimidated. Pedro Martinez of the Red Sox seemed to strike out a dozen Yankees every time he pitched against them, yet they had defeated Boston in five consecutive games started by Martinez over the 2000 and 2001 seasons. Even if Schilling somehow mustered a good fastball for Game 7, the Yankees could beat him the same way they beat Martinez—remaining patient, waiting through the off-speed stuff they thought Schilling would throw. Then, the Yankees figured, he would tire in the middle innings. "We thought he wasn't going to be as strong as he was before," said Jorge Posada.

Schilling and Damian Miller anticipated this strategy, however, and in Game 7, they planned to go after the Yankees with fastballs. "I knew that they got into bullpens," said Schilling. "The key was, for me, to get them into deep counts, where I'm ahead. Then I could use my split a lot." There was no reason to hold back anymore; after this night, Schilling would not throw a baseball for two months. "He kind of surprised us a lot," Posada said. "He came out throwing beautifully."

Schilling's first pitch to Derek Jeter was 94 mph, and all five pitches Jeter would see in his at-bat were fastballs, the last at 97 mph, nicking the outside corner for strike three.

Paul O'Neill followed, with three plate appearances left in a major league career of 7,318 at-bats. He had privately confirmed to several reporters that he would retire after the season; he wanted them to know this as they shaped their stories throughout the year.

It was time for him to go home to his three children, O'Neill thought. His father had not missed any of his games when he was growing up. As he pitched for Brookhaven High as a teenager in Columbus, Ohio, Paul would see Chick O'Neill's dusty truck and trailer in the high school parking lot and know his father was there. Paul O'Neill felt his children deserved the same from him. He had been away on a road trip when his five-year-old daughter Alexandra started school in the fall of 2001, and after Paul tried to get the reconstructed version of the event over the phone, he was sure he had been in the wrong place.

But O'Neill also asked the reporters for a little bit of wiggle room: *Please don't write about my impending retirement as if it was an absolute certainty,* he said, *because I don't want to have to answer questions about it the whole summer.* His plan was to go through the entire postseason without thinking or talking about the last games of his career, and then, when the Yankees finished their year, he could formally announce his retirement in a quick conference call.

O'Neill became more reflective as the season played out, however. In the midst of slumps, he would tell teammates he couldn't wait for the time when failure would stop gnawing at him, and on one particularly poor day, O'Neill remarked tartly to reporters how one day soon he would not have to relive his mistakes for journalists. It seemed to be as close to a tearful farewell as O'Neill would ever come.

He wanted to concentrate on the games to be played, but fans at Yankee Stadium increasingly focused on O'Neill's last days, their cheers for him lingering. When he jogged to his position for the top of the ninth inning of Game 5, for what was slated to be his final journey to Yankee Stadium's right field, the fans throughout the park stood and began chanting his name. O'Neill looked around, trying to figure out why the fans were cheering, and then he realized they were roaring for him. Uncertain how to react, particularly because the Yankees were trailing by two runs in the last inning of a World Series game, he tipped his cap, looked around the stands and assumed that with his acknowledgment, he would melt back into the background of the game.

But the fans continued to cheer until play continued, and between pitches O'Neill would lower his head and stare at the ground, trying to maintain his composure, glancing up at the grandstand. For four years, he had been telling Shane Spencer that he would retire and that Spencer could take over right field, and for four years, O'Neill had returned. But now Spencer understood it was real; O'Neill wasn't coming back.

The fans chanted for him again as he came off the field at the end of the half-inning. He slowed his trot and walked the last yards into the dugout, then waved his cap. "I didn't know what to do," he said later. "I didn't know whether to run and hide, or tell them to can it, or what to do."

After Alfonso Soriano ended Game 5 with a 12th-inning single, O'Neill lingered in the clubhouse, still wearing his pin-striped uniform long after many of his teammates had gone home. Gerald Williams walked past the right fielder's locker. "Wear it home, O'Neill," Williams said.

"There ain't no knocks in it anymore," O'Neill replied, laughing, lamenting, as always. O'Neill finally unbuttoned his jersey and dropped it to the floor at his locker. A batboy reached for it. "Wait, wait, wait," O'Neill said. He wanted to keep the jersey and pack it away still covered with the Yankee Stadium dirt. Uniforms looked better dirty, he thought.

The idea of playing in New York had once frightened O'Neill. He had begun his career with the team he loved as a boy, the Cincinnati Reds, and played under the man he idolized, Pete Rose. O'Neill would be among the players who ran onto the field to congratulate Rose on September 11, 1985, when he broke Ty Cobb's record for career hits. But Rose was suspended from baseball in 1989, and the Reds hired Lou Piniella. The new manager looked at O'Neill's six-feet-four-inch body, his graceful and sweeping left-handed swing, and wondered why he infrequently hit home runs. O'Neill had 16 homers for the Reds in 1990, when Cincinnati won the World Series. With Piniella prodding him to pull the ball more, O'Neill smashed 28 homers in 1991, but he stopped spraying hits and his batting average shriveled to .256.

After that season, Piniella bumped into Gene Michael, a former teammate and the general manager of the Yankees. *We've got this guy O'Neill*, Piniella told Michael, *and he hit some home runs last season.* "But you watch, he's going to hit 40 homers this season," Piniella said. "He might hate me by the end of the year, but he'll hit 40 homers." Michael understood Piniella, his manner and volatile temper, and knew what this meant: if Piniella thought badgering O'Neill would translate into more homers, then he would do it.

Michael could imagine Piniella circling the batting cage while O'Neill tried to take his pregame swings, talking loud enough for O'Neill to hear him. *Big fucking Paul O'Neill. Big guy with a big body like that and he can't hit home runs. Too fucking bad. What a fucking waste.* This was Piniella's way, push and push and push, and soon enough, Piniella expected, O'Neill would push back and respond. The best players always did. But Piniella may have underestimated the enormous pressure O'Neill already put on himself. Although the two men were very much alike in their temperament and competitiveness, Piniella did not seem to understand O'Neill. "I don't think he made anything harder," O'Neill would say years later. "The hardest thing that I was dealing with was inside me." But O'Neill was desperate to please his manager and understood that Piniella pushed him because he thought he could be a better ballplayer. If Piniella thought he wasn't good enough, O'Neill believed, he wouldn't have said anything.

When Michael heard Piniella's plans for dealing with O'Neill, he figured the right fielder would either thrive or disintegrate. In 1992, under greater pressure from Piniella, O'Neill batted just .246 and managed only 14 homers. He was almost 30 years old, his explosive on-field demeanor had become notorious among scouts, and there were questions about whether O'Neill's skills would continue to erode. His stock plummeted, and it became clear that he needed to get out of Cincinnati at the very least. Shortly after the World Series, Michael agreed to trade center fielder Roberto Kelly for O'Neill, a deal which, at face value, appeared curious. Kelly was younger and he was coming off a season of 28 stolen bases, a .272 average, and 43 extra-base hits. But Michael was convinced Kelly didn't have the skills to last as a center fielder; what's more, he was a right-handed hitter, and Michael had decided to restock the Yankees' lineup with left-handed hitters, like O'Neill.

When O'Neill was traded to the Yankees, Jim Bowden, the Cincinnati general manager, called to tell him, leaving a message on his answering machine. Nevalee O'Neill, his wife, heard the message and cried. Paul was crushed. They were both filled with the small-town trepidation of bringing their family to New York. The only optimism about the deal came from his father. *You watch*, Charles O'Neill told his son, *this will turn out to be the best thing that can happen to you*. "I don't know if he meant it," Paul O'Neill said. "But he was so believable."

The tension between O'Neill and Piniella would fester long after O'Neill left the Reds. Piniella became manager of the Seattle Mariners and O'Neill went to the Yankees; when the Mariners' pitchers hit O'Neill or knocked him down repeatedly, O'Neill and other Yankees were sure it stemmed from the Cincinnati days. The brushback pitches resulted in a brawl, inevitably, in Seattle in 1996. "I had Paul O'Neill in Cincinnati for three years," Piniella said then. "You know what? He was a crybaby over there every time they threw the ball inside on him. Pitchers knew it, so they frustrated him. What he has to do is step up there, hit a ball off the left-center-field wall like a man and that stuff stops. But we weren't throwing at Paul." Piniella continued, "Now, I was tough on Paul in Cincinnati. I was trying to make him a man. He cries all the time. Outside of that, I got no problems with Paul." O'Neill said, "I've had players on his team ask me what he has against me. If he wants to do something, why does he go through his players?" Jeff Nelson pitched five seasons for Piniella in Seattle and was a teammate of O'Neill's for five years in New York, and Nelson never fully ascertained the reasons for the tension between the two men—he knew only that it existed. After Seattle's Tim Davis had thrown inside to O'Neill in 1996, Nelson retaliated by hitting the Mariners' Joey Cora and was suspended. "Lou would say, 'Your big man O'Neill thinks I'm throwing at him, and I don't know why he would think that,'" Nelson recalled. "You never understood what was going on, and you wanted to know what the problem was. But I don't think Lou really knew, and I don't think Paul knew." O'Neill and Piniella would talk amicably in later years, chatting at the batting cages in New York and Seattle when others were around, but they never talked about what had gone wrong years before, O'Neill said.

Before O'Neill's first spring training with the Yankees, Michael met with manager Buck Showalter to discuss the player's experience in Cincinnati, and they agreed to give him some breathing room. There would be no talk of home runs or trying to take advantage of the short right field porch in Yankee Stadium. They would just let him play. Rick Down, the Yankees' hitting coach, found O'Neill easy to talk to, contrary to his reputation. The guy just wanted to work; he was insatiable, always wanting to take more batting practice to refine his swing.

O'Neill immediately developed a rapport with the Yankees' most established player, Don Mattingly, feeling as if he had already known him for years. They were both from the Midwest and had modest Midwestern sensibilities, finding little value in the fringe benefits of baseball, like fame and endorsements. Mattingly was, Showalter thought, the perfect role model for O'Neill as he began his time in New York; he nudged the newcomer subtly, teasing him, making him feel comfortable right away. Mattingly noted later that most players coming to New York face greater scrutiny than they have before, but O'Neill's circumstances were different. "Paul came from a situation where he was playing near his hometown, a lot of pressure, and whatever he did in Cincinnati wasn't enough," Mattingly said. "He got to realize that here, you just play your game. You don't have to do anything special, you just go out and hit and play hard, and he would be appreciated."

O'Neill would surpass all expectations other than his own. In his first season with the Yankees, he lifted a home run into Yankee Stadium's upper deck in right field, the ball ricocheting off the seats and rebounding onto the field. O'Neill rounded the bases and accepted congratulations from teammates in the dugout, but kept glancing at the place where the ball landed. My first upper-deck home run in Yankee Stadium, he complained to Down, and the ball didn't even stay up there. Whatever he did was not enough for him, Mattingly thought. He was always competing.

O'Neill had been the youngest of six children while growing up in Ohio, and his sister and four brothers all played sports, which meant that standout success was almost impossible until he was a teenager. Molly O'Neill, his sister, who would go on to become a food critic for the *New York Times,* used to write about the basketball games Paul had played against Robert, brother No. 4, in the afternoons. The winner was the first player to score 25 points, and Paul would reach 23 points, victory a single shot away. Robert would reel off consecutive baskets until he had 25 points, the flow of the game designed to defeat and, as siblings understand, to demoralize. The losses crushed Paul. "You cheater," he yelled, before calling their mother at work. "Mom, Robert cheated," he reported. But Paul would keep going back for more, demanding rematches, his sister recalled. "What's the matter, cheater?" he would say. "Afraid you won't get lucky again?" Defeat deterred him only temporarily, but each of his failures seemed to cling to him. Years later, O'Neill would recount his Little League devastations with great specificity; he had never been able to fully shed the frustration. He would pitch well and lose, and although his father would remind him that he had done well, the boy would be crushed. The bottom line was hard and clear.

He would never make his peace with baseball. The game seemed to devour O'Neill daily, one at-bat at a time. If O'Neill had a couple of good days, then he fretted about the bad streak that was sure to come, and any bad day—hell, any poor at-bat—infected his psyche. A three-hit day meant little to him if he grounded out weakly in his last at-bat; it was that last at-bat that would stay with him and grate on his mind. He was driven, unrelenting, and this was O'Neill's contribution to the emotional soul of the Yankees during the run of championships, David Cone thought; his daily fight became their fight. When O'Neill left, Joe Torre said, "A place in the heart of the Yankees will no longer be around."

Poor swings and slumps bothered other Yankees, too, but O'Neill reacted differently from almost anyone else on the team—or in the major leagues, for that matter—throwing his helmet after making an out, flipping his bat, complaining to umpires constantly. The fans in Yankee Stadium interpreted his demonstrations as a reflection of his desire to succeed, and even seemed to take comfort in them. When O'Neill popped up with the bases loaded, they felt like slamming a bat, and O'Neill did it for them. But in Boston, in Cleveland, in Seattle, fans regarded him as a boorish, whining brat, guilty of behavior that was unacceptable from even Little Leaguers. O'Neill would bounce his helmet or confront umpires, and opposing fans booed loudly. To fans in ballparks outside of Yankee Stadium, O'Neill became the foremost Yankee villain. Bernie Williams might beat the Red Sox or the Mariners with a hit, but he almost never showed emotion on the field; Williams's rants were done out of sight, where he could attack a bat rack in peace. But not only was O'Neill a Yankee in the eyes of fans around the country, he was a crybaby, an example of horrible behavior, and they let him have it. O'Neill, deep in his own torment, never seemed to notice. After making an out to end an inning, he would usually walk to the outfield, his head down, consumed by misery.

His outbursts fascinated and amused teammates. O'Neill would ground out or fly out weakly and talk to himself. "I'll never get another hit, I can't hit anymore," he would lament, and Jose Cardenal, the first-base coach, would turn away and cover his face, stifling laughter. O'Neill would still be talking to himself as he descended the dugout steps, sometimes waving for the television cameras at the end of the dugout to turn back to the action on the field. (There was little chance of that happening, because the television directors knew odds were good that O'Neill would put on a show in the dugout.) Few of his teammates dared to watch him directly, but they all were awed by his explosions and watched him surreptitiously, heads turned slightly—as if to check the outfield scoreboard—so they could see his next assault. O'Neill might attack the water cooler or throw his helmet or his batting gloves; it was not a matter of whether he would explode but how. When O'Neill approached the bat rack in the corner of the dugout nearest home plate, batboys leaned backward, as if bracing themselves against a coming hurricane, anticipating the ricochet of a helmet.

O'Neill's oldest son, Andy, played in a basketball league for eight-year-olds, and during one game, he missed a shot and then another and another, and as he ran down the floor, the boy began weeping. Nevalee O'Neill, sitting in the stands behind the coach, tapped her husband on the shoulder and said, "It's all your fault."

Paul O'Neill would go through a progression of emotions from at-bat to at-bat. Three at-bats without a hit and he would stomp back to the dugout, his head jerking with rage. Five without a hit and O'Neill would yank off his helmet and shout angrily. More than two days without a hit and he would begin launching his helmet, perhaps bouncing it with two hands if he made the third out of the inning, or spinning it through the air horizontally across the front of the dugout. Once the slump reached its apex, however, O'Neill was drained of his anger, disconsolate, dragging his body to the dugout, his chin seemingly stitched to his chest.

He was, in a sense, fortunate to play among tolerant teammates—from Torre to Martinez to Girardi. With another team, playing under different circumstances, O'Neill's preoccupation with his own failure could easily have been construed as selfish. Many ballplayers disliked it when a teammate acted as demonstratively as he did, feeling that the negative body language would inevitably drag down the team. Other players—including some of O'Neill's teammates—felt the same urge to throw their helmets, slam their bats, fire their gloves, but had long since conquered the instinct, partly out of respect for teammates.

But the other Yankees came to understand that O'Neill's explosions were rooted in his sense that he had failed them. He kept his own dissatisfaction in perspective whenever the Yankees won—which was most of the time—while acknowledging the successes of teammates. "He'd sit in the clubhouse after going 4-for-5 and he'd be saying, 'I let my team down,'" Chad Curtis said. "He'd be thinking about that one at-bat when he didn't get the hit, or the one ball he didn't get to in right field. Sometimes we'd be in the weight room after a game we'd won, and he'd be upbeat, even if he was 0-for-4. 'I'm sure glad the 0-for-4 didn't hurt us.' He was definitely team-oriented."

For all of his angst, O'Neill's frustration never fully conquered him. His rants were not entirely irrational, Homer Bush thought, because everything O'Neill screamed at himself was instructive, about keeping his front shoulder tucked, about swinging at good pitches. And if a temperamental umpire was calling balls and strikes and warned O'Neill about his outbursts, O'Neill was much less likely to turn and question a call openly. There were several occasions when he would raise himself up to his full six feet four and loom over umpires who had ejected him, but he always maintained a measure of control with the team's interest in mind.

He did not isolate himself when he played badly. Unlike Knoblauch, who seemed to internalize failure, O'Neill sought solace and confirmation from teammates and reporters. He sat at his locker hours before games, chair turned out, facing the open room, engaging anyone who passed by, and inevitably, as the conversations meandered from subjects ranging from the weather to the Mets' recent performance, O'Neill would toss in a self-deprecating remark. "The groundskeepers say the rain is going to delay the game an hour," a reporter told him. "The way I'm going," O'Neill retorted, "a hurricane sounds better."

O'Neill seemed to have an understanding of his inner torture, and used it. Jim Courier, the tennis star who won four Grand Slam titles, befriended O'Neill and thought he and tennis great John McEnroe—also infamous for his rants—deployed their emotion in much the same way, feeding off it. Rage against what they perceived as a bad call would increase their adrenaline and, in turn, their concentration. There was some speculation that McEnroe's outbursts were designed to unnerve his opponent, Courier believed, "but everything Paul did was strictly for himself. He was very much doing it in a tunnel." O'Neill compartmentalized his emotion much more than McEnroe, Courier believed. "McEnroe's intensity carried over to the rest of his life; what you see is what you get," Courier said. "Paul understood how to keep it bottled up inside the lines."

Many umpires tired of O'Neill's complaining. In a book published late in his career, Durwood Merrill, an American League umpire for 23 years, went so far as to rank O'Neill among the most prominent bitchers. But some umpires came to see O'Neill's griping as Courier did—a competitive mechanism. John Shulock, a longtime umpire, thought O'Neill's complaints and body language had little to do with how Shulock was calling balls and strikes and almost everything to do with how O'Neill was feeling about himself on a given day. "If I was a manager of a team and I had six or seven like him," Shulock said, "I'd be completely happy."

O'Neill liked much about his work—the friendships, the competition, being part of a team, the rhythms of summer—but some of his teammates were sure that the game of baseball gnawed at him. Derek Jeter believed O'Neill probably didn't enjoy the game in the same way that he did. Even if you had five hits in five at-bats, O'Neill thought, you still had the burden of proving yourself the next day. "When you're going through a bad time or bad day, I always had a problem of blocking that out, knowing tomorrow's going to be a better day," O'Neill said. "But when the race is over, if you know a sleepless night helped you work harder to do better the next day, then you did your best." It wasn't until the last days of his career that O'Neill began to look back and understand that his nine years with the Yankees had been the best part of his life.

"I hit the jackpot," O'Neill said. "I came here at the right time. I played with the right people. I was a little part of the right team. Nobody could ask for that, I don't think. You expect to win, but not the way we've won here."

He was a crucial piece of the Yankees' offense, batting .303 in nine seasons, with 1,426 hits, 185 home runs, a batting title in 1994, and four All-Star appearances. O'Neill kept his hands back in his swing, so that he could react at the last instant to a pitch—smashing outside fastballs to left-center field, spoiling nasty breaking balls by flicking them into left field, driving pitches down and in over the wall in right field. Ted Williams once told Yankees coach Don Zimmer how much he liked to watch O'Neill hit, and when O'Neill was in a spring-training slump in 1997, Williams phoned him and reminded him to hit to all fields, to not worry about pulling the ball. The words echoed for O'Neill: hit the ball on the button, his own father had told him.

O'Neill practiced his stance in hotel lobbies, at his locker, in the dugout, at his position. Standing in right field, O'Neill would wait until there was a lull in the action and raise his gloved right hand as if he was preparing to hit. He would lift his right leg, lower his chin—keep your head on the ball, Chick O'Neill had told him—and extend his arms. Then he would turn back to the infield again.

PAUL O'NEILL'S body began breaking down late in each of his last seasons, and he would play through October with injuries. O'Neill played the 1996 World Series with a torn leg muscle. Years later, Cone remembered watching O'Neill take a painkilling shot to play and, with the bad leg, make a running, lunging catch to get the last out of Game 5. He broke a rib crashing into a low fence near the end of the 1999 season and played with the injury throughout the postseason, swinging through wrenching pain, and he contributed to the first run-scoring rallies in Games 1 and 2 of that World Series.

O'Neill hurt his hip late in the 2000 season, and he fared miserably in the last weeks of the regular season, failing to collect any extra-base hits in his last 58 at-bats. He looked so bad at the plate that late in Game 1 of the AL Championship Series against Seattle, Torre yanked O'Neill in favor of pinch-hitter Glenallen Hill; the next day, O'Neill was dropped from third to seventh in the batting order. O'Neill's hip ached and his swing and balance were terrible, and opposing pitchers pounded him with inside fastballs. But Torre kept him in the lineup, and in Game 1 of the World Series against the Mets, he came to bat in the ninth inning, one out and nobody on base.

Armando Benitez was throwing for the Mets, his pitches hovering near 100 mph at a time when O'Neill was struggling to hit 90 mph fastballs. O'Neill's only advantage was that Benitez rarely pitched inside to left-handed batters, perhaps because of the angry reaction he had received at Yankee Stadium when he drilled Tino Martinez in the middle of the back in 1998. Or maybe it was because Benitez's crossfire throwing motion made it more difficult for him to throw inside to lefties.

Whatever the reason, Benitez pumped fastballs at the outside corner, and O'Neill quickly fell behind in the count, one ball and two strikes, barely hanging on. Benitez kept throwing fastballs, and O'Neill could barely get his bat around in time to slap foul balls into the stands on the third-base side. An off-speed pitch would have been a favor to O'Neill, so Benitez kept the pace up—but always outside, where O'Neill could at least extend his arms and swing defensively. This was not about looking to drive the ball; this was about surviving. Don't get yourself out, O'Neill told himself. A walk is as good as a hit.

O'Neill fouled off another and another and took a pitch out of the strike zone. Gradually, he began to gain traction, turning the advantage. With the count full, Benitez missed the strike zone on the 10th pitch of the at-bat, and O'Neill flipped the bat away and trotted to first base. It was an unbelievable, hard-fought at-bat. Torre would say afterward: "You could tell that he made up his mind that he wasn't going to give up."

Luis Polonia and then Jose Vizcaino hit singles, pushing O'Neill to third, and he scored the game-tying run on a sacrifice fly by Knoblauch. The Yankees would win in the 12th inning, O'Neill would bat .474 in the World Series, and many of O'Neill's teammates would view his walk as the turning point against the Mets.

In the first six games of the 2001 Series against the Diamondbacks, O'Neill had hit .250, 3 hits in 12 at-bats, despite his bad foot. Torre had benched O'Neill and Martinez, left-handed hitters, against left-hander Randy Johnson in Game 2, a decision that left O'Neill disappointed. He would never criticize Torre directly, and his opinion was tinged by his own competitive desire to play in every game. But as he chatted with a reporter before Game 2, he asked what the journalist thought of the choice. Although the question itself was not meant to be rhetorical, the fact that O'Neill posed it was an indication he really had hoped—and anticipated, perhaps—that he would play.

But there was no question that O'Neill would play in Game 7 against the right-handed Schilling, and he stood in the box, waving his bat, chin down, head on the ball.

Schilling, still wrestling with his anxiousness early in the first inning, fired a low fastball and O'Neill waited. Ball one. Schilling—who had thrown fastballs with his first seven pitches—tried a splitter. O'Neill jumped on it, slashing a line drive to right-center field, the ball splitting the outfielders, rolling toward the fence, in the deepest alley of Bank One Ballpark. He had a double, at least. But there was already one out, the Yankees were starved for runs, and if O'Neill could reach third base now, he might score on a groundout or a fly ball; Clemens could take the mound with an early lead. O'Neill raced around first, thinking about a triple.

O'Neill was an excellent base-runner, and under normal circumstances, he probably would have hit the inside of second base as he rounded the bag, driving himself toward third. But he was playing with a stress fracture in his left foot, and he stepped on the top of second, turning toward third. Arizona right fielder Danny Bautista had already thrown toward the infield, the ball reaching cutoff man Craig Counsell on one bounce.

Counsell turned and threw toward third. O'Neill could see third baseman Matt Williams setting up to the left-field side of the base, preparing to take the throw. O'Neill began straining in his sprint, his arms pumping, his torso leading his 38-year-old legs the way a farmer pulls a stubborn mule. His stride broke, slightly, before he tried to slide to the home plate side of third base. Counsell's throw was accurate, just as Bautista's had been, and Williams dropped a tag on O'Neill's right foot just before he reached the base—a close play, but O'Neill was out. He jumped to his feet immediately, just as the fans around him began roaring, and sprinted off the field. As Bernie Williams batted against Schilling, O'Neill paced the dugout, shouting in frustration. Williams flied to center to end the inning, and Schilling pumped his right fist slightly as he walked off the mound. "That's one," he muttered softly.

CHAPTER 4

GENE MICHAEL had a ticket for Game 7, and he would watch the first innings from the stands, but he understood that eventually he should make his way to the visitors' clubhouse, where his presence was required. Steinbrenner's superstition was powerful, and he needed his trusted amulets to ward off defeat. Michael, the director of major league scouting for the Yankees, would be seated alongside Steinbrenner and Dwight Gooden, a special assistant, in the visiting manager's office through the game.

Michael's relationship with Steinbrenner had roots 30 years deep. He had worked for him as a player, coach, manager, general manager, and scout, and like many of Steinbrenner's baseball lieutenants, he had fled the Yankees and then returned, in his case after spending two years with the Chicago Cubs. When Michael came back, he, like all Yankees executives, was intermittently shoved out of the loop. But Steinbrenner seemed to trust Michael's judgment on players above that of all other advisors.

Steinbrenner had turned to Michael in the summer of 1990 as he faced a suspension from baseball. He had been caught paying a known gambler for damaging information on one of his own players, Dave Winfield, and his lawyers began negotiating a sentence with Commissioner Fay Vincent. It was a good time for Steinbrenner to leave, anyway; he had run the team into the ground with rash decisions, and the Yankees were a laughingstock. "I want out of baseball," Steinbrenner told Vincent during deliberations over the penalty to be levied. "I'm sick and tired of it." He agreed to a suspension of indefinite length, knowing he could subsequently apply for reinstatement, but before he left the Yankees, Steinbrenner decided to replace his general manager, Pete Peterson.

At the time, Michael was working as a scout for the Yankees, and he phoned Steinbrenner to suggest former Dodgers pitcher Don Sutton as a candidate for general manager. Michael had been impressed by Sutton's intelligence, and he thought Sutton would satisfy Steinbrenner's standing desire for marquee names; Don Drysdale was another possibility, Michael thought. But Steinbrenner sounded completely disinterested. A couple of weeks later, Steinbrenner called back. "We've been thinking about your choice," Steinbrenner said. "But we keep coming back to one name."

Michael waited silently. "Aren't you going to ask me who it is?" Steinbrenner asked.

"OK," said Michael. "Who is it?"

"You," Steinbrenner replied, and Michael was stunned.

When Michael was introduced at a press conference, Steinbrenner told reporters, "I have great confidence in him," as he had said about other general managers and managers he had fired in the past. "No one is more knowledgeable in the organization." But a club official close to Steinbrenner thought the real reason the owner chose Michael was because he trusted Michael's motives. Michael might make decisions Steinbrenner didn't like, but Steinbrenner believed he would never make any decision without the best interests of the Yankees at heart.

Gene Michael had been the team's general manager before, during 1980, after Steinbrenner pried him off the field; Michael managed Class AAA Columbus in 1979. "Forget about managing," Steinbrenner had said, "and come up here with the other second-guessers." Now, in 1990, Michael was attracted to the challenge of rebuilding the Yankees, and he had some ideas of how the team could be improved. And with Steinbrenner out of the day-to-day operations, Michael would have the element most essential to restructuring the team: time.

There would be time for prospects to develop in the minors. Time for the youngest Yankees, like 21-year-old Bernie Williams, to evolve into productive major leaguers. Time for the organization to restock its pool of pitching. Steinbrenner would not be around to impetuously override the judgment of his baseball executives. He had changed general managers 14 times in his 17 years as owner of the Yankees, but now it appeared Michael would have carte blanche for at least a couple of years, maybe longer.

Michael was introduced at a press conference on August 20, 1990, and a reporter asked whether Michael would have taken the job if Steinbrenner had not been forced out of the game. Michael smiled. "That's not a fair question," he said. "I wasn't offered that." Twelve years later, Michael again declined to answer the same question. But friends inside and outside the organization thought the answer in both instances would have been no.

For many years, it seemed Michael made a mistake to make a career in baseball, because anyone who had seen Gene Michael play basketball and baseball knew that he was better at basketball. Michael himself preferred basketball. Almost six foot three and stronger than his slender build might suggest, Michael could shoot and play defense, and he liked basketball better because you could practice by yourself; a ball and a basket, and you were in business. Baseball required too many players. But he wanted to play professional sports, and baseball seemed like a more stable employment option; the major and minor leagues were better established. He signed with the Pirates in 1959 for a $25,000 bonus but never felt fully confident, the way he did in basketball. In an early game in the Carolina League, Michael faced a Durham Bulls pitcher named Wally Wolf and was completely overwhelmed by Wolf's fastball; nobody could hit that stuff, he thought. Wolf was subsequently promoted to Class AAA, where hitters pounded him, and Michael was appalled. If Wally Wolf can't get to the majors with that fastball, Michael thought, how am I going to hit major league pitchers?

Michael had a strong third season in the minors, though, batting .324

and stealing 36 bases, and in that winter, as 1961 became 1962, he played basketball in Akron and was recommended to the Detroit Pistons, who had lost a couple of guards to injuries. Michael was offered a two-year contract that would have offset his baseball signing bonus. But this was before players had agents and lawyers to represent them in negotiations, and Michael knew that his baseball contract specifically forbade him from pursuing a basketball career. "Nowadays, you see players get out of that kind of contract all the time," Michael said years later. "But I was scared, I was naive."

He was misled, too, by the high batting average he posted for the Hobbs Pirates. His offense continued to fluctuate in the summer that followed—that year with Hobbs, as it turned out, would be the best of his professional career, something of a fluke—and he kept taking college classes, working toward his degree. Michael tended to take more classes after his worst seasons, fewer when he played better.

When a minor league teammate named Jim Price met Michael for the first time, he was struck by how tall and skinny Michael was. "Either you're a human one iron or a stick," said Price, and forever after Michael was widely known as Stick. Michael spoke with a hearty midwestern accent and laughed easily. His thick hair often looked windblown when there was no wind, and he tended to wear caps that didn't quite fit him. He often finished his sentences with a chuckle, guffawing at an anecdote or at himself. "You could look at him and underestimate him," said Pat Gillick, who played against Michael in the minor leagues, long before Gillick became general manager of the Toronto Blue Jays. "And the whole time, he would have his hand in your pocket, getting the best of you. He was always heads-up, always in the game."

He demonstrated a wider understanding of the game very early in his career, even as he struggled to hit. Michael was playing for the Class B Kinston Eagles and his team was getting pounded by a young Red Sox prospect named Rico Petrocelli, who would later go on to star for Boston. Playing shortstop, Michael noticed Petrocelli's whole approach to hitting was based on the ball-strike count: when he was ahead in the count, two balls and no strikes or 3-1, he would wait for fastballs—and only fastballs—and crush them. When he was behind in the count,

Petrocelli would wait for breaking balls. It was a common approach, but Petrocelli was uncommonly disciplined in adhering to this strategy, and Michael informed the team's catcher, Harper Cooper, who scoffed. Catcher and shortstop argued, until an annoyed Cooper gave in and told Michael he should call the pitches from his position. Years later, Michael vaguely recalled the system they used—he stood a little straighter for fastballs, placing his hand on his knee for a breaking ball. Petrocelli began making outs.

Michael reached the major leagues for the Pirates in 1966 and was quickly conquered by curveballs and sliders, hitting just .152 in 33 at-bats. The Pirates traded Michael and Bob Bailey to the Dodgers for shortstop Maury Wills before the 1967 season, and Michael batted .202 in 98 games, his career path established. He would hit .229 with 15 homers in 11 seasons, surviving because of his fielding and other intangibles. Peter Gammons, the *Boston Globe* baseball writer who covered Michael at the end of his playing career, found him to be unexpectedly competitive and tough. Yankees catcher Thurman Munson and Red Sox catcher Carlton Fisk had gotten into a brawl at home plate in 1973, after Michael had missed a squeeze bunt and Munson, charging from third, had smashed into Fisk viciously, with a resolve that was not entirely spontaneous. For months, Michael had been prodding Munson by placing pictures of Fisk in his locker, and Munson, aware that Fisk was more photogenic and perhaps a better player, was furious, partly because he did not know who was taping the pictures. Michael knew, however, and as the scrum evolved, Michael came face-to-face with Fisk and fired punches at the Boston catcher, defending the Yankee pinstripes.

Bouncing from team to team at the end of his career, Michael was 37 years old when Boston dumped him a month into the 1976 season, before he even had an at-bat. He had only vague notions of what he would do with the rest of his life. Michael had made a steady wage in baseball, but he wasn't wealthy; maybe he would teach someplace, coach in college or high school.

Marty Appel, the Yankees' media relations director at that time, contacted Michael and told him that Steinbrenner wanted to talk. The two chatted at a function in Shea Stadium's Diamond Club. "I think you should stay in the game," Steinbrenner told Michael, adding that some of the Yankees' coaches had thought he was unusually intelligent. Michael was still unsure what Steinbrenner had in mind, whether it was broadcasting or coaching or working in the front office; he only knew he had a job with the Yankees. In 1978, Michael joined Billy Martin's coaching staff, but because Martin had no prior relationship with Michael and because Steinbrenner had sponsored him, Martin was suspicious. "Billy thinks Gene is a spy for George, that he's one of the guys telling George stuff," Sparky Lyle wrote in his 1979 book, *The Bronx Zoo*. "Billy doesn't know for certain, but he knows that he doesn't like him. If Billy can keep his job to the end of the year, he'll fire Gene at the end of the season." Once, when the Yankees were in Detroit, Michael was forced to dress with the players, rather than with the other coaches. "I don't know what's wrong," Michael told Lyle. "They just don't like me anymore." Martin and Michael later settled their differences, Michael recalled. "Billy trusted me only when he knew I didn't want to manage for George," said Michael.

Michael eventually did manage for Steinbrenner, though, for two brief stints during the 1981 and 1982 seasons. Michael went to work for the Chicago Cubs in 1986, returning to the Yankees as a scout only after he resigned as the Cubs' manager in 1987. When Michael became general manager of the Yankees again on August 20, 1990, the team was a mess, a jumbled collection of ill-fitting parts; they would finish that season last among seven teams in the American League East, with 67 victories and 95 losses. Michael had a strategy for rebuilding the franchise.

He wanted to restock the Yankees' lineup with left-handed hitters, to take advantage of the close right field fence—314 feet down the line and 385 feet in right-center, compared to left field, where the fence seemed to curl out from the foul line and extend into Queens. Seven of the nine regulars in the team's lineup in 1990 were right-handed, and Don Mattingly, one of the two lefties, was suffering from back trouble that would sap the power he had had earlier in his career. Most of the Yankees in the Hall of Fame were left-handed hitters: Babe Ruth and Lou Gehrig, Bill Dickey and Yogi Berra, Reggie Jackson. Roger Maris had been a lefty, Mickey Mantle a switch-hitter. Yankee Stadium had been built to

Steinbrenner didn't see it that way. "This team is messed up," he told
Michael shortly after he returned from his permanent ban, which had
been reduced to 2½ years. "The players are messed up; everything is
messed up. This was in good shape when I left."

"That's why we had the first pick in the '91 draft, right?" Michael shot
back. "Don't be a wiseass," Steinbrenner replied.

For the next few years, Michael would hold together the framework
he had built, but it wouldn't be easy. Steinbrenner was forever impatient,
temperamental. He would demand change and Michael would argue,
vehemently. "There was a mutual respect between him and George, because Stick would stand up for what he believed, and George knew
that," said Showalter. "You had to show him how passionate you were
about a decision. Now, you were going to be held accountable for it, but
Stick didn't have a problem with accountability. He had the same thing
we were looking for in our players."

Because Steinbrenner was boss, Michael often had to wage clandestine battles, using creative tactics in the face of a stronger enemy. Before
Bernie Williams established himself, Steinbrenner once ordered Michael
to collect offers from other teams for the young outfielder and then trade
him to whoever dangled the best deal. Michael employed a tactic worthy
of Rommel: he called executives with the other 25 teams but never mentioned Williams, then reported back to Steinbrenner that yes, he had
talked with every team in baseball, and no one had expressed any interest in Williams. He had succeeded in holding off Steinbrenner, and
though Michael almost traded Williams in 1994, talking for weeks with
the Montreal Expos about a possible swap for Larry Walker, Williams hit
a few homers and was again saved. Michael phoned Montreal GM Kevin
Malone: *Thanks for your interest, but we're keeping him.*

Michael was not afraid to trade young players; there was no set rule
against dealing a prospect for a veteran player. But patience was para-
mount, he thought. You had to give a young player time to develop, to
learn, to adjust, and if you didn't, you would cheat yourself of the opportunity to make sound judgments. He had swapped Roberto Kelly for
Paul O'Neill when Kelly was 28 and younger and faster, and had taken
some criticism. The swap of a blossoming young player for a veteran who

favor left-handed hitters—Ruth, at the outset—and it made no sense to
Michael for the Yankees to be predominantly right-handed.

Michael planned to build his offense on the foundation of on-base
percentage. He wanted to acquire players who would draw walks as well
as get hits. If there were more runners on base, Michael believed, it naturally followed that more runs would be scored. This was an elementary
concept that had not yet gained leaguewide recognition, and it was
partly a by-product of the shrinking of the strike zone. Umpires no
longer were calling strikes at the bellybutton, or even pitches at the belt.
"If you throw it above the sack"—the scrotum—"then it's borderline,"
said a National League pitcher. The average number of pitches per at-bat
would rise steadily, and so would walks. Babe Ruth and Ted Williams
drew more walks than other hitters in their respective generations, but
primarily because pitchers refused to throw them strikes. By the late
1980s, however, the best hitters were making walks an integral part of
their offense. Wade Boggs, an All-Star third baseman for Boston, had
won the American League batting title in 1986 with a .357 average, but
he also drew a league-high 105 walks. By the turn of the century, the inability to draw walks would be viewed as a liability.

But in the early '90s, Michael was ahead of the pack in building a
lineup of hitters with high on-base percentages—a group of hitters who
would force opposing starting pitchers to work deep into ball-strike
counts and perhaps tire in the fifth, sixth, or seventh inning. The
strength of most pitching staffs was the starters and the late-inning relievers, and if the Yankees could wear out the starters, they could then
feast on the soft underbelly of major league pitching—the middle relief.

The Yankees gradually added left-handed hitters, with the notable exception of Mike Stanley, a right-handed backup catcher who had been
cast off by the Texas Rangers after the 1991 season. Stanley hit .249 in
1992, and before the next season, Michael gave him a two-year contract,
a move that appeared to be based in no logic whatsoever. But Michael
recognized that he had good plate discipline, and in 1993, Stanley—30
years old—batted .305 with 57 walks. Wade Boggs signed with the Yankees in 1993, batting .302 with 74 walks in his first season. Paul O'Neill,
a tough left-handed hitter, was added in '93. Mike Gallego, a five-feet-

seven-inch middle infielder with a small strike zone, joined in 1992. In 1990, the year Michael became general manager, the Yankees drew 427 walks; in 1993, they collected 629 and scored 218 more runs than they had three years before.

Michael had his own strong sense of what kind of player could succeed in New York, and amiability was not a factor. Along with Buck Showalter, who became the Yankees' manager in 1992, he rid the team of players they thought detrimentally selfish—bad teammates, like Mel Hall. To Michael, it really didn't matter if a player was an asshole so long as his antics did not become a serious distraction for the other players. Michael wanted players who demonstrated an ability to block out everything going on around them and focus on the task at hand. "Deep thinkers," he called them, although in a sport in which almost everything could be quantified by some type of statistic, it was unclear how deep thinkers might be identified.

But Michael had a knack for recognizing them. Other scouts who had seen O'Neill throw helmets and rant while with the Reds were certain he would fail in New York, unnerved by nosy reporters or Steinbrenner or the fans who would boo him as a matter of course. Michael, on the other hand, watched O'Neill and interpreted his intensity as evidence of a player deeply committed to his work, preoccupied with the pursuit of success.

Steinbrenner had once landed the best free agents, signing players like Reggie Jackson and Goose Gossage in the first years of the system. But Steinbrenner's bizarre treatment of Winfield and other players, as well as the team's disintegration in the 1980s, changed the way free agents viewed the Yankees. The team was neither successful nor glamorous, and a veteran player signing with the Yankees had to assume there was a fair chance that sooner or later, he would become a target of Steinbrenner's criticism. Free agents flirted with the Yankees but merely used the team to boost their market values. It became an amusing rite of fall: an attractive free agent would express interest in playing for the Yankees, driving up his own asking price, and then sign elsewhere. By the mid-'80s, the Yankees were struggling to lure the premier free agents, a problem that would last for almost a decade. Before the 1992

season, Yankees executives—presumably serving Steinbrenr not permitted oversight of day-to-day operations of the tear vented Michael and jumped in late in negotiations with Danny Tartabull, compelled by public-relations fears after signed Bobby Bonilla. But Tartabull was overhyped: injury-pro subpar outfielder, Tartabull signed for $25 million over five y was a disaster, and he was dumped before the end of his c Shortly after the 1992 season, the Yankees pushed hard to sig Maddux and failed; Maddux signed with Atlanta. The Yankees perception problem with free agents. But that all changed with J Key, Michael believed.

Key pitched for the Toronto Blue Jays for nine seasons, worl steadily, usually winning 13 to 17 games when he was healthy. But impact went beyond his record. The left-hander was viewed as a serio professional and a competitor, tested in the postseason—a natur leader, in the opinion of Pat Gillick, the Toronto general manager. Ke had thrown three scoreless innings in the 1992 playoffs before winning twice in the World Series, and despite his history of injuries, he was one of the premier free agents in the off-season. A country kid from Huntsville, Alabama, Key had thrived in the calm of Toronto, and when the Yankees began wooing him, questions arose among scouts about whether he would like pitching in New York, if he would be bothered by the big city. But Gillick didn't think anything would bother him: "He was just one of those guys who competed no matter where he was." The Blue Jays offered Key a three-year deal, and the Yankees topped them with an offer of four years and $17 million. But Key would also be swayed by what he had seen of the Yankees in 1992. Since Showalter had become the manager, Key had seen the roster shifting, the personality of the team changing. "The so-called bad guys were getting weeded out," Key recalled years later. "I just felt like Buck had gotten the organization going in the right direction."

Key went 18-6 in 1993, his first season, and the Yankees went 88-74. They led the league in hitting with a .279 average, their roster had many more young players, and, said Gillick, it was apparent that Michael was building something good, something that might last.

seemed to be fading smacked of Steinbrenner, circa 1985. But Michael had watched Kelly for several years and decided he had peaked, while O'Neill had not realized his potential. Over the next nine seasons, O'Neill would drive in 858 runs, Kelly 327.

Michael had been talking to the Detroit Tigers about a possible trade for left-handed pitcher David Wells in the early part of the 1995 season, and the Tigers had expressed interest in Mariano Rivera, then a young and unproven pitcher who had undergone elbow surgery in 1992, followed by a lengthy rehabilitation. Rivera threw with varying success, compiling a 5.81 ERA in six starts at Class AAA Columbus in 1994. His array of pitches was considered to be a bit above average—a good changeup and slider, a mediocre fastball that usually clocked 88 to 90 miles per hour. Michael was prepared to trade Rivera, in the right deal. But after Rivera pitched for Columbus on June 26, 1995, Michael read the reports the next morning and was stunned: Rivera's fastball had been clocked at a consistent 95 mph, sometimes touching 96 mph. Skeptical of those results, Michael called the Columbus coaching staff to make sure its radar gun was operating properly. Yes, he was assured, the reading is accurate. Still doubtful, he phoned Jerry Walker, the Tigers' scout who had seen the game. Michael chatted amiably, asking about other players and other teams, and then idly inquired if Walker had noticed what Rivera's radar readings were. Consistent 95 mph, Walker told him, and he touched 96. There was no way Mariano Rivera would be traded that summer, Michael decided. Talent existed within him that the Yankees had not seen yet; they had to be patient.

Stump Merrill was the Yankees' manager when Michael took over, and he ran the team through the 1991 season before being replaced by Buck Showalter. The lasting memory some beat writers had of Merrill came from spring training in '91: as he spoke with reporters after an exhibition, Merrill finished his meal and employed a game-used sock to clean his teeth. Showalter, on the other hand, was impeccably dressed, looking as though he just stepped out of a Nordstrom catalogue. When he appeared on a baseball card for the first time, he was disturbed by a particularly prominent pore on his nose.

Showalter's meticulousness extended to the decoration of his office.

A calendar on which he could organize his pitching rotation—and those of the Yankees' opponents—was mounted on the west wall. His lineup cards were written so neatly that they appeared to be computer-generated (in contrast to Merrill's nearly illegible scribble). Jack Curry, the beat writer for the *New York Times*, noticed that the major league media guides behind the desk were always arranged in alphabetical order. Showalter worked extraordinary hours, sometimes sleeping in his office and spending almost his entire waking day at ballparks, meeting with coaches, reviewing statistics and charts. He once complained about gaining weight, and when an acquaintance suggested he might work out more, Showalter said it wasn't possible. *When I'm on the treadmill or riding an exercise bicycle*, he explained, *I'm wondering what Tony La Russa—* the manager of the Oakland Athletics—*is doing at that exact moment to get better.*

Showalter changed the conditions and the culture of the Yankees' clubhouse, making everything first-rate. The weight room was improved, a family room was installed for the players' young children to play in during games, more attention was paid to appearance. The clubhouse looked great, and while players might have lingering concerns about their safety outside of the Yankee Stadium gates, life at the park seemed much more tenable. Make being a Yankee a great thing, Showalter told the players. Eliminate the excuses; make this a great place.

He paid attention to the evolution of the whole organization and was aware of development at every level. When a young minor league pitcher injured his arm and required surgery, Showalter penned a letter, encouraging the player—Mariano Rivera—and assuring him he had a bright future in baseball, with the Yankees. There were team meetings before every series to review the scouting reports of the opponents, and while some players increasingly grew weary of Showalter's micromanaging, they understood that the Yankees would never lose a game because their manager wasn't prepared.

Showalter, like Michael, carefully weighed the effect that players had on their teammates. He wanted players who cared about being part of a team, players who were sincere about playing well. When Showalter watched videotape of the games, he would check how the players reacted to the success of teammates. Because the home dugout in Yankee Stadium was angled toward right field, players on the bench would have to leap forward to follow the flight of a ball hit into the right field corner, and Showalter saw that when other Yankees drove balls to right, Mel Hall never moved from his spot on the bench. "You can afford to have one asshole if you surround him with 24 good guys," Showalter once told a friend. "But if you have more than that, then the assholes are going to befriend those who might be good guys, and pretty soon it's a problem." Showalter was instrumental in bringing in strong professionals like Spike Owen, who were not necessarily great athletes but were considered to be great people, and who treated teammates with respect. He wanted players who were accountable. During the 1995 season, Showalter relieved starting pitcher Jack McDowell, and as he faced the bullpen in left-center field, he heard a loud roar from the crowd. "Stano, what was that?" Showalter asked Mike Stanley, his catcher. "Well, let's put it this way," Stanley replied. "Jack just flipped off New York." McDowell had flashed the middle finger to the fans. But as the manager considered juggling his rotation to keep the offending pitcher from starting in Yankee Stadium, McDowell said no, he wanted to pitch at home, to take the heat he had created. It was the kind of attitude that Showalter loved.

After years of having managers with loose control, the Yankees needed someone rigidly structured. Showalter had never played in the major leagues and had battled and scrapped for everything he had gotten in his professional life, ascending because of his tenacious concern with detail. But that trait, some players believed, fueled his obsession with control and worries about what was being said privately and, in particular, what was being said about him. Managers traditionally exit first from their spots at the front of the buses and planes, but Showalter would wait in his seat to allow the rest of the team to depart before he left, all of them pinned by his stare; it was as if he was trying to see how they reacted to each loss, to each victory, to him. He would pull the beat writers aside, ask them questions, and then offer information, beginning in a conspiratorial tone: "Just between us girls . . ." Of course, it didn't take long for them to figure out he was feeding other writers the same information. Some felt Showalter treated prominent national columnists with much more deference than the beat reporters who covered the team daily, a dangerous habit in a city with such heavy newspaper crossfire.

The Yankees' winning percentage improved from .438 in Stump Merrill's last year to .619 in the strike-shortened season of 1994; there was a wide consensus that the Yankees were the best team in the American League that year. The next year, they would make the playoffs, winning the AL's first wildcard berth. But after they lost to Seattle in a crushing five-game series, surrendering the tying and winning runs in the bottom of the 11th inning of the decisive game, many of the veterans, weary of their manager's controlling nature, thought it was time for Showalter to go. The players had always had faith in Showalter's managing, said Jim Leyritz, even if they felt he didn't always know how to deal with his players. "What happened in the playoffs was that he made some decisions where it looked like he was protecting himself," said Leyritz. "A lot of guys started to lose confidence in him."

Steinbrenner, furious about the loss to Seattle, seemed ready to make changes anyway. Showalter's contract was about to expire, and while Steinbrenner's well-honed instinct was to fire the manager, the owner recognized his popularity; Showalter, after all, had received the loudest cheers during the pregame introductions at Yankee Stadium just before the series with Seattle began. But they would part ways—a mutually arranged divorce, executives in the organization thought. Showalter indicated he could not accept Steinbrenner's decision to fire hitting coach Rick Down and others on his staff, but the departure was also convenient for Showalter; he would have tremendous job options elsewhere. The departure was widely criticized, and Steinbrenner blanched at the public outcry over his decision to hire Joe Torre as the new manager. About a month after the change, Steinbrenner arrived on Showalter's doorstep in Pensacola, Florida, and asked him to take back his old job. *You just hired Torre as your manager,* Showalter said, and Steinbrenner assured him he would find another job for Torre, make him a vice president or something.

Showalter declined. He had been given the opportunity to mold the franchise in Arizona, making decisions on everything from the outfielders to the uniforms to the design of the infield. Showalter wanted the Diamondbacks' home to look unique, so that if a fan turned on the game or saw a highlight, he would know immediately, just by looking at the field, that he was seeing a game from Arizona's Bank One Ballpark. Showalter also wanted the Diamondbacks to have built-in advantages playing on their own field. So it came to be that Bank One Ballpark was the only field with grass laid down between the outfield fences and the warning track—a feature that fooled opposing outfielders repeatedly—and became the first modern park in the majors with a yard-wide corridor of dirt running directly from the mound to home plate, cut into the infield grass. "Fucking Buck's strip of dirt," Kevin Towers, the San Diego general manager, said, laughing.

Steinbrenner targeted Michael, as well, after the playoff loss to Seattle, tired of the constant dissent. "Why should I pay this guy to argue with me?" Steinbrenner asked an acquaintance. He told Michael he would have to take a pay cut, from $550,000 to $400,000, and also offered him a job overseeing the team's major league scouting for $150,000—a golden parachute. Michael had contractual permission to talk with other teams if another GM job became available, and almost immediately, Baltimore owner Peter Angelos expressed interest in hiring him. But Steinbrenner called Angelos and asked him not to pursue Michael. Angelos, who was trying to convince a bloc of owners to stand against the shift of a team into Washington, D.C., needed Steinbrenner's support and respected his wishes.

Michael's demotion to the scouting job, after five seasons of rebuilding the franchise into a contender, cemented Steinbrenner's reputation as an impossible boss. A half dozen executives from other teams declined to interview for the job, before former Houston GM Bob Watson took the position. Steinbrenner promised Watson he was backing away from baseball. "I took the man at his word," said Watson, who would last little more than two seasons.

Michael's quality of life improved greatly after Watson took over; he no longer had to field the daily manic phone calls from the owner, and yet he continued to wield enormous influence within the team's circle of executives. Like all of the Yankees' officials, Michael would occasionally migrate into Steinbrenner's doghouse—as when he encouraged the Yankees to re-sign David Cone to a one-year, $12 million deal in 2000, and Cone won just four games—but Steinbrenner retained an abiding trust in his judgment. Steinbrenner would continue to ignore standard baseball protocol and deny the requests of other teams to interview Michael, including an overture by the Boston Red Sox; to placate Michael, Steinbrenner would increase his salary to over half a million dollars, an exorbitant fee for a scouting executive. Although Steinbrenner had demoted Michael, there was no way he would ever allow the person most responsible for building the dynasty to join a division rival.

CHAPTER 5

BEFORE THE BOTTOM of the first inning of Game 7 of the 2001 World Series, Roger Clemens hauled his unique set of accessories to the mound. He pitched games with a mouth guard, and his body was always covered with medical wrap. He was heavily muscled, particularly in his legs, making him susceptible to strains and tears, and the wrap seemed to hold his body parts together and keep everything in line. The first time Jorge Posada worked with Clemens he had slapped the pitcher on the back and felt the wrapping; it was as if he was a mummy, Posada recalled. Like a swimmer, Clemens had the hair on his arms, legs, and chest removed, and before each game would cover much of his body with a heat balm—potent stuff with an antiseptic smell that reached the infielders.

He pitched and prepared with a linebacker's mentality, and used the days between his appearances to build physically and emotionally toward the next game. By the time his day in the rotation came around, Clemens was often so loaded with adrenaline that he would fight himself early, rushing his delivery in a frenzy of legs and arms, his eyes wide. At the outset of Game 2 of the 2000 World Series, Clemens had been in a furor, muttering obscenities to himself on the mound, staring down the Mets' batters.

In the first inning, he shattered Mike Piazza's bat with an inside fast-ball, and when the barrel tumbled to the mound, Clemens picked it up and flung it along the ground into foul territory, barely missing Piazza, who was trotting to first base, not realizing he had hit the ball foul. This instantaneous reaction created an eternity of controversy.

The Yankees' makeshift press area in the postseasons was a converted employee cafeteria, a modest-size room made even smaller by the square columns that extended from the floor to a low ceiling. A small stage was built inside a horseshoe of folding chairs, and managers and players sat at a table on the stage, underneath hot TV lights, and spoke into a microphone as they answered questions. Scores of reporters wearing fall sweaters and jackets packed the windowless room, and by the time Torre came to face the reporters on the night of the bat-throwing incident, the air was stagnant.

The manager was bombarded with questions about Clemens, his state of mind, and his true intention when he threw the bat. Though usually calm in these settings, Torre began to lose his temper, finding the tone of the questions objectionable.

Clemens had beaned Piazza in July, and there had been weeks of anticipation leading up to the rematch. The Mets' catcher had suffered a concussion, and even before Clemens faced the Mets in Game 2, Torre was furious about how television networks kept replaying the beaning, feeling the whole incident was overblown. From the stage, he looked down on the sea of reporters, and as the questions grew more pointed, Torre snapped back, particularly when it was suggested that Clemens tried to hit Piazza with the splintered bat.

"Why would he throw it at him?" Torre barked. "So he could be thrown out in the second game of the World Series? Does that make sense to anybody? Or is that too shitty a story to write?"

When Ira Berkow of the *New York Times* responded by talking about Clemens's history as an intimidator, Torre stood up and walked away from the microphone. "I'd never seen Torre lose his cool," Berkow recalled. From his seat in the upstairs press box, *New York Daily News* columnist Mike Lupica saw Torre start to melt down on a closed-circuit television and raced to an elevator to get downstairs to the press room. "I had a feeling he was going to get up out of that chair, get up and leave," Lupica said. "But I knew there was a part of him which knew that leaving an empty chair there, in front of all those reporters, was not going to look good."

And leaving would not help Clemens, who was supposed to follow Torre into the interview room; what Torre did best, as manager of the Yankees, was to relieve his players of as much pressure as he could, to support and defuse and deflect. Torre returned to his seat and continued.

He could have done what many managers and coaches would do— embrace his player while keeping him at arm's length: *I'll support Roger, he's our ace, but you'll have to ask him why he threw the bat*. But Torre kept sparring with reporters.

Lupica came into the room and asked a question. Torre answered sharply, defending the indefensible. If he had been the opposing manager, Torre allowed, he would have been angry. But as Clemens's motive and intent were questioned, Torre planted himself squarely in defense of his player's character. By the time Clemens took his turn at the microphone, the tension in the room seemed to have dissipated. "Right or wrong wasn't the issue for Torre," Lupica recalled. "I think his feeling was, 'This is what I'm supposed to do, this is where I'm supposed to be.'"

By the obsessive-compulsive standards of managers and coaches, Torre was not a hard worker. He did not sleep in his office or analyze videotape until his eyes hurt; instead, he relied upon a basic set of statistics. He did not develop or espouse new or radical theories. He was not fluent in Spanish, like many of the younger managers who had learned a second language in an effort to communicate better with players on the increasingly diverse rosters. Torre went to lunch and dinner with family and friends, spent time at home, and usually arrived at the ballpark a short time before the players. The Yankees were loaded with veteran All-Stars, which meant he didn't have to do much teaching. If there was a nine-to-five manager in the majors, Torre was it. But what he did, probably better than any other manager in baseball, was to tend to the minds of his players, work to understand their personalities, and ascertain how he could help them relax.

What Torre knew from his own experience—he had already spent 18 years as a player and 14 years as a manager when he took over the Yankees in 1996—was how long the seasons could be and how frustrations or expectations or even an isolated failure could devour a player. He could recognize or anticipate the symptoms of a possible problem, and sometimes Torre worked like a bulldozer, clearing out the emotional path for the player. Jorge Posada, the Yankees' catcher, had shared his position with veteran Joe Girardi for three seasons, and Posada was aware of the lingering doubts in the organization about whether he could handle the job himself. Torre, knowing the position would be turned over to Posada full-time in 2000, had the option of starting Girardi in Game 4 of the World Series in '99 but went with Posada—reasoning that Girardi had been on the field when the Yankees won the World Series in '96 and '98, and now it was Posada's turn. A few days later, when the Yankees were honored at City Hall after their victory parade, Torre introduced a handful of players, mostly the established stars. And then he called on Posada. "Tell them what we say at the end of our meetings, Jorge," Torre barked into the microphone.

"We grind it!" Posada yelled to the crowd, turning a fist and grinning, and the crowd roared back. Mark Newman, the Yankees' vice president, watched this and thought that was Torre's first managerial move of the 2000 season.

The Yankees were struggling at one point in 1999, and Torre called a meeting in the cramped visitors' clubhouse of Boston, telling the players to stop pressing. "Jete, you're trying too hard," he said, beginning with the shortstop as he went around the room. "Brosius, you're swinging too hard." He looked at Chad Curtis, the intense outfielder who had been told time and again during his career that he was too aggressive. Curtis cringed. If he is getting on those guys for swinging too hard, Curtis thought, he is going to lay into me. "Chad," Torre said, "you keep doing what you do," immediately disarming Curtis of his apprehension. In the years that followed, Curtis thought about that meeting, what Torre said, and how he had chosen to say it. Torre probably understood how many times Curtis had been told he was swinging too hard, and probably knew that Curtis was too far along in his career to be changed, and within a meeting in which he addressed more than a dozen players, he said the perfect words to Curtis. Torre had a gift, Curtis decided: "Social genius."

Torre's long and successful playing career—2,342 hits, 252 homers, and 1,185 RBIs—gave him a deep reservoir of credibility with his players, who appreciated Torre's steady demeanor. If a pitcher allowed a hit or a batter struck out, Torre remained placid; he never reacted to a player's mistake when its roots were purely physical. The most talented and dedicated hitter could prepare for hours before a game, smash the ball in every at-bat, and still go hitless. Slumps were inevitable, even for the greatest players. Torre often referred to his own experience in 1972, the season after he batted .363 and won the National League Most Valuable Player Award. He started slowly and never got rolling—at least not in any way similar to the way he had in '71—and finishing the year with a batting average 74 points lower. Failure was ingrained in the sport, and Torre understood he would only increase the pressure on the player by grimacing or mouthing curse words within range of the cameras that would capture images for *SportsCenter*.

He empathized with players and generally liked them, which was not always true of managers trying to motivate athletes much younger and wealthier than themselves. Some managers were embittered by the younger generation, said Todd Zeile, who played for Torre in St. Louis and New York, "but Joe was very comfortable and satisfied with what he accomplished." When Torre played with the St. Louis Cardinals, he and pitcher Bob Gibson would listen to Enos Slaughter come in on Old Timers Day and talk about how much different and better it was when he had played. Torre and Gibson agreed they didn't want to hear about "when we played," and as a manager, he did not fall into that pattern. "Players are people, and too often we talk about them as dollar signs," said Torre. "If they're not producing, then they're not doing their job. I base my opinion on a player on the effort, rather than the bottom line. Because I hit .360 and I hit .240, and I'd like to believe I tried hard both times. When you're around people, when you're around players, on a day-to-day basis, you know when they're playing hard and when they're not."

Brooklyn born and raised, Torre also understood that playing in New York, with the intense focus on daily successes and failures, was different from playing anyplace else. A batter could go hitless for a week or a month in San Diego and the fans would be forgiving. In Yankee Stadium, a player who hit a bases-loaded groundout in the first inning and then struck out in the fourth was on probation for his at-bat in the sixth. It took years for even the best Yankees to gain complete acceptance from the New York fans, who grew to despise Steinbrenner in the 1980s but then took his demanding attitude as their own in the '90s: Win today, win all the time. Andy Pettitte once mused that Mariano Rivera was his only teammate who had not been booed in Yankee Stadium; Bernie Williams, Paul O'Neill, Derek Jeter all had been targeted at one time or another.

The tradition of the team, Steinbrenner, and the enormous expectations of the fans created performance pressure on the players, Torre knew, and so he worked to relieve pressure in his clubhouse. Goose Gossage, the Yankees' closer in the late '70s and early '80s, worked for the team in spring training in his retirement. He watched Torre manage the team for a time before telling Torre how he wished he could have played for him—someone who would defuse powder-keg issues and serve as a buffer between Steinbrenner and the players. Billy Martin, the Yankees' manager for some of the years Gossage was with the team from 1978 to 1983, tended to exacerbate problems instead of solving them. Torre didn't get as much credit as he deserved, Gossage felt, for the cocoon of comfort he created for the players. "Playing with everything here in New York is difficult," said Gossage. "The pressure that goes with the tradition of the Yankees, the media, and then you throw George into the mix. I wish we had Joe. We had Billy, and that was not good. That was gasoline on the fire. We had Reggie [Jackson] and Billy, and that was the opposite of Torre."

The media horde presented a daily minefield for New York managers. Torre often said he never read stories about the team, a remark that amused his own players, who saw him go through an armful of newspapers during his daily workouts. It would have been a mistake for any manager of the Yankees or Mets, one veteran player said, not to know what was being written. And Torre easily handled media relations, always placing the interests of his players—even those he did not like—above those of the omnipresent reporters. He would give good or bad news to a player directly before telling reporters, a simple courtesy that many other managers did not extend. That way, a pitcher would not walk into a clubhouse and hear from reporters, rather than his manager, that he was being dropped from the rotation.

Torre understood that to publicly deny an obvious problem was a waste of time and would only subject himself and the team to ridicule, so he would be direct in assessing a player's mistake or slump with reporters. But after giving a technical explanation of the problem, he would use his appraisal to nudge perception. If a player, such as O'Neill, happened to be struggling, Torre's critique usually would include a subtle compliment: he's pressing too hard, Torre would say, which reinforced the idea that O'Neill cared deeply. He remained polite with reporters, never ducking questions, but he was not known as someone who chronically leaked stories to curry favor. He shielded his players as best he could from reporters when the players were struggling, and stepped aside to give them full credit when they played well, in the same calm, understated manner.

Beneath the steady demeanor, he knew that his standing as manager of the Yankees—as Steinbrenner's manager—was inherently tenuous. He had managed mostly bad teams and teams unwilling to spend big dollars on players, and he fully recognized the incredible chance that managing the Yankees represented late in his career. And while he was attuned to the needs of his players, he was also an opportunist—perhaps like all great managers and coaches—with a smart and nuanced understanding of how to manipulate. He was honest but could bend the truth, and could be nasty or ungracious to foster his own success.

Early in Torre's first season as manager, a ball fell between Paul O'Neill and Bernie Williams, and Torre removed O'Neill from the game. Michael Kay, half of the team's radio broadcast team, asked Torre in a postgame interview if he made the move to punish O'Neill. Torre did not like the reporter's tone; Kay, always direct, thought it was a natural question. The next day, Torre approached Kay in the clubhouse, with about a dozen players around, and shouted at him, accusing Kay of trying to create animosity in his clubhouse. "I don't need you to be Rona Barrett around here," Torre barked, invoking the longtime gossip columnist. Kay eventually settled his differences with Torre, but ultimately, he decided that the manager had used him—which Torre later acknowledged—by yelling at him in front of the players to show how tough he could be; rather than yell at O'Neill or Williams, better to sound off at a broadcaster and still make your point. Torre also was aware that Kay had been close to his predecessor, Buck Showalter. "I don't know if I trust you," Torre told Kay, who thought the remark—and the entire episode—revealed Torre as insecure at his core, like most first-year Yankees managers, but distinguished by his extreme shrewdness.

Despite his savvy, Torre had ways of betraying his feelings on the field. When he changed pitchers, he rated their performance with a set of almost imperceptible mannerisms often so subtle that the players did not always notice. When pleased with a pitcher, he might give a short clap of his hands as he neared the mound, look the player in the eye as he reached for the ball, and add a compliment: *Nice job, Coney*. If a pitcher simply had a bad day, battling while getting knocked around, Torre would pat him on the back as he descended the mound: *Nice effort, hang in there*. If Torre thought the pitcher had thrown passively, nibbling at the edges of the strike zone and allowing too many walks, he wouldn't look at him as he took the ball and wouldn't pat him on the back. When a young pitcher was pounded, perhaps losing his composure as the crowd began calling for a reliever, Torre sometimes bounced up the steps of the dugout, moving quickly onto the field just as the previous play ended: I am getting you out of the game as quickly as possible. "But unless you saw the guy every day," said Mike Stanton, "you couldn't tell the difference."

Players also sensed slight differences in how he felt about them as players and how much he trusted them. Derek Jeter, of course, existed in that special place in Torre's heart, along with David Cone and Paul O'Neill and Joe Girardi and Mariano Rivera and some players who weren't stars, like utilityman Clay Bellinger and pitcher Allen Watson, who had managed to earn the full measure of his trust. Some other players, including some veterans, believed Torre allowed them a smaller margin for error than he did his group of favorites.

During the 1999 World Series, in Atlanta, NBC reporter Jim Gray had a contentious on-field interview with Pete Rose directly in front of the Yankees' dugout. O'Neill, who had idolized Rose as a child growing up in Columbus, Ohio, and had played for him in Rose's last years as manager, was incensed; other Yankees were upset as well. To the players, Rose's accomplishments were staggering, and most could not understand why there was any debate about if he should be in the Hall of Fame. Whether or not he had bet on baseball, they knew what was required to accumulate 4,256 hits, through the injuries and malaise inevitable in more than two decades of long seasons. A group of Yankees agreed, during the trip back to New York, that Gray had been out of line and that they wouldn't talk to him for the remainder of the World Series. After Curtis hit the game-winning home run in Game 3, he told Gray of this embargo on the air; Gray was embarrassed and livid. Torre subsequently told reporters, in the same room in which he would defend Clemens a year later, that there had been no team meeting.

NBC was paying boatloads of money for World Series broadcast rights, and now one of its reporters was being rebuffed; network executives went ballistic, pressing Major League Baseball officials, who, in turn, came down on Torre. The Yankees' manager called a meeting of his players before Game 4. You can't say not speaking to Jim Gray was a team decision, Torre said, when it wasn't. Before Curtis could respond, Tino Martinez and other players quickly corrected Torre: many of the players had conferred, Martinez said, and this is what they had agreed to do. "OK, I didn't realize that," Torre said, and he backed off, though he asked the players to cooperate with Gray for the rest of the Series.

Curtis was not an integral player, and he was unpopular among some teammates. Earlier in the year, he had an on-field run-in with Jeter, and some teammates were uncomfortable with his intense religiosity; in fact, he would be traded in the off-season. After the meeting about Gray broke up, Curtis walked into Torre's office and asked him to publicly correct the record about what had taken place among the players; after all, when Torre initially told reporters there had been no meeting, Curtis had been left hanging. But Torre said nothing in his defense, Curtis recalled, never exonerating him. "I kind of felt like he could have done that," Curtis said, years later. "But I guess what is done is done." It was hard to imagine Torre treating Jeter, O'Neill, or other more renowned Yankees in the same way.

Inconsistency, particularly in pitchers, grated on Torre. Randy Choate had first been promoted to the major leagues in 2000 because executives thought he could develop into a strong left-handed specialist. He threw sidearm, and his breaking ball made left-handed hitters flinch. But Choate was erratic, and sometimes Torre would not use him for more than a week at a time, and when he would finally get into games it was in mop-up situations, against right-handed and left-handed hitters, a role that did not suit his stuff. Then, in his third year with the Yankees, Choate had gotten the team out of a jam and Torre met him at the top step of the dugout with a fist extended—his way of congratulating players. *That's the second time I've gotten the fist from Joe,* Choate told a reporter excitedly. "Some players might feel like they're entitled to respect and trust when they walk in the door, but Joe is one of those guys whose trust and respect you have to earn," said Todd Zeile. "Not that he's going to scorn anybody, but he certainly wants people to know the way he runs a club, the way he runs a clubhouse, and the things he expects out of you. To earn a benefit of the doubt with him, you have to do exactly that—earn it."

This ethic could be hard on the youngest players, like Shane Spencer or Ricky Ledee, and some of Torre's colleagues wished he were more patient. If a rookie went hitless for a couple of games, Torre was apt to take him out of the lineup. Late in Spencer's five-year stint with the team, the outfielder complained about never getting an extended chance to establish himself. Young players on other teams, Spencer noted, could take the field with the comfort of knowing they might get months, or even an entire season, to win or lose a job. But Torre didn't think this way—and probably couldn't think that way—as manager of the Yankees. Every loss could be the beginning of a losing streak, and as far as New York fans were concerned, two consecutive defeats constituted the seeds of a slump. Three consecutive defeats and the reporters were sure to call Steinbrenner, who was apt to take shots at the players and add more pressure to the situation. Four or five straight losses—well, then there would be complete panic surrounding the organization. Torre bore down intensely, recognizing opportunities when he could go for the jugular, and when the team lost, he made changes with his movable parts. Most of Torre's lineup was set, with Jeter, Williams, O'Neill, Martinez, and when the Yankees dropped a game or two, shifting Spencer or Ledee was one of the very few moves he could make, and Torre would do so, just to make a change.

A manager in Milwaukee or Kansas City might watch patiently as a young pitcher got pounded, knowing that all the experience would some-day pay off. San Francisco's Dusty Baker was roundly criticized for managing in the 2000 playoffs with a regular-season style: rather than use closer Robb Nen in a tie game that went into extra innings, Baker held out Nen for the possibility the Giants might take the lead later. This is the way we did it all year, Baker explained, after the Giants were quickly eliminated. Torre was more aggressive in pursuit of victories, never allowing himself to be constricted by established patterns or roles. In the mid-'90s, for example, the culture of closers dictated that they would pitch only the ninth inning, but Torre and Rivera changed that. If a Yankees lead was in its greatest peril in the eighth inning, Torre reasoned, then Rivera was most valuable in the eighth. He used Rivera to get four or five outs in some regular season games, and if the score was tied going into the ninth inning at home or on the road, Rivera would almost invariably throw the ninth, and probably the 10th; this gave the Yankees time to score the tiebreaker.

In the midst of the Yankees' 125-win season in 1998, they fell far behind Philadelphia on a July afternoon; Hideki Irabu gave up five runs before recording an out in the fourth inning. The Yankees were 57–20 at the time, and this particular game had little value within the broad scope of the long season. But the Yankees scored a run in the fourth inning and another in the sixth, cutting the lead to 5–2, and Torre sensed the Phillies were vulnerable, ready to collapse. He summoned Mike Stanton, who typically pitched when the Yankees were ahead or tied, for the seventh inning, believing that if Stanton could contain the Phillies, the Yankees would come back and win the game. It was an unusual strategy for any manager, let alone the manager of a team on a record-setting pace, and Bob Watson remarked in later years that this decision contained traces of Don Zimmer DNA—the unconventional thinking of Torre's trusted bench coach, the willingness to take a chance. Stanton allowed single runs in the seventh and eighth innings, but the Yankees scored three runs in the eighth. Now the score was 7–5, and after the Phillies added a run in the ninth, the Yankees tied the game in the bottom of the ninth when Tino Martinez hammered a three-run homer; then they went on to win in the 11th, 9–8.

Torre openly lobbied for changes on his roster, acknowledging to reporters where he thought there could be improvements—a No. 5 starter, perhaps, or a left-handed hitter off the bench. His comments exasperated some club officials; most managers made do with what they had rather than publicly air their wish lists. They wondered whether Torre appreciated how much talent he had at his disposal. "Other contenders are looking for a No. 2 starter, and our biggest problems are a No. 5 starter and the No. 8 hitter," said one executive in the summer of 2000. Torre, the officials thought, would have served the organization a little better if he committed fully to the players on the roster and tried to make it work. When he publicly cited weaknesses on the team, some executives believed, the players focused on having those weak links replaced rather than simply performing better. But Torre seemed to feel, one member of the organization noted, that as manager of the Yankees, he was entitled to the best; if he was to win every game, then he had to have the necessary weapons.

And Steinbrenner always provided for his manager. Rudy Giuliani, who came to know both Steinbrenner and Torre through his dealings with the team, felt that they made an exceptional management team—Steinbrenner the strict father figure, perhaps the only owner with enough stature to effect discipline in his organization, and Torre, "who happens to be masterful at loyalty and sticking with players and knows the game really well."

Torre and Steinbrenner shared an interest in horse racing and often made friendly conversation about topics other than baseball. They were able to maintain the camaraderie in no small part because Bob Watson, the Yankees' general manager for Torre's first two seasons, served as a buffer between the two men, screening the angry phone calls that had once unhinged Billy Martin. Similarly, Brian Cashman served as something of a sparring partner for Steinbrenner, taking the owner's verbal abuse until Steinbrenner had worn himself out.

But others in the organization thought that the relationship succeeded because Torre, with his keen insight into people, knew how to manage Steinbrenner. When Steinbrenner complained to a reporter about a player or the way the team was performing, Torre would respond, "He's the owner and he can say what he wants." And at times, that's what Steinbrenner wanted, for everybody to remember who was in charge. Previous Yankees managers had dreaded phone calls from Steinbrenner, but Torre would seek out the contact, phoning the owner even when it seemed his dissatisfaction might be simmering. When he spoke of that relationship, Torre referred back to his military service. "I've always had the capacity to calm George," he wrote in his book, *Chasing the Dream*. "I talked to him the way I did my nervous troops back in basic training in 1962. . . ."

Torre could also play on Steinbrenner's insecurities, his worry that he probably didn't know as much about baseball as his employees. Steinbrenner had long been an outsider—an outsider who wanted to be on the inside. When they were together, Torre would sometimes laugh off Steinbrenner's assessment of a player or something that happened in a game—not with blatant disrespect, according to witnesses, but with just enough sarcasm to remind Steinbrenner that he really didn't know what he was talking about. It was an effective way, a mutual friend thought, to manage up: while Torre deferred to Steinbrenner publicly, he seemed to intimidate him privately.

After the Yankees won the World Series in 1996, Torre seemed to move beyond Steinbrenner's reach. In 2002, *Newsweek* published the results of this poll question: which sports figure would be best able to lead the country? Torre finished second only to Michael Jordan, an extraordinary measure of popularity for someone who was not a current player. If Steinbrenner fired Torre, he would touch off a major public backlash, risking the goodwill he had won back since the championship run began. Steinbrenner's friends were sure he hated this loss of control. He was the owner of the team that was winning largely because of his investments of money and ambition, yet Torre, not Steinbrenner, was a beloved figure, a near deity in the sports-crazed culture of New York; it was Torre, not Steinbrenner, who got most of the credit. "Even if he fired me, he can't do anything to me," Torre mused in the spring of 2001. "To me, what I've accomplished is pretty special. Yeah, I guess you could say he's stuck with me. In two ways: he stuck *with* me, and now he's *stuck* with me."

From time to time, Steinbrenner would take subtle shots at Torre, mentioning that he hadn't won any championships before he came to the Yankees—Steinbrenner's Yankees—and that he needed to remember why he was winning. As he began negotiations with Torre on a new contract before the 2001 season, Steinbrenner told reporters, "Here's a guy who has won four out of five for you. Sure I want him. He's a great one. But you've got to always remember one thing—we keep reminding him jokingly—this is an organization. This isn't me, this isn't Joe. . . . He was in three other jobs, and he got fired from all of them. Suddenly, you become a genius? Yes, he did. He's a genius. But he understands how to handle people, and he's got a good organization of people around him. As long as he understands that, he'll be fine."

In his first six seasons as manager, Torre never reacted to the slights, repeating his mantra that Steinbrenner was the Boss, crediting him with creating the Yankees' powerful dynamic. But Steinbrenner's shots would become more forceful. Slowly but inevitably, the relationship between the two deteriorated, like a strain between neighbors—one jealous to the point of distraction because of his neighbor's beautiful home, the other finally fed up with the fact that the guy next door keeps sneaking over to curb a dog on the corner of his lawn.

Torre protected his players from Steinbrenner, not necessarily from the owner's wrath, but from the day-to-day anxiety that he created. Torre managed the team to win every day, but, as one executive noted, he never made the team feel as if any particular game was bigger than any other. Steinbrenner might chirp in the newspapers about how crucial an upcoming series against the Red Sox appeared to be, but Torre never emphasized a game against the Red Sox more or less than any other game. With Martin and previous managers, there had always been a daily crisis, pressure that weighed on the players, but with Torre, this was minimized. He had few rules, asking only that they play hard. Only occasionally did he need to arch his thick black eyebrows to get his point across. "If you deserve the Stare, you'll get it," infielder Homer Bush said in 1998. "He'll give the Stare to anybody."

The players, even those who never felt the full measure of Torre's trust, believed he treated them as people, as men with the usual range of human experience and concerns about family and work. He would joke with Luis Sojo as he passed by the player's locker, listen when Shane Spencer approached with a personal problem. He would write them notes in the off-season and send players home for funerals.

Torre once reminded the players in a team meeting to make sure they ran out every ball; he had seen some things he did not like. Young out-fielder Ricky Ledee listened, his mind flashing back to the game the previous day: Ledee had hit a fly ball to center field, running as hard as he could out of the box, rounding first and nearing second base when the ball was caught.

Ledee was sensitive, insecure. When Ledee was 12 years old, he had gotten into an argument with his father, Antonio Ledee, a musician. His father was about to depart on a trip and asked for a kiss good-bye; Ricky refused. Antonio was killed in a car accident, and the boy, haunted by his last exchange with his father, made up his mind he would never be mean to anyone again. He fretted about how others thought about him, and as Torre spoke in the meeting, he wondered if Torre had noticed his effort. Just then, Torre looked at Ledee and said, "Ricky, I saw you run hard. I believe in you. I believe in you." Years later, Ledee would vividly remember Torre's words of affirmation.

Torre helped to ease Roger Clemens's transition to the Yankees. During his tenure with Boston and Toronto, Clemens was one of the few rival players genuinely disliked by the Yankees—Cleveland's Jaret Wright and Baltimore's Jerry Hairston were two others—but the team embraced Clemens when they dealt for him at the outset of spring training in 1999. That first year, though, Clemens would struggle to get comfortable in his new surroundings.

Joe Torre and Mel Stottlemyre had always known him as a power pitcher, someone who pumped fastballs to get ahead in the count before finishing off the batter with a 90 mph splitter; instead, Clemens was relying more on his off-speed stuff, spinning sliders. During games against the Yankees, he had dominated the field, shouting encouragement to his infielders and mixing in neck-high fastballs as reminders of what he might do. But what Torre and the rest of the Yankees saw in the first months of 1999 was Roger Lite. He appeared much more quiet, more reserved. Historically a little rough with opponents, Clemens seemed on his best behavior, as if he wanted to fit in with the more polite Yankees. Torre would long suspect, as well, that he was secretly nursing some leg injuries. At the end of July '99, Clemens, the winner of back-to-back Cy Young Awards in '97 and '98, had an ERA of 4.78. It got to the point, Andy Pettitte recalled, where you were sitting in the dugout and thinking, C'mon, let's see it.

Torre and Stottlemyre kept encouraging Clemens to relax, to be himself, and trust his fastball again. As Clemens heard more and more boos in Yankee Stadium, Torre would acknowledge his struggles to reporters but also kept referring to the pitcher's long record of success, making it clear he expected Clemens to come around, almost sounding as if he was speaking to him through the newspapers. Torre continued this campaign until Clemens regained his dominance and his animated style in the middle of 2000.

AT THE OUTSET of Game 7 of the 2001 World Series, Clemens flung his full intensity at the Diamondbacks, but without the reckless frenzy that sometimes derailed him early in games. He was pitching with a bad shoulder and hamstring, but injuries seemed to make him focus, concentrate on keeping his body and mechanics in control. Opening the bottom of the first inning, he pumped a 95 mph fastball for a strike with his first pitch to Tony Womack, Arizona's leadoff hitter, and when he tried his first split-fingered fastball, the ball sank at 91 mph and Womack popped up to short center field. One out. "Right out of the gate, I had it," Clemens recalled months later. "I knew I had it, and I knew it was going to be a great challenge; I had to just keep momentum on our side."

Craig Counsell, the Arizona second baseman, was the second hitter for the Diamondbacks, his hands lifting the bat high over his head in his stance. The count was 1-1, and Posada signaled for a fastball. Clemens rejected the suggestion but reassuringly, a slow shake of his head: no, no. Posada ran through other signs, and when he signaled for a splitter, Clemens nodded emphatically, still in rhythm: YES, YES, you got it. Counsell swung over the splitter and whacked a hard ground ball along the first-base line. Tino Martinez tried to glove the bouncer but dropped it, chasing the ball into foul territory as Counsell and Clemens raced toward first base.

There were land mines in this play for Clemens. He had become more susceptible to leg injuries as he had aged, and when he had to cover first base, competing in a sprint against the base-runner, all of the muscles in his legs tightened, sometimes straining, sometimes pulling. Pitchers covering first base usually curled the end of their routes, so that they could run parallel to the baseline without blocking the runner. But because Clemens was losing speed in the last years of his career, he often ran a straight line to first base, a path that put him on a collision course with the batter. Opposing base-runners usually tried to avoid him because of his size, but sometimes they spiked him inadvertently. Clemens was at the greatest risk when covering first base, and after he finished these plays, Torre and Stottlemyre would watch him closely, bracing themselves as they looked for a telltale limp.

Now, with Counsell rushing down the first-base line, Clemens reached the bag, stretched for the flip from Martinez, and dropped the ball as Counsell slid into the bag, his spikes nicking the back of Clemens's left foot and right calf. Clemens walked back to the mound, head down, assessing the damage. Everything was OK.

Counsell took his lead from first, and Luis Gonzalez stood in to hit. The count to Gonzalez reached 2 balls and 1 strike—a good count for the base-runner to break from first base, because of the diminished chance of a pitchout. Clemens threw to first three times, trying to keep Counsell close, then challenged Gonzalez with fastballs, including five straight at 95 mph. Gonzalez hit three foul balls, and it wasn't until the seventh pitch of the at-bat that he grounded weakly to first base; Counsell advanced to second. Two outs.

Clemens's plan against Matt Williams, the next hitter, was just as transparent. He got ahead in the count and began throwing splitters, Williams fouling them off three times after he reached two strikes. Clemens's face began to glisten with sweat.

Williams finally swung over a splitter, Clemens's 21st pitch of the inning. The Diamondbacks hadn't scored, but they had made Clemens work hard, with the play at first and the pickoff attempts and all the foul balls. Schilling, who had thrown only 12 pitches in the top of the first, quickly retired the Yankees with just seven pitches in the second inning, striking out Martinez, getting Posada on a fly to left, retiring Spencer on a drive to the center field warning track. So far, so easy for Schilling.

Clemens lugged his accessories back to the mound for the bottom of the second.

CHAPTER 6

LUIS SOJO stood at the railing of the Yankees' dugout as he watched Game 7, his major league career just about at an end. After trying in vain over the years to find a replacement for him, the Yankees had finally found someone younger and faster, Enrique Wilson, who would grow into the role in which Sojo had excelled.

Sojo was 36 years old, but even when he was younger his hitting style was probably the ugliest in the game. When he swung, Sojo looked like someone falling out of a boat, the upper half of his thick body tilting forward awkwardly, his rear end sticking out, the bat appearing too heavy in his hands, as if it were a 12-foot oar. He almost always managed to make contact when he batted, though, and he had terrific hands and a strong arm, and could sit for weeks and still play confidently. He had an acute sense of humor, too, and was easygoing and gregarious and loved the game, qualities that made him enormously popular within the Yankees' family.

When the Yankees let Sojo go after the 1999 season and looked for another utilityman, Bernie Williams's wife, Waleska, lobbied Brian Cashman to bring him back, telling him how much Sojo and his family were missed and what a positive influence he was. For the 2000 season, however, the Yankees committed to giving D'Angelo Jimenez a chance to be the utilityman, and Sojo signed with the Pittsburgh Pirates, one of baseball's many struggling small-budget franchises.

The Pirates had been one of the best young teams in the early 1990s, winning the National League East three consecutive seasons, but could not afford to keep stars Barry Bonds and Bobby Bonilla, who signed big-money deals with other teams. The franchise declined: as Sojo joined the Pirates, Pittsburgh had endured seven consecutive losing seasons, and in that time, the team's payroll had increased from $20.5 million to $30.1 million. The payroll of the plush Atlanta Braves, by comparison, had grown from $46.9 million to $94.6 million.

What Sojo saw in Pittsburgh stunned him. The Pirates' players, he thought, operated day to day with absolutely no expectation of success, no belief they might actually make it to the postseason and contend for a championship. The Yankees were obsessed with playing deep into October, but the Pirates seemed to have the hope beaten out of them, Sojo thought. "They had a lot of young players who did not have the mentality to win," Sojo said, "because they just didn't know what it takes." The Pirates had some decent talent, Sojo believed, and because they were members of the weak NL Central, he thought it was enough to contend—with young slugger Brian Giles, catcher Jason Kendall, pitchers Jason Schmidt and Kris Benson, a decent defensive infield. "But sometimes I think they just didn't care," said Sojo. "We win, we lose, they don't give a shit. They just didn't think they could win. For a couple of months, we're a few games back out of first place. When I see that, I'm thinking, 'We've got a chance to win this thing.' It's the type of thing that gets you pumped up. But what I saw is they just didn't care."

This malaise and hopelessness were taking root among many small-budget teams during this era, when teams were increasingly defined—and defining themselves—by the size of their payroll. The problem seemed to be slowly eroding the popularity and credibility of the sport in many cities. When teams like Kansas City, Tampa Bay, Pittsburgh, and Detroit competed against the large-market teams, they were like a local hardware store vying against Home Depot. All they could do, it seemed, was find their niche in the marketplace, maintain a payroll commensurate with their modest revenue stream, and try to hold on. But the integrity of Major League Baseball's product, at least in smaller cities, was diminishing.

Traditionally, most of the patrons of their business—the fans—bought tickets expecting legitimate competition. When Royals manager Tony Muser spoke at public functions and addressed frustrated fans, he would not pretend the Royals were a team on the cusp of greatness. Instead, he talked about Kansas City's talented young players and promised that they would always play hard. It was a tactic that many teams began to adopt around Major League Baseball at the turn of the 20th century: market the game. Your team might stink, but you could always sell baseball, they thought.

But attendance and television ratings continued to sag. Most fans did not seem to view baseball as art, as many league executives would have it; rather, they held fast to the expectation that there should be competition, and the reality was that each year, fewer and fewer teams seemed to have a legitimate chance to win the World Series. In 1999, all eight of the teams that made the playoffs ranked among the 10 highest payrolls.

The budget of the Kansas City Royals was $36 million in 1998—about half of what the Yankees would spend that season—and the financial divide between the two teams would grow to more than $100 million in the next few years. Muser was sure this affected the morale of his players. When he had played in the 1970s, Muser thought, even the worst teams had reason to be optimistic in spring training; a good trade, a hot young pitcher, and a fast start could close the gap quickly. Two decades later, however, the payroll disparity made for an unbridgeable gap on the field.

The Yankees could spend millions of dollars on the back end of their rotation and millions more on proven middle relievers and catchers. Those were luxury items for low-budget teams, which filled half their rosters with unproven players or fringe major-leaguers—inexperienced pitchers, in particular, who usually were still learning "and had no idea what they were doing," said Rey Sanchez, the shortstop for Kansas City. For teams like the Royals, the disparity did not manifest itself solely in their inability to pay stars like Jeter or Clemens, but also in the fact that they could not afford to surround their young players with established veterans. "A smaller-market club has younger players, and younger players have less experience," Muser said. "They don't have all the attributes they should to create the type of morale they need. They couldn't say, 'We can beat these guys, we can beat the Yankees.'" When the Royals played the Yankees, Muser said, "it was almost like there was a feeling on the club that we were beaten before the game started. Our players didn't believe we could beat the Yankees."

One or two low-budget teams might have a legitimate chance to contend from year to year—"window of opportunity" became the small-market mantra—but by 2001, almost all of the low-budget teams, like Kansas City, would open each season virtually assured they could not compete over the long summer. Muser and other managers in the small markets would try to convince their players that the club was in a developmental mode, that the franchise was building toward something good. But each year, these clubs would shed blossoming players to meet budgets, the theoretical finish line always moving further out of reach. "It was David against Goliath," said Phil Garner, who managed the Milwaukee Brewers and the Detroit Tigers for a little over 10 seasons. "I never felt like I never had a chance, but what I said was that if you put a gun to my wife's head and asked, Did we really have a chance to win? I would say you were betting a long shot."

The Milwaukee players attributed everything rotten in their small-budget existence to what they called "the Brewer Factor." If the postgame meal was terrible, it was the Brewer Factor. If a flight was particularly bad, or the team lost five games in a row, or the adoring women in the lobby of the team hotel were not particularly good-looking, it was the Brewer Factor. A writer working on a story on the Brewers once saw a veteran player step out of the Milwaukee clubhouse late for pregame stretching, and when the writer mentioned the player might get in trouble for this offense, the player smirked and shook his head. "The Brewer Factor," the player said. It really didn't make a bit of difference in the standings if any of the Milwaukee players arrived on time.

The financially powerful teams hoarded pitching, which had not always been possible before the advent of free agency in 1976. There had been some instances in which teams sold off their best pitchers, the Philadelphia Athletics dealing Lefty Grove to the Boston Red Sox in the midst of the Depression being the most notable example. But weaker teams often kept their best pitchers because of baseball's reserve clause, which tied players to their teams indefinitely. The hapless Washington Senators always featured Walter Johnson, the Phillies had Robin Roberts, the Cleveland Indians boasted Bob Feller and Bob Lemon, and the pathetic Brooklyn Dodgers teams had Dazzy Vance for more than a decade. Free agency changed that. In 1999, the three teams with the best cumulative earned run averages in each league were among the highest 12 payrolls, a reliable trend.

The low-budget Oakland Athletics were an exception, developing three excellent young starting pitchers simultaneously: Mark Mulder, Tim Hudson, and Barry Zito. But while most executives with other teams admired the Athletics' success and the aggressiveness of General Manager Billy Beane, they did not look at Oakland as an inspiration for how a championship-caliber club could be built cheaply. Rather, the Athletics were widely viewed as an aberration, the flukey recipients of the extraordinary good fortune needed to have three young pitchers mature into stardom and remain injury-free at the same time. And the Athletics had, in fact, wanted to draft right-hander Ben Sheets instead of Zito in 1999, picking Zito only after failing to reach a contract agreement with Sheets before the draft. Sheets developed arm trouble that slowed his development in the first seasons of his career; if the Athletics had been able to pick him instead of Zito, they would have been like many low-budget teams, lacking depth in their rotation. The team had not necessarily anticipated such greatness in Hudson, either, drafting him in the sixth round, after they had taken seven other pitchers, including first-round disappointments Chris Enochs and Eric DuBose. Oakland would reach the postseason in four consecutive seasons from 2000 to 2003, but they failed to win a single playoff series, their erratic October play often reflecting the lack of experience on their roster.

The franchise had paid a heavy toll along the way, enduring terrible seasons in order to be in position to draft Mulder second overall in 1998 and then Zito ninth overall the next year, seasons that further damaged the popularity of the team. Oakland went 65-97 in 1997 and 74-88 the next year; their attendance ranked last and then next to last in the American League. Even when the Athletics began winning, the franchise seemed to be viewed with some skepticism by fans: Oakland's attendance would barely creep over two million, substantially less than in the late '80s and early '90s.

Scott Brosius, who played the first seven years of his career with the Athletics, recalled the frustration the Oakland players felt whenever the Yankees made a midseason deal for a star player. "You'd be like, 'Hey, they got *this* guy?'" Brosius said. "All of a sudden, when I got to the Yankees, my tone changed. They traded for Chuck [Knoblauch], and I was like, 'All right.' As good as it felt buying players, it can be just as frustrating being on the other side. The bottom line in Oakland was, we knew that when we played the Yankees, if we did everything right—everything—we might win two of three games. We *might*. And that's a tough way to go into a series. We weren't on even ground."

More instructive, and more daunting, was the small-budget model of the Cleveland Indians. The franchise was a wreck, failing to appear in the postseason for four decades, its attendance rarely climbing over 1.2 million. John Hart took over as general manager in 1991, and the Indians developed a formidable cast of young position players, signing them to long-term deals that enabled Cleveland to control the players through their arbitration-eligible years. The Indians had a manageable middle-class payroll and a dangerous team when they opened Jacobs Field in 1994, a beautiful park, which fans filled. The labor war that wiped out the World Series that year hardly dampened the enthusiasm for the Indians, who went 100-44 in 1995, their attendance averaging 39,483 per game. The team would win its division in five of the next six seasons, play in the World Series in 1997, and finish first or second in the AL in attendance in six consecutive seasons, selling out a major-league record 455 consecutive home games. Before the 2002 season, however, club ownership determined that it could not maintain the spiraling budget, which had climbed from $16.1 million in 1993 to $94.4 million. The Indians had operated their franchise extraordinarily well, done everything the right way, and yet determined they could not sustain a payroll as high as the Yankees' or other high-payroll teams' while absorbing enormous financial losses. They could not keep up.

Within two years, the Indians cut their payroll to roughly $60 million, and attendance fell by more than 50 percent. "We had an owner who allowed us to stay within our means, but when we got to that $85 million mark [in payroll], we started going in the red, and that's even with sellouts," said Hart. "What happens with fans is that they start to back off a little bit, because they've had their heart broken before." Hart thought the fans' patience for rebuilding a franchise had diminished greatly; they would not subsidize a low-budget loser.

The window of opportunity for the small-payroll teams continued to shrink as the disparity increased, Hart and others thought. The big-budget teams could make mistakes, cover over problems with cash, while less prosperous teams could be crushed by one mistake. As San Diego attempted to make the playoffs in August 1998, Padres general manager Kevin Towers placed a waiver claim on Toronto reliever Randy Myers, believing that Atlanta might grab him. But the Blue Jays did not withdraw Myers from waivers, as Towers expected; instead, they sent the pitcher and his $6 million annual salary to the Padres, and for the next two years, Myers was an unmovable albatross on the San Diego roster, accounting for 13 percent of their budget. Low-budget teams that made mistakes—like the Pirates and Kansas City—destroyed any chance they had to contend. Richard Jacobs, the Indians' owner, told Hart that competing financially with the Yankees and other high-payroll teams was like walking into Lake Erie against taller contenders: your hat will start to float a lot sooner than those of the guys from New York.

The players understood: if you wanted to have a chance to win and get paid, you went to the Yankees or another high-payroll team. Chuck Knoblauch, drafted and developed by the Twins, forced his way out of Minnesota after the 1997 season, demanding a trade; the Twins were compelled to make a deal with the Yankees, who had the resources necessary to make the trade. Roger Clemens would do the same thing, pushing Toronto to deal him after the 1998 season. Except for Ken Griffey Jr.'s trade to Cincinnati in 2000, there were no examples, on the other hand, of talented players demanding they be dealt to low-budget teams.

The Yankees made Tony Muser's job as Kansas City manager all but impossible. But he liked watching them play, admiring their ruthlessness. You could punch a stopwatch when Jeter rolled a harmless grounder to shortstop and find that he ran just as hard to first base as when he smashed a line drive into the right field corner. If Jeter had been the exception among the Yankees, there still would have been incredible value in his effort, Muser believed—a star playing with consistent passion. But all the Yankees seemed to play this way, from Bernie Williams to Tino Martinez to Joe Girardi, concentrating on their at-bats against the Royals as if they were in the postseason. It was a show of respect for Kansas City, Muser thought, that the Yankees took the games against the Royals so seriously, and respect for the game itself. "They never bullied anybody," Muser said. "They were never pompous. They came to beat you, and you knew that, but they never played the role of the neighborhood bully."

Muser would find himself defending the Yankees when friends complained about their enormous payroll. "Yeah, they have money, and yeah, they have talent," Muser said. "But don't overlook the effort. Their inner heart is effort." The Yankees made it a point to shrink their egos, Muser thought, and worked to play together, concentrating on accomplishing whatever was necessary to win each game. "That was impressive to me," said Muser. "They could play little ball"—advancing runners with ground balls, running aggressively on the bases—"and that takes intelligence. They could play big ball, too. There was no selfishness that was portrayed. There's always jealousy, because they're winning and you are not winning—that's a human tendency. But in the big picture, you respected them for how they played."

In his time with the Pirates, Luis Sojo missed the Yankees badly, missed the feeling that each game mattered, the expectation that they were going to win that day. When the Yankees reacquired him in August 2000, he felt as if he had been rescued, and he played an important role in the last weeks of the season. In Game 5 of the World Series against

the Mets, Torre double-switched Sojo into the lineup in the eighth inning. Jose Canseco, with 446 career home runs, was on the bench to
pinch-hit, but Torre used Sojo, feeling sure that he would make contact.
Sojo would come to bat against Al Leiter in the top of the ninth inning,
the score tied, two runners on base and two out, and bounce a single
through the middle. Posada scored the eventual championship-clinching
run, Brosius followed when the throw home hit Posada, and a couple of
hours later, Sojo grinned happily at his locker, his short, bristled hair
shiny with Champagne. If the Yankees didn't want him back for the
2001 season, Sojo said, he would retire. He would never play anywhere
else. Never again.

CHAPTER 7

STEVE FINLEY led off the bottom of Game 7's second inning against Roger Clemens, swiping his left foot through the dirt of the batter's box and taking a practice swing before staring out at the mound. Clemens wore a shadow of beard; as a kid, he had loved the feeling of his step-father's scratchy face, so he would let his facial hair grow for each of his starts as a token of remembrance. He wasn't entirely motivated by nostalgia, though: the beard made him look a little more sinister, and like everything Clemens did, it seemed designed to intimidate hitters. He stood on the mound with his feet set apart, six feet four, his massive 235 pounds shifted slightly on one hip, in the stance of a gunfighter. He wore a black glove—not soft brown, but black—and as he glared at the catcher for the sign, he held his hands directly in front of his face, so that hitters could only faintly see his hazel eyes, hidden underneath the bill of his cap. Clemens gnawed on his mouth guard, his jaw grinding underneath his cheeks. Then, as he released the ball, the lips on the right side of his mouth curled back like a Doberman's. Batters never knew for sure whether Clemens was going to buzz his fastball across the outside corner or just underneath their chin.

But despite his swagger, Clemens was pitching Game 7 injured. He had strained his shoulder lifting weights weeks before, and the inflammation extended from his right collarbone to just above his bicep. Most of the time, Clemens preferred to feel the aching, so he could have a greater understanding of what was happening inside his body. But before Game 7 he took some medication for the swelling and some for the pain—the first time he had done that in his career, Clemens would say months later—and he was surprised at how good he felt, throwing easily. His first fastball to Finley in the second inning was 94 mph, too high. He came back with a sinking fastball, and Finley smashed a grounder toward shortstop. The ball was hit with a lot of topspin and skidded across the dirt when it bounced in front of Jeter, staying low. But Jeter jabbed his glove at the bouncer, grabbed it, and threw to first base. One out.

Clemens at 39 was still very much the same hard-throwing pitcher he had been when he had first come to the majors in 1984. As a 22-year-old rookie for the Boston Red Sox, he had struck out 126 batters in 133.1 innings—8.5 strikeouts per nine innings—and in 2001 Clemens had struck out 213 batters in 220.1 innings during the regular season, 8.7 strikeouts per nine innings. Many of the great power pitchers who had reached the majors at the same time as Clemens, or after—Dwight Gooden, David Cone, Jose Rijo, Bret Saberhagen—were either fading or retired altogether, their stuff diminished, but Clemens had gone 20-3 for the Yankees in 2001, a performance that would win him his sixth Cy Young Award.

John Elway and Michael Jordan, great stars in other sports, had finished their careers like Clemens, still excelling at an advanced age. Clemens, however, would never be the object of such broad affection. He was disliked by some opponents, booed in Boston for leaving the Red Sox, flatly despised by Mets fans. He was an endangered species in an era of offense, a pitcher who was willing to fill the role of villain and knock down some hitters.

But Clemens's persona and raw power obscured his precision and intense pursuit of his craft. He often talked as if somebody was trying to catch up with him—hitters on other teams, pitchers chasing his record of success—and constantly sought an edge.

When there were no runners on base, most pitchers would take just one sign from a catcher—one finger for fastball or two fingers for a curveball, and so on; whenever an opposing runner reached second base, most pitchers would then switch to a sequence of three signs, to prevent the runner from stealing the signals. But Clemens asked his catchers to give a sequence of signs *all the time*, regardless of whether there were runners on base; scouts thought he was the only major league pitcher who did this. Clemens figured that somehow, somebody would probably be watching him, trying to steal his signs and break him down.

He honed his mechanics incessantly, with a primary goal of standing tall over the rubber so he could throw on a downward plane. He had once gone to Birmingham, Alabama, to be tested at the American Sports Medicine Institute's laboratory, where cameras surrounded him and recorded his motion in minute detail. Glenn Fleisig, the director of research, who had pinpointed flaws in the mechanics of thousands of professional and amateur pitchers—an arm angle, the placement of the hand—found Clemens to be entirely exceptional. Each piece of his delivery was in almost optimal position.

Clemens loved to think about pitching and talk about pitching, and some members of the Yankees' support staff greatly enjoyed watching games with him because he would tell them what he was seeing, in the hitters and in the pitchers. Even though some of the staff had been around baseball for years, they felt he opened a portal to a higher level of understanding. He took nothing for granted and his attention to detail was extensive, like some slop-throwing lefty who had to carefully pitch to the weaknesses of hitters. He gave himself every possible chance to succeed, Stottlemyre thought, from his workout regimen to his study of the opposing hitters and the umpires, and even his own catchers. "He factored all of that in," Stottlemyre said, referring to Clemens's written and mental notes. "Kept it all right there in his computer." The Yankees' pitching coach believed Clemens was as close to being a machine as was humanly possible. Torre thought Clemens occasionally was overprepared, concerning himself too much with the vulnerability of the hitters when he could have simply overpowered them. But this was part of the package of his greatness: Clemens as perfectionist wanted to win the mental battle as well as the physical challenge.

He worked on his conditioning year-round, running miles for distance and time, burning through thousands of stomach crunches and hundreds of sets of shoulder exercises. Clemens had a powerful arm and a strong frame suited for pitching, but what most impressed teammates and rival players was his mental drive. Andy Pettitte was a decade younger than Clemens and could already feel himself looking forward to the time when he could go home for good and play golf. He joined Clemens in his workouts—a career-altering choice, Pettitte thought, because it raised his level of preparation dramatically—and he marveled that his older friend cared so much after two decades in the majors. Torre thought Clemens had somehow maintained a young boy's desire to play baseball instead of allowing the game to become drudgery.

Each time they throw a baseball hard, pitchers damage their arms, tearing their bodies microscopically, the damaged cells leaking fluid. Calcium slowly collects in those places where there is tearing and leaking, affecting the muscle in the same way that ice cracks a sidewalk. The calcium hardens and impedes movement, the muscles weaken, and the explosive movements of the legs and shoulders are retarded, affecting the pitcher's ability to cock his arm before he throws, to accelerate his hand forward, to decelerate in his follow-through. Arm speed is lost, pitching speed is diminished. This is the toll of aging, inevitably extracted.

Except in the case of traumatic injury, the slowing of the fastball is generally gradual, maybe two or three miles per hour every few years. A pitcher who throws 95 mph at age 31 throws 90 mph at age 36. Tom Seaver, the Hall of Fame pitcher who was Clemens's teammate in Boston in 1986, estimated that if you once threw 75 good fastballs per game, you probably were down to 15 good fastballs late in your career.

But as he neared his 40th birthday, Clemens's fastballs were still in the mid-90s. By working out so much, trainer Gene Monahan thought, Clemens was like a race car, "keeping his body lubed, the whole thing running smoothly. He couldn't do what he does if he wasn't as dedicated as he is in fighting back. . . . He's putting the so-called aging process on hold."

Mentally, Clemens was just as resilient and relentless, sometimes frustrating reporters by refusing to acknowledge his own poor performances; if he walked five and allowed seven runs in three-plus innings, he was still apt to declare that he threw the ball well. But it was apparent that while Clemens was outwardly defensive, never conceding anything to outsiders, he was much more truthful with himself and worked to make necessary adjustments. And Clemens asked pitching coach Mel Stottlemyre, generally tactful to the point of fibbing a little, to be completely frank with him—"brutally honest," Stottlemyre said. If he thought his fastball was a little short, Clemens wanted to know so he could factor that into the decisions he made early in the game. If Clemens thought he was losing control of the game, he would make adjustments.

One of the tools of change he used was the brushback pitch. He would use it to rattle a batter who kept leaning over the plate and fouling off pitches low and away, or sometimes he would do it in retaliation for one of his own teammates getting hit. But most often, it seemed, Clemens used this tactic simply to instill fear, to change the competitive dynamic. Roberto Alomar once ducked underneath a Clemens fastball, and as he kneeled on the dirt in the batter's box, he stared toward the mound angrily. The ball had been behind Alomar's neck, the kind of pitch that hitters fear most because their instinct is to duck backward. Clemens looked at Alomar, his face blank.

At times, the intimidation tactics were even more direct. In 1997, when Clemens was with the Toronto Blue Jays, he reached second base at Shea Stadium, and the Mets repeatedly ran pickoff plays, forcing Clemens to keep lurching back to second in an attempt to wear him out. Finally, Clemens turned to shortstop Rey Ordonez and informed him that if the Mets tried another pickoff, Clemens would smoke him with a fastball. (The exchange did not escalate from there.) Before the Yankees traded for him, they viewed Clemens as a master of the cheap shot, someone who might throw at hitters whenever he got frustrated, without fear of retribution; the designated hitter rule ensured that Clemens would never have to bat. He had drilled Derek Jeter with a pitch during a spring training game in 1998, and after Scott Brosius had repeatedly gotten hits off him during the regular season, Clemens had hit him in a September game, a pitch that eventually led to a bench-clearing fracas.

On June 9, 2000, Mets catcher Mike Piazza launched a grand slam off Clemens and then added a single, giving him 7 hits in 12 at-bats against Clemens, with three home runs. Teammates assumed Clemens would change his strategy the next time he faced the Mets a month later, and sure enough, he threw high and inside to two of three batters he faced. Piazza led off the next inning. "Everybody knows Mike's had success against me," Clemens would say later. "I wanted to pitch him inside." This was more than inside: Clemens hit him just above the bill of the cap with a 92 mph fastball, and Piazza flopped onto his back, his body limp. As the Mets screamed at Clemens from their dugout, he squatted on the mound and looked down at the dirt.

Later, Clemens tried to call Piazza from the Yankees' clubhouse, using the phone in the trainer's room. He would never beg for forgiveness, of course; it was not his way to concede anything, to acknowledge any weakness. He just wanted to check on Piazza. But when Piazza was told who was on the line, he uttered a profanity and made it clear he would not accept the call, and at a press conference the next day, Piazza said he could no longer respect Clemens. "I thought it was definitely intentional," Piazza said. "I could respect the fact that he's throwing inside. I could respect the fact of getting hit, getting hit in the ribs or the body. I know that's a part of the game. I accept that and don't have a problem with that. But I feel there's a difference between that and almost ending my career."

Over time, Clemens became angry that Piazza had not only rejected his apology but had vilified him. Years later Clemens said, "So many guys have been hit in baseball, and we only know of one that held a press conference." Torre thought this illustrated a difference between Clemens and some of the intimidating pitchers of past generations: while the likes of Bob Gibson and Don Drysdale were remorseless and didn't care what other players thought, Clemens wanted opponents to respect him and was sensitive to how they perceived him. If Piazza had acknowledged Clemens in some way, both players might put the incident behind them. But Piazza said nothing—"Why the fuck should he?" Mets manager Bobby Valentine once asked—and the tension festered, building to their highly anticipated confrontation in the 2000 World Series.

Clemens pitched exceptionally in his last two starts that fall, throwing what he believed to be the best game of his career in the AL Championship Series, against Seattle. Clemens usually needed an inning or two to harness his fastball, and as he settled in, his velocity would rise from 92–93 mph to 94–95 mph. But Clemens's first fastball against the Mariners in Game 4 was 96 mph, a neon announcement that he had great stuff. He felt terrific throwing in the cool temperature he loved—it was 56 degrees—and driving his legs on a mound that both he and Pettitte liked to work on. (As large pitchers, they had found that the front apron of some mounds tended to crumble underneath their constant pounding during a game, but this mound, constructed with clay from the Pacific Northwest and a Mississippi mud composition called Gumbo, held together.) He struck out Stan Javier and Al Martin to open the game. Alex Rodriguez batted third for Seattle, and Clemens hurled a 97 mph fastball in the vicinity of A-Rod's jaw. Rodriguez fell backward, spinning away from the plate. He stared at Clemens. At the Yankees' dugout. At the pitcher again.

Clemens threw his next pitch in almost the exact same spot, driving Rodriguez away from the plate again. Clemens allowed one hit, in the seventh, when Martin pulled a line drive into the right field corner, just over the outstretched glove of Tino Martinez; from the mound, Clemens could hear the ball nick off Martinez's mitt. That was the only hit the Yankees' pitcher would allow. He struck out 15, at least one in every inning, his fastball reaching 99 mph. Edgar Martinez said after the game that he had struck out on a pitch he never saw. Seattle catcher Joe Oliver would later say he thought Clemens essentially beat the Mariners when he threw those two inside pitches to Rodriguez.

His next start was against the Mets, in Game 2 of the World Series, and before Piazza even came to bat in the first inning, Clemens seemed to be in a competitive froth, muttering to himself. He fired an inside fastball to Piazza, and Piazza's bat disintegrated, spraying splinters, with the barrel tumbling toward the mound.

Clemens lowered his glove and intercepted the bat, then turned and whipped the barrel sidearm across the foul line, a few feet in front of Piazza, who had started running toward first. The Mets catcher turned and looked at Clemens, wide-eyed with shock. Clemens asked home plate umpire Charlie Reliford for a new ball, but Piazza had begun walking toward him. "What's your problem?" Piazza asked aloud as players from both teams started surrounding the two; there was some shouting and jostling but no fight.

Clemens said after the game that he initially confused the bat for the ball, and he had meant only to discard the bat and throw it into the on-deck circle. But some of his teammates thought there was more to it than that. David Cone tried to imagine what was going through Clemens's mind, after months of buildup. Clemens, he thought, had just reacted emotionally after wrecking Piazza's bat. "It was like he was saying, '*Get that shit out of here!*'" Cone said. "He just grabbed the bat and threw it away without thinking. . . . I think he was just overloaded, over-pumped, overhyped up, like a middle linebacker starting a University of Texas football game. The thing that was lost in the shuffle was what an incredible pitch it was—100 mph, right on the thumbs." Cone didn't believe Clemens ever intended to hit Piazza with the bat. He was not quite in control, perhaps, but not quite out of control, either.

As that inning ended, Clemens continued talking with the home plate umpire, smiling, and then retreated to the Yankees' clubhouse, where Stottlemyre saw him; he was shaking, perhaps realizing how close he had come to being ejected. Clemens calmed himself, refocused, and allowed only two hits in eight scoreless innings, striking out nine. The bizarre incident was the primary topic of conversation after the game, and as Valentine answered questions about Piazza and Clemens, he paused and mentioned what an unbelievable game Clemens had pitched—an afterthought, almost. Nobody wants to applaud the quick draw of the black-hatted gunfighter.

But injuries would rob Clemens of his dominance in the postseason of 2001. Pitching against Oakland in Game 1 of the Division Series, he had strained a hamstring and had to work carefully to keep from exacerbating the problem. Before he pitched Game 5 of the Division Series against the Athletics, Clemens agreed with Brosius and Martinez that he would not field any ball hit in front of the mound; they would have to take everything. The Yankees won that game and also his next start, in Game 4 of the Championship Series against Seattle. His hamstring gradually improved, and he beat the Diamondbacks in Game 3 of the World Series, beginning the Yankees' comeback in New York.

With the Yankees leading the best-of-seven series 3 games to 2, Pettitte started Game 6 with a chance to close out the World Series. But the Diamondbacks ripped him for four runs in the first two innings, and kept piling on, building a 12–0 lead after three innings. Stottlemyre sought out Clemens in the sixth. "Well, it looks like we're going to have a Game 7, so why don't you go," Stottlemyre said. Clemens dressed and took his family to dinner. With everyone painfully aware the weight of the World Series would fall on him the next night, the table was mostly quiet, but Clemens's head was cluttered with thoughts. He had no idea how he would pitch to the Diamondbacks; their hitters seemed to be on everything. But he put that aside and made a few jokes, and the atmosphere at the table finally lightened a bit. His family went horseback riding on the morning of Game 7, while he stayed in his room and studied videotape before going outside and stretching on the grass of the golf resort where the Yankees were staying; his sore shoulder, he discovered, felt great.

With one out in the bottom of the second, he faced Arizona right fielder Danny Bautista, getting ahead in the count 1 ball and 2 strikes. But Clemens, anxious to close out Bautista, threw two splitters low and then fired a head-high fastball for a walk. Mark Grace, a good contact hitter, was next to bat for Arizona, and Arizona manager Bob Brenly signaled for a hit-and-run. Bautista broke from first, and Grace punched a fastball into left field, a single; Bautista stopped at second base.

Runners at first and second, one out. Arizona's No. 8 and No. 9 hitters, Damian Miller and Curt Schilling, were due to hit, so Clemens could still easily pitch out of trouble, if he stayed in control.

But he rushed his first pitch to Miller, a fastball sailing high. Posada stood and lifted both hands at Clemens, palms out, giving a traffic cop's signal: just slow down.

The two had worked together for all but a handful of Clemens's starts as a Yankee, and they were well matched emotionally. Posada pushed himself, was hypercompetitive and desperate to succeed, and had made the All-Star team for the first time in 2000. He was naturally right-handed but had been a switch-hitter since he was eight years old. His father had made him bat left-handed, explaining that it would be an advantage, and the boy endured 21 consecutive strikeouts as a left-handed batter, sometimes playing in tears, until he hit a home run on his 22nd at-bat. He waved to his father, who was coaching the opposing team, hoping for a sign of approval. Jorge Posada Sr. also did not want his son to use an aluminum bat or play basketball or other sports that might distract him from baseball.

Posada played in the middle infield when he was drafted in the 24th round by the Yankees in 1990, but the club officials eventually decided to convert him to catcher, and he devoted himself to adapting to the position, as he had to switch-hitting.

He was patient at the plate, drew walks, hit with power, and had a strong throwing arm; by all indications, he was becoming the heir apparent to Girardi. But his ascension to the role of the Yankees' No. 1 catcher had taken years, perhaps too long, and his competitiveness worked against him as he waited. He fretted about mistakes long after they happened, a habit that made him prone to slumps, particularly on defense. If he dropped a pitch in the first couple of innings, he tended to drop others during the course of the game; his passed balls came in binges, and never more so than in the first months of the 1999 season, when Don Zimmer was filling in for Torre as manager. Zimmer had managed the Cubs when Girardi was a young catcher breaking in, and Posada accurately sensed Zimmer favored Girardi; they knew each other better. The plan before spring training had been for Posada to catch about three-quarters of the games, but once the season began, Girardi seemed to be playing a little more than planned and Posada a little less. Posada felt more pressure to play better on the days he did start, and so he pressed and made mistakes. He began fumbling pitches at an alarming rate, and he was hitting terribly, batting .189 in his first 143 at-bats. Posada had 10 passed balls by June 13, and Yankees executives decided to have his eyes checked, on the off chance there was an unknown root to his problems. But nobody really expected the optometrist to find anything; the problem was that his overpowering desire to succeed—the same drive that transformed him from a Class A prospect to a catcher with excellent tools—was gnawing at him. Torre met with Posada shortly after returning to the team. "Look around," he told the catcher. "O'Neill suffers from it, Tino suffers from it, they all go through it."

In Posada's first years with the team, some of the pitchers had found him too willful. If David Cone shook off his sign, he seemed to take it as a personal rebuke, Cone thought, when it was not that at all. Cone had the responsibility of pitching the game, and therefore, he thought, he ultimately needed to decide what the best pitch was, not the catcher. It was just business, not personal, but Cone wasn't sure if Posada understood that.

Posada sometimes annoyed pitchers by arguing questionable strikes with the home plate umpire while batting; they were sure that an umpire fed up with Posada's complaints would take it out on the Yankee pitchers. It was part of a catcher's responsibility, they thought, to quietly absorb the bad calls when he was batting and serve as the pitcher's advocate when he was catching.

Posada's passion was still unrefined in his first seasons with the Yankees. During a game on a hot Fourth of July in 1999, Greg Kosc, the home plate umpire, was having a terrible day defining the strike zone, interpreting some pitches down the middle as balls and calling strikes on breaking balls far outside. Kosc, a heavyset man generally disliked by the players because of what they perceived as his arrogance, was drenched in sweat, and as the day progressed, he curled cold towels around his neck. His calls seemed to get worse from inning to inning, and Posada seethed, feeling Kosc had made mistakes both when he was batting and when he was catching. Finally, during the seventh inning, Kosc was removed from the field, his arms dangling over the shoulders of fellow umpire Larry Barnett and Yankees trainer Gene Monahan. Posada continued to fume after the game. "The bottom line, the [umpires] are not in shape," Posada said to a reporter. "It was hot—I can understand it's hot. You've got to be able to go through the game. They're not prepared, they're not in shape; it's a shame. He gets hot, the zone gets bigger. One doesn't go with the other." What Posada did not know was that Kosc had been taken to a hospital, where he was held overnight for heat exhaustion and dehydration. Cone and Girardi saw Posada's comments in the paper and immediately saw the potential for retribution from umpires, and they confronted him and told him to apologize. Posada walked the 100 feet from the Yankees' clubhouse to the umpires' room the next day and, finding that Kosc was still out sick, passed on his apology to Barnett. "There was a lot of frustration inside of me," said Posada.

The 1999 season would be difficult for Posada, but Clemens had made it easier for him early that year, embracing him as he had always done with his catchers. Early in spring training, Clemens bumped into Posada in a weight room and said he wanted him to be the catcher when he won his 300th game. "This guy is a Hall of Famer, and he was saying things to me he didn't need to say," said Posada, who emerged from the talk pumped up, inspired. He caught the majority of Clemens's starts that season, before the pitcher asked for Girardi late in the summer to work through some of his own struggles, in his first summer with the Yankees. Before Game 4 of the World Series against Atlanta, with the Yankees on the verge of a sweep, there was some sense that Girardi would catch. Posada went to Clemens, told him he wanted to be the catcher for that game, and the pitcher agreed.

Clemens invested himself in teammates in this way, and when he pitched, they invested themselves fully in him, their energy level rising. Tino Martinez loved to watch him before games opening the black trunk that contained his glove and mouth guard and protective cup, and pulling on his jersey, fully prepared to take the mound. "You know he's getting fired up, he's going through this whole routine," Martinez said. "He's telling you where he wants you to play certain hitters. He's so focused on that game that when you see him walking around, everybody in the clubhouse is ready to play."

Most pitchers, conditioned to hide their response to mistakes made behind them, mostly divorced themselves from the performance of the fielders, preferring to focus on their own task; Clemens, on the other hand, was fully engaged with the infielders, shouting to them, pumping a fist when they made great plays or even routine ones. If network television wanted some serious reality television, Clemens once joked, they might have put microphones on him and Martinez and Jeter and the other infielders to hear the running comedy and byplay; they would have been a ratings winner, he thought.

When a fielder made a solid play to end an inning, Clemens would wait in front of the dugout to acknowledge him as he came off the field, like a star summoning a supporting actor to the stage for a solo bow. If someone fumbled a grounder at a crucial moment or misplayed a pop fly, Clemens never showed frustration. Without even glancing at the offending fielder, he would march back to the top of the mound to tend to business: *Don't worry, I'll pick you up.*

The week after the All-Star break in 2001, the Yankees slogged through a horrendous schedule. They played a late-afternoon game in Florida on July 14 and an early-afternoon game in Philadelphia the next day, followed by two extra-inning night games against the Phillies. They finished the latter of these at 11:18 p.m. and were due to start a day-night doubleheader in Detroit about 15 hours later. The plan was to call up Class AAA pitcher Adrian Hernandez to throw the first game of the doubleheader, but Hernandez began feeling queasy a few hours before the game; he had the flu, forcing Torre and Stottlemyre to scramble for a replacement.

Many of the Yankees drifted groggily into the clubhouse about 90 minutes before the game after four or five hours of sleep. Clemens, scheduled to pitch the next day, walked in with a semicomatose stare, exhausted, his face still puffy from a major pillow collision, his hair vertical.

But Clemens's head cleared quickly when he heard about Hernandez's illness. His competitive sensibilities were offended: the idea that a kid pitcher would bail out on a major league start at the last second bugged him. It didn't matter that he was sick; when it was your turn to pitch, Clemens thought, you took the damn ball. "You get a chance to pitch for the world champions, you pitch," he said later. So Clemens found Torre and Stottlemyre and volunteered to throw in Hernandez's place. At first they thought he was joking. "Give me the ball," he said. "I'm serious. Give me the ball."

He downed a banana and a couple of spoonfuls of cereal. The news that Clemens, with 18 years in the majors and 272 victories, had stepped forward to pitch in Game 1 rocketed through the Yankees' clubhouse, instantly energizing the other players. "You're in the clubhouse and you see that, and you're going, 'Let's go!'" Tino Martinez recalled. The Yankees scored twice in the first inning, and again in the second, and after Clemens began tiring in the muggy afternoon heat and allowed four runs in the fifth, the Yankees came back with three runs in the sixth, battling for him. With two outs in the sixth, Clemens walked a batter, and Torre headed to the mound. "About out of gas?" he asked with a smile. Clemens insisted that he could continue, but Torre relieved him, and as Clemens departed, the fielders on the mound gave him appreciative slaps on the back. The Yankees went on to win, 8–5—the ninth in a streak of 16 consecutive victories compiled by Clemens that season. As far as Martinez was concerned, it was one of Clemens's greatest games for the Yankees. "It's just another thing you put in your personal notebook about how much respect you have for the guy," said Paul O'Neill.

Yankees reliever Mike Stanton had played with Clemens in Boston in 1995 and knew from his experience that summer how he related to his teammates. After Clemens was traded to the Yankees, he surprised his new teammates, Stanton thought, with the way he engaged people and extended himself, and disarmed others with his humor. "He's just as personable as anybody could be, but that was not his persona," said Stanton. "In some ways, he had the same makeup and energy as O'Neill."

Speaking in a Texas drawl, Clemens had a language all his own—Rogerspeak, some of the Yankees called it. A *bowling ball* was an inside fastball. *Cancel Christmas* was used when something bad happened: We had a lead in the fifth, and then, cancel Christmas. When Clemens played catch from a short distance as part of his workout routine, he called it Williamsport, after the home of the Little League World Series. If he thought a home plate umpire was not calling balls and strikes with the respect due a pitcher of his stature, Clemens might say, "Check the media guide"—where his exceptional record was printed. "Throw some shoulders," he would say, to encourage the hitters to generate some offense. A *cement mixer* was a hanging slider that spun badly. If he struggled to remember the name of someone outside of the team, he referred to that person as Shemp—the fourth member of the Three Stooges; everybody knew Larry, Moe, and Curly, but nobody could remember Shemp. After these expressions gained currency, Clemens had about two dozen of them put on T-shirts, which he handed out in the clubhouse.

He organized outings for teammates, got concert tickets, arranged dinners, set up tee times for golf. When the Yankees played two exhibition games in Houston before the start of the 2000 season, Clemens and his wife hosted the team in a bash at his estate. Some of the Yankees later noted how Clemens had worked to make it an event and not just a meal, hiring a full band to play and getting the place all done up. "You couldn't stand him when he was on the other side of the field," Jeff Nelson mused, years later. "And then when you played with him, he was one of the greatest teammates you ever had."

Now, facing the Diamondbacks in Game 7 in 2001, the fate of the Yankees' dynasty was in his hands, and Clemens would need both his good fastball and splitter to get through the second inning. There was one out, and Danny Bautista took a lead at second base, as Mark Grace stepped away from first; the count on Damian Miller was 1-0.

Clemens threw a fastball, low, and Torre, at the rail of the dugout, arched his eyebrows, concerned. Miller was not a good hitter and Schilling was on deck, but Clemens was having trouble finding the strike zone. He threw another fastball, over the outside corner, and Posada dropped the ball. But Steve Rippley, the home plate umpire, called a strike anyway.

Miller fouled off a 96 mph fastball, bringing the count to 2-2. Clemens had a chance for the strikeout and went to his split-fingered fastball, the pitch he often used to finish off hitters. At 91 mph—harder than the fastballs of most major league pitchers—the ball dropped under Miller's swing, for a third strike. Two outs. Clemens overthrew a couple of fastballs to Schilling, the count reaching 2-2, and when Posada suggested a splitter, Clemens shook him off; he wanted to throw nothing but heat. He pumped a 95 mph fastball through the strike zone, finishing the inning.

But Clemens, sweating and breathing hard, had thrown 20 pitches in the inning, laboring 10 minutes. Schilling went out to pitch the top of the third inning and needed only nine pitches and a little over three minutes: Soriano flied out, Brosius fouled out, and Clemens struck out. Schilling and Clemens were in the same race, but it seemed as if Clemens was running uphill.

CHAPTER 8

THE YANKEES had to keep Game 7 close early because Curt Schilling wasn't going to give up much, and because the Yankees weren't a team well suited to win a high-scoring game and rarely had been during Torre's tenure.

From 1998 to 2001, in an era when home run records were being overwhelmed, no Yankee hit 35 or more homers in a single season. The team led the American League in runs in 1998, with 965, but in 1999 they ranked third, and then ranked sixth in 2000 and fifth in 2001. The foundation of the team, Joe Torre and Brian Cashman agreed, was not the offense but the pitching. Most of the primary personnel decisions were made in an attempt to either upgrade the pitching or prevent the pitching from being compromised.

When Toronto general manager Gord Ash phoned Cashman on the eve of spring training in 1999 and offered Roger Clemens in a trade for David Wells, reliever Graeme Lloyd, and second baseman Homer Bush, the Yankees' executives and coaching staff conferred and reached a unanimous conclusion (with Steinbrenner abstaining, an excellent position to hold if the deal turned out badly): Clemens would be an improvement over Wells. Clemens was coming off back-to-back Cy Young

Awards, and he was a seasoned power pitcher who showed no signs of slowing down.

Plus, Boomer Wells was a pain in the ass.

Wells had compiled an 18-4 record the season before, and in his two years with the Yankees, he had won all five of his postseason starts and had thrown a perfect game. He was a left-handed pitcher with exceptional control, and based on tools alone, only Randy Johnson was better matched to Yankee Stadium, a place forever kind to lefties. But Wells was troublesome and inconsistent; throughout his career, these were the only constants in his personality.

Pat Gillick, then the general manager of the Toronto Blue Jays—the first of Wells's many teams—was sure that if Wells had been more disciplined, he would have been one of the game's greatest pitchers, someone who might have won 300 games. But from the outset, managing Wells was a nightmare. Discipline had been a foreign concept as he grew up in a single-parent home in San Diego, and when he began playing professionally, managers and coaches had to push him hard to adhere to training regimens, and he pushed back. If the pitching coach called for 10 wind sprints in the outfield, Wells might do five, if he did any at all. His eating habits were atrocious, he drank copiously, and his weight ballooned. He tended to think of himself as the beleaguered victim of anal retentive geeks. But his habits constantly put his bosses—from Gillick to Toronto manager Cito Gaston to Torre to Stottlemyre—in the position of having to demand accountability from him, which would, in turn, anger Wells. He would defend himself with his respectable statistics, but Gillick and others recognized his far greater gifts and were frustrated by the waste, his unreliability, and selfishness. Most years, he was a pitcher with grade A ability who was getting a lot of C minuses. In a tense meeting in 1998, Wells once accused Torre and Stottlemyre of not having any faith in him, but in a sense, they and others believed more in David Wells than he did.

His bloated body camouflaged exceptional athleticism; former Orioles pitcher Mike Flanagan noted that it would have been impossible for Wells to function around his own bulk if not for his agility. Even when he swelled close to 275 pounds, he could stretch and bend like a gymnast, touching his knee with his chin. And Wells still moved with a bounce that scouts recognized as a mark of the best athletes. In the off-season, he joined pickup basketball games with Blue Jays teammates, and though he hadn't been on the basketball team in high school, he was among the better players. He could run and move well and jump—everything that you would expect he couldn't do, said pitcher Todd Stottlemyre, one of his teammates.

Wells didn't seem to care much about the competition, however, unusual among professional athletes. He seemed to be on the court to socialize, Flanagan recalled, to have a good time with buddies. His demeanor was often the same when he pitched; Wells sometimes chatted with opposing hitters in midgame, swearing good-naturedly at them after they fouled away a series of pitches, joking with them if he allowed a particularly long home run.

He'd resisted coaches and managers his entire life, and yet he reached the majors with a nearly flawless pitching motion—smooth, his hands and torso and legs precisely where they needed to be. This made no sense, Flanagan thought, considering Wells's background and his generally negative attitude toward coaches. He delivered strikes like a conveyor belt, no matter his size or his blood alcohol level. And his left arm was blessed with the kind of durability, Torre thought, that was bestowed upon only a handful of pitchers in each generation. Later in his career, as Wells's back problems began manifesting themselves, he could still throw freely and easily, without impingement or pain in his shoulder or elbow. He was known as a physical wreck because of his girth, but in truth, he was a physical marvel.

Day to day, however, he could be completely unreliable. Before Wells was called up to the major leagues, Gillick had grown weary of his conditioning problems and mandated regular weigh-ins, levying a $20 fine every time he was too heavy. "At Gillick's command, team trainers actually began lugging heavy medical scales on all our road trips for the sole purpose of having me step up and be measured like some prized heifer at the county fair," Wells recalled in a book published late in his career. "It was humiliating. It was demeaning. And obviously, it got to be a real pain in the ass."

During one game with Toronto, Wells had become furious when the coaching staff began calling pitches from the dugout, and when Manager Cito Gaston had gone to the mound to confront him, the pitcher whipped the ball into foul territory and stalked to the dugout. In 1993, he was a 29-year-old lefty, oozing with talent, but the Blue Jays cut him. He and Gaston could not coexist.

He bounced to the Detroit Tigers and the Cincinnati Reds before being traded to the Orioles before the 1996 season. Early that season, he developed a case of gout—an accumulation of uric acid often related to drinking—in a big toe. He was given medication and told to stay off his feet and avoid alcohol, but the team was in Chicago, the greatest party town for major league players. Wells skipped the medicine and got intoxicated, walking from bar to bar, and the next morning he could barely move. He was out of action for 10 days.

After he came back, he struggled early in a game against the California Angels and was overcome by frustration. His fastball lagged and his curveball flattened out; it was quickly apparent that he had quit competing. In the broadcast booth that day was Sparky Anderson, who had been Wells's manager in Detroit; Anderson was the only manager who really reached Wells, but their relationship was more of a treaty than a typical player-manager alliance. Recognizing Wells's affection for alcohol, Anderson told him that he could do whatever he wanted for three days between his starts, but two days belonged to Anderson: the day before he was scheduled to start, and the day he took the mound. Wells adhered to these terms, went 11-9 for the Tigers in 1993, and began to turn around his career. But he was still capable of inexplicable immaturity, and after watching Wells give up in the game against the Angels, an appalled Anderson confronted him the next day in the Baltimore clubhouse. "I can't help but listen to the man—he's been a great inspiration," Wells said four days later. "When I played for him, he pretty much put me in my place. He taught me how to be a man. He sees what's going on, he knows when you're not giving it your all, when you're giving up, and I think I've been giving up lately. My heart really hasn't been into it."

But he tended to quickly forget advice and admonitions from Anderson and others, and had to be reminded to work, to stay in passable physical condition—and it wasn't Torre's style to badger players. After Wells signed with the Yankees for 1997, there were problems almost immediately. He broke his hand in an altercation outside a San Diego bar before spring training began and was diagnosed with gout as camp opened. Then, in an interleague game in Florida in mid-June, Torre desperately needed him to pitch deep into the game to rest the Yankees' overtaxed bullpen. But after a questionable call went against Wells, he allowed a home run and was in a foul mood when he came to bat in the second inning. It was hot, and Wells always hated pitching in those conditions. "You're horseshit," Wells told home plate umpire Greg Bonin. The umpire, who either didn't hear Wells clearly or was trying to give him a chance to back off, asked Wells what he had said. "I said you're horseshit," Wells said again, and with a resigned look on his face, Bonin threw him out of the game. It appeared as if Wells had worked to get himself ejected, and Torre was incensed. He called the act "unprofessional"—for Torre, the worst possible epithet—and didn't speak to Wells for three days. David Cone was more direct, following Wells into the clubhouse. "Are you just quitting on us?" Cone screamed, closing in on him. "Because you know that's your reputation, that you're just a fucking quitter." Wells and Cone shoved each other as Darryl Strawberry watched but did not intercede right away. Other players wanted to confront Wells, too, Cone thought, and they wanted to see what Cone would do. Strawberry finally stepped in and broke it up, and later, Cone went for a beer with Wells and made his points more civilly. But there would be more trouble.

Later that month, Wells walked onto the mound with a vintage Yankees cap worn by Babe Ruth in 1934. Wells, who loved memorabilia related to Ruth and the Yankees, had paid $35,000 for the hat and he wanted to wear it in a game, an act that endeared him to Yankees fans but greatly annoyed his manager, who ordered him to take it off after the inning, pinning him with the Stare.

Wells's willpower seemed to wane quickly when he pitched in some day games—teammates suspected that sometimes, he was still recovering from the previous night's adventure—or on warm days, a problem that the Yankees' brass thought was due to his poor physical condition. Late in that season, there would be an angry clubhouse confrontation with Steinbrenner, and after Wells pitched badly in August and September, Torre refused to commit to using him in the playoff rotation. He did get to start Game 3 in the Division Series against Cleveland and pitched exceptionally, as he always did in the postseason. But the Yankees lost the series, and Wells would forever believe that if Torre had just pitched him twice against the Indians, they would have won. Wells seemed to think Torre made his decision because of his disrespect for Wells.

There was, however, something likable about Wells, in a high-school-buddy sort of way. He was brash and crude and funny, as loyal to friends as he was disloyal to employers. When the Yankees and Orioles traveled around, Wells's childhood pals from rough corners of San Diego would show up at the park and be happily welcomed. Yankees fans had an open affection for his unpretentious manner, from the oval shape of his body to his unbuttoned jersey to his habit of adjusting his protective cup after virtually every pitch. "He wasn't a stuffed shirt," one fan told the *New York Times* after the Clemens trade was completed. "He rolls up his sleeves, chugs his beer, and rides a Harley." Some of his teammates found him immature and labored to tolerate his profanity, loud music, and flatulent humor, but others liked him. Although Wells and Mike Mussina had completely different personalities and had minor clashes as teammates, Mussina still found it hard to dislike Wells. He was not malicious, and at heart, Mussina thought, Wells was just a big kid. When Wells's book came out years after the trade, Clemens didn't take much of it seriously, believing Wells to be something of a harmless loudmouth. "I call him Eli," Clemens told reporters with a smile. "Because if he talks for more than 30 seconds, 'e lying."

After Cone and Wells fought and reconciled in Florida, they began spending more time together. At first, Cone's motivation was professional: if sharing drinks with Wells meant that he might be more accountable to the rest of the team, Cone thought, it would be worth his time. But Cone came to sincerely like Wells, seeing some innocence in him, and also came to have some effect on him. Early in the next season, Wells labored in the sweltering heat of Texas and nearly blew a nine-run lead. Torre, close to his breaking point, yanked him out of the game and suggested afterward that Wells was out of shape. Wells made plans for retaliation, intending to tell reporters that Torre's managerial reputation was overblown: if Torre was so good to players, Wells wanted to say, then why would he complain about my conditioning to the media? When Wells told Cone of his plans, though, Cone challenged Wells to reach a more honorable resolution. "If you got a problem with him," Cone said, "then be a man and go in his office and hammer it out face-to-face." Wells did so, stepping into the visiting manager's cramped quarters in Minnesota's Metrodome to speak to Torre and Stottlemyre, and the three men talked for 40 minutes, clearing the air. Seven days later, Wells pitched the 14th perfect game in major league history, and he would finish third in the AL Cy Young Award balloting, behind Clemens and Pedro Martinez.

Wells won eight of his first nine postseason decisions in his career, and even his friends on the teams he played for could offer no explanation for his October dominance. He wasn't a cutthroat competitor, like Cone or Greg Maddux. Maybe he just liked the feeling of pitching well in the postseason, Mike Flanagan theorized; with one great game, he could generate the response and respect that were so difficult to maintain over a long regular season. Or maybe Wells had a perfect makeup for October: he never took anything too seriously and wasn't bothered by the pressure as other pitchers might be. He had big-time ability and would apply himself in the postseason, and he pitched exceptionally.

But those days were overshadowed by his inability to consider how his actions might affect others. When a fly ball fell between Derek Jeter, Ricky Ledee, and Chad Curtis late in the '98 season in Baltimore, Wells turned toward the Yankees' dugout and raised his hands, as if to say, *Are we trying?* Jeter saw this and, astonished, he berated Wells, profanely telling him this kind of gesture was not acceptable on this team, and Wells sheepishly apologized to Jeter. But years later, Ledee, not one to hold a grudge, still remembered that while Wells had taken the time to speak to Jeter, he had not done so with him. "What I remember is he apologized to one of the guys," Ledee said. "And one guy, he did not apologize to."

As the Yankees prepared for spring training in 1999, Wells's contract was close to expiring, and the club executives were already beginning to pick up some disturbing vibes. They heard through the Tampa grapevine—the area where Wells lived in the off-season—that Wells was focused on getting a contract option for 2000 exercised before camp opened, and if he didn't get what he wanted, he intended to show up out of shape and make a nuisance of himself. If the situation had involved almost any other player, the Yankees might have perceived this as an idle threat and ignored him, but with Wells, team executives thought, it was something to be taken seriously. As club officials met at a restaurant in Tampa on the eve of spring training and discussed trading Wells for Clemens, some of them talked about what might happen the next day if the trade was not made: Wells would report to spring training, and his weight would be an issue again, and that would probably be the first of many Boomer headlines of the year. Everyone agreed his poor condition made him a physical time bomb.

After Steinbrenner excused himself from the decision making, the others went around the table and answered the question: Would you make this trade? Torre agreed with all the others: Absolutely. Brian Cashman called Gord Ash and noted the time on his watch when he completed the blockbuster trade: 11:42 p.m. Torre and Cashman decided to wait till Wells strolled into the clubhouse in the morning to inform him of the deal. "Boomer, I need to talk to you," Cashman said, leading the pitcher into Torre's office. "First day and I'm in the principal's office," Wells said, grinning, assuming they were going to tell him to shave his goatee. Then Cashman told him the news. "Wow," Wells said, expressionless and stunned, as if he'd been popped in the chin.

The trade devastated Wells, and for several years he thought Torre was the driving force behind the deal; it did not seem to occur to him that he was at all responsible for his departure. Wells would pitch well in the first two years after the trade, and when Torre managed the 2000 All-Star Game, he picked Wells to start. But in 2001, while pitching for the

Chicago White Sox—his seventh team in ten seasons—Wells broke down and required back surgery. In the first three years after the trade, Wells went 42-25. Clemens was 47-21, but more important, was still healthy, still dominant.

A FEW months after Wells was dealt to Toronto, Torre fought hard to keep another left-hander on the Yankees' staff from being traded—a pitcher who was struggling badly at the time. At the end of July, Andy Pettitte was 7-8 with a 5.65 ERA, pitching with his confidence in tatters. But he was 27 years old and healthy, and Torre kept thinking about Game 5 of the 1996 World Series: with the Yankees and the Braves tied at two games apiece, Pettitte had dueled John Smoltz to a standstill, shutting out Atlanta into the ninth inning—on the road. That game, Torre thought, had been one of the seminal moments of the championship run. Yes, he's struggling now, Torre argued, but how can we give up on someone who responded to stress the way he did in that game?

Pettitte was vulnerable to his own frustration and self-doubt, but blocking out the rest of the world was easy for him. He would tilt his neck and lower the bill of his cap when he stared into home plate to focus on his target, his eyeballs rolling upward ghoulishly. This created a tunnel effect, blocking out the stands behind home plate so he could see only the catcher's glove. Pettitte never seemed bothered by jeering fans, the opposing hitter, the possible ramifications of the game. He operated like a plow horse, preferring to have his catcher drive and steer him, trusting him to call the signals. If the catcher flashed one finger for a fastball, Pettitte nodded his head robotically, gripped the ball, and threw homeward. Two fingers for a curveball, another nod, and Pettitte threw.

Cone and Mussina were control freaks by comparison, calling their own pitches, shaking off signs repeatedly until the catcher flashed for something they wanted to throw. Clemens was a compromiser, taking his own ideas into the process with a willingness to listen to suggestions. But Pettitte just nodded. Jimmy Key, the left-handed pitcher who had been Pettitte's mentor in the first seasons of his career, thought Pettitte relinquished control not because of an inability to make his own choices, but because of an abiding confidence in his own ability as a pitcher: if he executed his pitches properly, it really didn't matter what the signs were.

Pettitte's simple method for pitch selection fit his personality, because there was an earnest simplicity to him, probably one reason why Torre and Stottlemyre would fight to keep him in the summer of 1999. He was wide-eyed, gregarious, and had few interests other than his work, his religion, and his family. Pettitte uniformly blamed himself when he pitched badly, several times explaining to reporters that he was consumed by the melancholy he felt while away from his kids. Few players would have admitted to such feelings, and coming from some it might have sounded like bunk; not with Pettitte. His wife once returned to the family's home in Texas to prepare for the birth of a child, leaving him alone in their New Jersey apartment, and Pettitte fell into a monthlong slump, which ended as soon as his children returned.

In a sport where most players deceived themselves or their manager or reporters at one time or another, Pettitte was absolutely honest. Cone could look into Torre's eyes and tell him he felt good even when he really didn't. When Torre asked Pettitte the same question, the pitcher would turn his head and glance off in another direction, his body language betraying his feelings.

Shortly after the Yankees resumed play in the aftermath of the September 11 tragedy, Bernie Williams was beaned by Chicago pitcher Kip Wells. Williams fell to the ground writhing, and for a brief moment appeared seriously injured, before he got up and was taken out of the game. While the Yankees didn't necessarily believe Wells hit Williams in the head intentionally, the baseball code clearly called for retaliation. But Pettitte was pitching, and it was not in his nature to retaliate; he was probably as close as anyone in baseball to being a conscientious objector, a stance which sometimes annoyed teammates. In fact, in the first week of the 1998 season, a team meeting had been called after Pettitte failed to retaliate for inside pitches in a game against Seattle; the relievers on the team—Jeff Nelson, in particular—always felt as though they had to take care of dirty business.

But as Williams was taken off the field with a concussion, everything felt a little different. Emotions had been shaken since the terrorist attacks, the players were on edge, and Williams's initial reaction to the beaning had been particularly frightening—he had been sprawled on the ground, head in the dirt, his legs kicking wildly. Magglio Ordonez, Chicago's best hitter, came to bat in the bottom of the first inning, and against almost any other pitcher, he might have expected to get plunked. But this was Pettitte, who never threw at anybody. And yet Pettitte fired a fastball against his hip; Ordonez dropped his bat and trotted to first base, understanding the code. After the game, a reporter asked Pettitte if he had thrown at Ordonez intentionally. Pettitte turned his head and looked down. Almost all pitchers answer this question by saying they were trying to throw inside, or that a pitch got away. Pettitte kept looking down. "I don't want to talk about that," he said quietly.

Jim Leyritz became Pettitte's personal catcher in 1995, and this arrangement would last through the 1996 season: Leyritz called all the pitches, Pettitte obediently responded. "Hey, dude, shake me off at least once," Leyritz joked to Pettitte, "so it makes it look like you're doing something out there." The Yankees traded for Joe Girardi before the 1996 season, but Pettitte, a creature of habit, preferred his old catcher. Only after Leyritz was traded did Pettitte come to trust Girardi, and he then preferred Girardi to Jorge Posada. When Torre tried mixing Posada in more, Pettitte seemed almost incapable of functioning, balking at the new catcher's pitch suggestions, shaking off signs. He would grow comfortable with Posada, but only after Girardi departed.

Girardi was easy to trust. There was a 1950s-style purity to the way he competed for the Yankees and treated his teammates, and though he averaged only two homers and 38 RBIs in his four seasons with the Yankees, he was widely regarded as one of the team leaders. Don Zimmer, who had been Girardi's first manager with the Chicago Cubs and also his bench coach when he played with the Colorado Rockies, had strongly promoted Girardi as Bob Watson explored a trade with the Rockies after the '95 season. There is much more to his value than his offensive production, Zimmer told the Yankees' executives. Girardi would run to and from his position every inning, and whenever there was a ground ball in the infield without runners on base, he would charge up the first-base line, following the runner to back up in case the throw went past first baseman Tino Martinez. Girardi would run out every grounder and fly ball. (As most of the Yankees did. Torre would receive much credit for the way he managed the players, but the intensity of Girardi, Jeter, Martinez, Williams, and the others relieved him of a burden other managers faced daily: rarely did he have to address the simple matter of hustle.)

When the Yankees began installing Posada as their primary catcher in 1998, Girardi worked closely with him, talking to him during games, encouraging him; even when Posada lobbied for more playing time, there was never tension between the two. The Yankees planned on letting Girardi leave as a free agent after the '98 season, but Torre talked Steinbrenner into exercising an option on him for the next year; he thought that Girardi was crucial to the team and that Posada—while a much better offensive player than Girardi—still needed more time to develop defensively. Girardi would make $3.4 million as a backup catcher in 1999, playing in 65 games, and after he signed with the Cubs the following winter, third-base coach Willie Randolph would call to thank him for his professionalism and unselfishness over the years. "He's probably one of my top ten all-time teammates," Randolph said.

Behind the plate, Girardi operated with great empathy, bending his personality to fit the needs of the pitcher. David Cone commanded his own games and mostly wanted his catchers to get the hell out of his way, and Girardi would defer, never arguing over pitch selection. Cone wanted to get the sign quickly but cleanly, to maintain a rhythm, and Girardi would let him set the pace. (Early in Posada's career, he tended to give signals so quickly that Cone would be nodding yes just as Posada moved on to the second sign, and Cone would have to step off the rubber to clear up the confusion.)

When he caught Pettitte, though, Girardi, a graduate of Northwestern, did the mental heavy lifting, and the left-hander went 18-7 with a 2.88 ERA in 1997 and 16-11 the next year. But Pettitte began to labor in his games, and Gene Michael thought his passivity indirectly led to his problems. In 1996, he developed a nasty cut fastball, a pitch that banked sharply into the hands of right-handed hitters, and over the next two seasons, as he mastered its movement, Girardi came to rely on it. If he

needed a first-pitch strike, Pettitte threw the cutter. If there were runners on base, he threw the cutter. Michael believed Girardi was an excellent catcher, but he thought he had inadvertently abandoned the
left-hander's other strengths. Pettitte had a good curve and changeup,
but by the middle of 1999, he had only minimal command of both those
pitches, essentially because he hadn't thrown them enough, Michael
thought. He's got to start throwing his curveball more, Michael insisted
in organizational meetings.

But by the summer of 1999, Pettitte threw almost nothing but cutters
and sinkers. His record dropped to 5-7 and his earned run average was over
five runs; he was lost. With Pettitte eligible for arbitration after the season,
George Steinbrenner ordered Brian Cashman to phone other general managers in late June to ask them to prepare their best offers. A reporter approached Pettitte and said he was preparing a story about the trade
possibility. "I've heard trade rumors before, and they're not going to trade
me," Pettitte said, grinning. "Why would they trade me?" Because of arbitration, the reporter explained; you've struggled the last couple of years, and
they're worried they're going to have to pay you a lot more money in arbitration next winter. Pettitte's smile evaporated as he puzzled over the process.
"If I'm having a bad year, why would I get a raise in arbitration?" he asked,
posing a logical question that had stumped baseball owners for years.

Laura, his wife, wondered about his mental state, as well. They had
met in high school, in Deer Park, Texas, and she had sat on alloy bleach-
ers as he pitched prep games; later, she would watch him in the minor
leagues. Now, with the Yankees apparently prepared to trade him, Laura
asked Andy if he had the same fire he had before. "You're crazy," he responded, amused and stunned by the question.

But the doubts gnawed at him and fed into his insecurity. He tortured
himself on the mound, complaining about his mistakes so loudly, Girardi once said, that you could hear almost every word from home plate.
Because he relied on sinkers and cutters, Pettitte produced a lot of
ground balls and, in turn, allowed a fair number of hits; such is the nature of the sinkerball pitcher. But this reality rarely diminished his own
harsh self-critique.

In his last start before the trade deadline, in Chicago's Comiskey

Park, Pettitte was unnerved. With runners on base and two strikes in the fourth inning against Chris Singleton, a left-handed hitter with the White Sox, he began throwing a cutter, then for some reason dropped his elbow in middelivery to throw sidearm. (Afterward, Pettitte admitted he had no idea why he tried this.) Singleton slammed a single, and Pettitte was replaced and left the field wondering if he would ever pitch for the Yankees again. Steinbrenner, his patience characteristically exhausted, was getting pressure from advisors in Tampa to promote Ed Yarnall, a left-handed pitching prospect who was throwing well for Class AAA Columbus, and to create a spot in the rotation by dealing Pettitte. Cashman settled on the parameters of a trade with Philadelphia: pitcher Adam Eaton, outfielder Reggie Taylor, and a third, lesser prospect to be drawn from a list. Ed Wade, the Phillies GM, was certain that Cashman was sincere, and that they were closing in on a trade.

But Cashman, Torre, and Stottlemyre didn't really want to deal Pettitte, and the day before the trade deadline, they implored Steinbrenner to hold off. We've got to hang on to our pitching depth, Cashman argued; he believed that Pettitte would come around before the start of the playoffs, but even if he didn't, the Yankees still had time to insert Yarnall in the rotation by the end of the year. Torre talked about Pettitte's experience and what he had done for the Yankees in past years, in Game 5 in '96. Torre had nothing against Yarnall, but he never had much faith in unproven prospects, no matter how much they dominated in the minor leagues; what counted most for him were experience and success in big games, and Yarnall had neither.

Steinbrenner assented, once again putting himself in a position to second-guess the move if it didn't work out. "Our manager seems to think things are all right," Steinbrenner told reporters. "I have great confidence in our manager."

The natural order in his life restored, Pettitte won seven of his last 10 decisions in the regular season, and he prevailed in both of his playoff starts. He would begin to join Clemens in his workout regimen, and after seven seasons with the Yankees, Pettitte's career record was 115-65.

• • •

WHILE PETTITTE rebounded, David Cone won only four games in 2000, and for the first time in years, the Yankees' rotation appeared somewhat thin, an injury or two away from becoming a serious concern. There was some discussion in the organizational meetings after the 2000 season about pursuing Cleveland outfielder Manny Ramirez, the best offensive player on the market.

But Cashman and others again insisted the major investment should be in pitching, and the Yankees committed $88.5 million to a six-year deal with Mike Mussina, a free agent pitcher who for most of his life had hated the idea of going to New York City. He had grown up in central Pennsylvania, in Montoursville, and as a boy had gone to Yankee Stadium with his father. To the Mussinas, New York City was a place of too many cars, too many people, too many buildings. In Montoursville, many streets were named for trees, and it took no more than 10 minutes to get anywhere. When Mussina rode his bike across town to Indian Park, most everyone he saw knew him or one of his parents.

As a boy, he had spent hours throwing a ball against a wall in the basement of his parents' home, aiming at a box made with tape, and rattling a radiator when he missed badly. On Saturdays, he would watch *The Game of the Week* on television and try to imitate the pitchers he saw—maybe Tom Seaver or Nolan Ryan. Most of the mechanics he would take to the majors were self-installed; he taught himself how to throw a knuckle-curve when he was a teenager, and he tinkered constantly with pitches.

He would play catch with his father until he was 12, when Malcolm Mussina—Big Mike, as he was called within the family—decided his son threw too hard. But the boy was perfectly comfortable throwing alone or kicking a football up and down an empty field or shooting baskets by himself. If a friend called Mike and asked him to go somewhere, that was fine, his mother recalled. But he was never going to pick up the phone; he preferred privacy. He would go on to pitch in front of thousands of people but found solitude in the competition. "I'm still by myself when I'm on the mound," he said. "It's still me against that guy at the plate. I know I'm good enough to beat him, so I'm going to beat him. . . . It's just me doing something I'm comfortable doing."

Mussina attended Stanford, where he could play baseball year-round, and graduated with an economics degree in 3½ years. He signed with the Baltimore Orioles and went 147-81 in 10 seasons, packing up his truck and returning to Montoursville each fall. He married a girl from his hometown, coached football and basketball in the off-seasons at his old high school, and bought an isolated house in the middle of the woods, 10 minutes from his parents' home.

His contract negotiations with the Orioles broke down after the 2000 season, and he began talking to other teams, with a primary criterion being proximity to Montoursville. The Yankees were near enough, and they had the money to pay him.

Mussina signed with the Yankees and went 17-11 in his first season, winning the pivotal Game 3 of the Division Series against Oakland and beating Seattle in the AL Championship Series. The Diamondbacks ripped him in Game 1 of the 2001 World Series, but he started Game 5, featuring a split-fingered fastball—a pitch he had thrown only a few times before, out of concern for his elbow—and struck out 10, pitching well.

While he was being recruited by the Yankees the previous fall, Clemens had called and talked enthusiastically about how much fun it would be to try to win him a ring, chatting for so long about the possibility that Mussina had to politely break off the conversation. Now, months later, in Game 7, Clemens was in a position to win a ring for Mussina and the other Yankees.

Clemens had thrown 41 pitches in the first two innings, and the Diamondbacks pressured him again in the third, making him work till sweat dripped down his face. After Tony Womack struck out, Craig Counsell singled through the middle, Clemens jabbing his glove at the ball as it went past the mound and bounded into center field. Before Clemens threw to the next hitter, Luis Gonzalez, he fired to first base twice and stepped off the mound to look Counsell back to the base.

Gonzalez struck out, swinging underneath a waist-high 95 mph fastball, but Matt Williams bounced a chopper off home plate and toward third base, where Scott Brosius barehanded the ball and threw to first—too low. Martinez knocked it down, keeping it in front of him. Runners at first and second, two outs, and Steve Finley, who was swinging better than any of his teammates, coming to the plate. Clemens had already thrown 57 pitches and wasn't yet out of the third inning; Schilling's pitch count was only 28.

With the count 1 ball and 1 strike, Clemens threw a splitter, a bad one, which drifted into the strike zone, belt high, at 87 mph, not much to it. Finley fouled it back. Clemens puffed his cheeks, breathing heavily, shook off a sign. Posada jogged to the mound, and he and Clemens talked, the pitcher speaking into the back of his glove so that no one could read his lips. They decided on a high fastball and agreed that Posada would not give a sign after he squatted behind the plate. Clemens pumped a 96 mph fastball and Finley took it, too high. Ball 2.

Posada thumped his glove with his fist, calling for a splitter down, a logical follow-up after the high fastball on the previous pitch. Finley stepped out of the box, and Clemens shook his head slightly at Posada; wary of Counsell, who was watching hawkishly from second, Clemens sent a subtle message to his catcher: *Don't give another sign when he gets back in the box.*

Clemens crammed the ball between the middle and index fingers on his right hand, the grip for the splitter—Mr. Splitty, he called it—and this time, it dove low and outside, underneath Finley's swing. Clemens had six strikeouts, and Game 7 was still scoreless through three innings.

CHAPTER 9

SOME OF the Arizona players had entered Game 7 of the 2001 World Series knowing that they would face a lifetime of regret if they did not beat the Yankees. Many of the Diamondbacks were playing in the World Series for the first time, and for most of them, it would be the last. Arizona had the oldest team in baseball. First baseman Mark Grace had 14 seasons in the majors, third baseman Matt Williams 15. Randy Johnson was 38 years old, reliever Greg Swindell 36 years old, infielder Jay Bell 35. Twenty-nine-year-old right fielder Danny Bautista was the only member of the starting lineup under 30. Reliever Mike Morgan was 42 years old and had pitched in the majors for half of his life, 21 seasons; the Diamondbacks were his 12th team.

For all their age, the Arizona players had little experience with post-season success. Craig Counsell, the second baseman, was the only member of the active roster with a championship ring, won with Florida in 1997. Williams had twice played for losers in the World Series, in 1989 and in 1997, and center fielder Steve Finley had been the San Diego center fielder in the 1998 World Series, when the Yankees swept the Padres. Schilling had pitched against Toronto in the 1993 World Series while with the Phillies.

But in the months leading up to this World Series, almost everything had fallen into place for the Diamondbacks. They had managed to stay relatively healthy through the regular season in spite of their age, and they had beaten St. Louis and Atlanta in the National League playoffs. Then they had outplayed the Yankees for almost the entire World Series— dominated them, for the vast majority of innings.

And yet Arizona had been pushed to Game 7, the outcome very much in doubt in the top of the fourth inning, with Schilling and Clemens trading zeros. "I don't mean this to be bragging or egotistical or anything, but I feel like we outplayed them in every game in that series," Diamondbacks manager Bob Brenly recalled months later. "And to lose a Game 7 in a series like that, where you feel that you've outplayed the other team in every ball game—that would be devastating."

Johnson thought the Diamondbacks were like the Yankees in many respects, with an understated style. Arizona's veterans competed without showing up their opponents, played hard, and played well: "Professional players who respected the game," Brenly said, "and who respected their teammates."

And because of Schilling and Johnson, the Diamondbacks had superlative pitching—the postseason advantage the Yankees had always enjoyed before meeting Arizona. Brenly would spend much of the postseason talking down the notion that the Diamondbacks were a two-man team, as any good manager would have. But in reality, the duo had made Arizona's success possible, by giving the Diamondbacks an attribute no other team had: two pitchers who could consistently overpower opposing teams. Atlanta had John Smoltz, Greg Maddux, and Tom Glavine, but while Smoltz had an electric and overwhelming repertoire, hitters could at least feel confident they could put the ball in play against the more conventional Maddux and Glavine. The Yankees had Clemens, Pettitte, and Mussina, but Pettitte gave up a lot of hits and Mussina outmaneuvered hitters, rather than blowing them away. Johnson and Schilling effectively emasculated opposing batters, whose only real chance was to outlast them, staying close until the Arizona bullpen took over in the last innings. The Diamondbacks finished the regular season 22 games over .500, with a record of 92-70, and Schilling and Johnson combined to go

31 games over .500, with a 43-12 record. They struck out 665 batters in 506⅓ innings, allowing just 418 hits and 110 walks, and commonly drew comparisons with the Dodgers' 1960s tandem of Sandy Koufax and Don Drysdale. The Diamondbacks had 10 postseason victories behind them as they played Game 7 against the Yankees, Johnson and Schilling accounting for eight of those.

Both had been late bloomers. Randy Johnson was 6 feet 10, with the wingspan of a condor, and threw extremely hard, but while he was armed with the tools to dominate, he initially had control problems and did not make his major-league debut until he was 25, breaking in with the Montreal Expos. He would walk 26 batters in 29⅔ innings for Montreal in 1989 before being dealt to Seattle. Though he was almost 30 when he finally gained full command of his pitches, no other left-hander could match his raw stuff: his fastball neared 100 mph, and his slider seemed to move laterally across yards, rather than inches. He was so tall and his arms so long that he seemed to be handing the ball to the catcher as he finished his delivery, mechanics that intimidated batters, left-handers in particular; they were unaccustomed to facing hard-throwing left-handers, let alone a 6-feet-10-inch lefty who threw with a relatively low arm angle that made it seem as if he was whipping the ball at their ribs. Most managers benched their left-handed batters when Johnson pitched. John Kruk, a lefty, had faced him in the 1993 All-Star Game, and when Johnson playfully whizzed a fastball high over Kruk's head, Kruk had flapped the collar of his jersey, as if his heart was beating fast and he needed air. Kruk bailed out of the batter's box on subsequent pitches, striking out weakly. "For two days, I couldn't sleep, thinking about the guy," Kruk would say. Johnson had arrived on the national stage, and he would go on to win five Cy Young Awards, including four after signing with Arizona as a free agent after the 1998 season.

Schilling had signed his first professional contract with the Boston Red Sox in 1986, but he was traded to Baltimore just two years later, and the Orioles dealt him to Houston prior to the 1991 season; after one year with the Astros, he was again traded, to Philadelphia. During Schilling's short time with the Astros, Roger Clemens was at the Houston Astrodome, working out in the off-season, and was told that Schilling idolized him and wanted to meet him. Clemens had heard that Schilling was wasting his talent; the kid didn't work hard, people said, and he acted unprofessionally. So Clemens said that while he was happy to talk to Schilling, he didn't want to waste his own time, either. "He had great tools, and I mean, he was pissing years away," Clemens recalled. If Schilling wasn't serious, Clemens figured, then why bother?

But Schilling wanted to change and insisted on the meeting. Clemens was direct, telling the young pitcher that he was essentially cheating himself and his family. Schilling listened. "It was like getting a third eye," Schilling told Tyler Kepner of the New York Times. "I looked at the game with a whole new approach, outlook, respect. I just realized I couldn't do things the way I had done them and put my head on the pillow at night and say I'd done everything I could. There was just so much more I could do."

Schilling improved his conditioning, got serious about his work, and refined his gifts, and his style became a virtual carbon copy of Clemens's: blazing fastballs complemented by diving split-fingered fastballs and sliders, all thrown with exceptional command. He had walked only 39 batters in 256⅔ innings in 2001, with 293 strikeouts.

Now, in Game 7, he was pitted against his idol. Clemens usually worked in a mental vacuum in his games, concentrating on his own challenges and ignoring the other pitcher, but there was a moment when Clemens stood in the on-deck circle and looked out at Schilling. "It was like I was facing a double," said Clemens. "He says stuff about talking to me and what that meant to him, but he's the one who made the changes. He's the one who made the decision to quit what he was doing and get serious."

Schilling had thrown only 28 pitches the first time through the Yankees' lineup—just 28 pitches for nine outs. He had thrown nothing but fastballs to Derek Jeter in the first inning, but as the two matched up in the fourth, Schilling changed his pattern, mixing in some splitters. Jeter fouled off one, then another, the count 2 balls and 2 strikes. Schilling went back to his fastball, 94 mph, and Jeter drove it to right field—right to Bautista, for the first out.

Then Schilling fell behind against Paul O'Neill, 3 balls and 1 strike—

the first time any Yankee hitter had reached a three-ball count. Finally, they were making him work a little. O'Neill took a 95 mph fastball over the outside corner for a full count, then fouled off a fastball. As Schilling fired his next pitch, O'Neill started his hands early, trying to keep up with the fastball he anticipated, but Schilling had thrown a splitter, the ball diving down. Badly fooled, O'Neill tried to adjust his swing, his upper body collapsing forward like a folding chair; no chance. Bent forward in his awkward follow-through, O'Neill looked out at Schilling and grinned in disbelief: *Full count and you throw a nasty splitter.* He returned to the dugout, pushed his bat into the rack, and shook his head slowly. Schilling had faced 11 hitters and gotten 11 outs.

Next up was Bernie Williams, who had once come to Bank One Ballpark seeking a job. After the 1998 season, he had talked with the Diamondbacks as a free agent, touring Arizona's park with his former manager, Buck Showalter. Jerry Colangelo, the Diamondbacks' owner, had not made a formal offer but had indicated to Williams's agent, Scott Boras, that he could put together a $100 million package, deferred money included. Unbeknownst to Williams, as he walked around Bank One Ballpark, the Yankees had decided to let him go. After years of waiting for Williams to blossom into a superstar, they had moved to sign volatile baseball wrecker Albert Belle in his stead.

Williams's progress in the majors had been steady and gradual, rather than explosive. He was 22 when he made the majors, in 1991, 27 years old when he broke the .300 barrier for the first time, 28 when he first hit more than 20 homers in a season. In 1998, Williams won the American League batting title, hitting .339, but he got hurt that summer, as well—he seemed to get hurt every year—and his power numbers of 26 homers and 97 RBIs were solid but not overwhelming. Belle, meanwhile, had hammered the American League that year, smashing 49 homers, driving in 152 runs, and hitting .328, and after that season he became a free agent. The Yankees wanted him instead of Williams and went full bore in pursuit of the sport's worst citizen.

It was taken as fact in baseball circles that Albert Belle was nuts. He'd been disciplined repeatedly during his career, for firing a baseball at a fan who'd been razzing him about his history of drinking, for blasting into Milwaukee infielder Fernando Vina, for swearing at NBC reporter Hannah Storm during the 1995 World Series; if Belle had been suspended every time he swore at a reporter, he might have missed several seasons. He slurped coffee constantly and seemed to be in a perpetual caffeinated frenzy. Few escaped his anger: on some days he would destroy the postgame buffet that was laid out in the late innings, launching plates into the shower, and after one poor at-bat in Boston, he retreated to the visitors' clubhouse and took a bat to teammate Kenny Lofton's boombox. Belle preferred to have the clubhouse cold, below 60 degrees, and when one chilly teammate turned up the heat, Belle walked over, turned down the thermostat, and smashed it with his bat. His nickname, thereafter, was Mr. Freeze.

The Indians billed Belle about $10,000 a year for the damage he caused in clubhouses on the road and at home, and tolerated his behavior only because he was an awesome slugger. He clubbed 36 home runs in only 106 games before the players' strike in 1994, and hit 50 homers in 143 games the next season. Belle's stance, more open than most right-handed batters', allowed him to see the pitcher better, with both eyes focusing directly on the mound, and he stared with an expression better suited for a bouncer. He dropped his hands slightly as he began his swing, as if he were cocking a sledgehammer, and powered his bat through the strike zone. There was more to his hitting than transferred rage, however. Teammates thought Belle was an extremely intelligent batter, apt to notice virtually imperceptible tendencies in pitchers—the slight wriggling of a glove that indicated a split-fingered fastball, for example. In the 1996 playoffs, when Belle was with Cleveland, he battled Baltimore pitcher Armando Benitez, fouling off fastball after fastball, before anticipating a slider and hitting a game-winning home run. Belle told teammates he had noticed that Benitez cocked his wrist a little differently when he threw a slider. Benitez, an effective regular-season closer, seemed haunted thereafter and developed a crushing tendency toward postseason failure.

Belle accumulated a staggering 399 total bases for the White Sox in 1998, cementing his market value, and exercised a contractual clause to negotiate with other teams. Yankees executives thought he would make a much greater impact on offense than Williams: the team was already stacked with left-handed hitters, and the right-handed Belle would balance the lineup, they figured, and give them their first pure power hitter since Reggie Jackson.

Joe Torre would have the responsibility of coping with Belle's temper, a task that Belle's former manager, Mike Hargrove, told others he regarded as almost impossible. But Torre loved the idea; he loved sluggers, and since he had become manager, the team had absorbed a handful of personalities previously thought to be troublesome—Knoblauch, Wells, Strawberry, and others. Torre was confident that Belle could be integrated seamlessly into his clubhouse, embraced and protected by veterans like O'Neill and Martinez and Cone. Torre and Cashman flew to Arizona to meet with Belle, played golf with him, and found him to be charming, deferential, precise, obsessive. His Mercedes was spotless, and he was devoted to his workout routine and meal schedule. The meeting confirmed what they believed, that Belle was intense but hardly unreachable, and they sensed he wanted what they wanted: success. Cashman began negotiating with Belle's agent, Arn Tellem, and Yankees officials agreed the team would be better with Belle. The Yankees had never thought of Bernie Williams as an elite player, as Williams knew.

When he had signed with the Yankees, on his 17th birthday, the organization's scouts and minor league executives could see right away that Williams possessed awesome physical potential. He ran like a 100-meter sprinter, drawing his knees high, pumping his arms and hands—track had been his primary sport in high school—and his large six-foot-two frame convinced them that he would develop eventually into a very good power hitter. But even after he became an All-Star, some of the skills other players developed through repetition eluded him. Despite his excellent speed, Williams was a poor base stealer, never developing a knack for reading a pitcher's move to home plate, and by the time he broke for second base, the ball was usually headed for home plate, and the opportunity missed. Williams would win four Gold Gloves, but some staff and club officials who watched him play daily did not think of him as an exceptional outfielder. His first step was sometimes in the wrong direction, and as a result he took circular routes to fly balls, and balls hit in the gap occasionally carried over his head when they shouldn't have.

Early in his career, there were larger questions about whether he could ever be a great player. Williams was extremely sensitive by baseball standards, and the hard clubhouse humor bothered him. His father, Bernabe Williams Sr., had always been reluctant to draw attention to himself, preferring his children to skip parties and avoid situations in which others would focus on them, such as speaking out in public.

So Bernie Williams would go out with friends, and after an hour or two, the family station wagon would appear: time to go home. He already felt different from other children—he was much larger, with gangly legs—and was petrified of rejection, and his father's reticence made it easier for him to withdraw. Bernie began playing Spanish guitar, strumming alone on the porch of his family's home in Puerto Rico. Years later, music continued to be an emotional outlet for him, and he would spend hours playing in the corner locker in the clubhouse. Paul O'Neill played the drums and sometimes got together with Williams to play, trying different styles and different songs. But no matter what they played, O'Neill noticed, eventually Williams would wind up playing the blues.

Bernie Williams's parents had demanded that he treat others the way he would want to be treated, and what he wanted more than anything was to be left alone. But it could not be that way in a baseball clubhouse, where players teased one another constantly about anything that seemed out of the norm—big ears or a big head, a thick accent. The vast majority of the players laughed along with the teasing, even when they were upset, because they knew that if they reacted strongly, they would invite even more abuse. Williams was, in many respects, a perfect target, because he was very different—large, soft-spoken, with extremely thick eyeglasses. And he never fought back. When Williams was a rookie, outfielder Mel Hall teased him relentlessly, attacking and attacking. Gene Michael saw Hall drive Williams to tears one day and warned him that unless he backed off, he would be released. Michael asked Hall why he was so vicious to Williams, but Hall never really offered a reason.

Hurt covered Williams's face when he was teased, and angry thoughts welled in his mind, he recalled years later. He'd think about ways to hurt his tormentors. The teasing might have stopped if Williams had thrown punches, but he would remain silent, any instinctive and vicious retorts choked off in his throat, until he would finally muster the only words he could: "I can't believe you said that to me, man."

That represented an explosion for Bernie Williams, and he felt sickened by his own inability to respond. "Sometimes you really want to hurt people with what you say, but it's always a burden on your mind," Williams explained, years later. "Yeah, it's terrible, man. It hurts not to be able to express the feelings the way you want to feel them. You don't want to finesse them and make them come out in a civilized way. You just want to go out there and really say what you feel."

Williams's sensitivity only fed concerns in the organization about whether he could develop the toughness required to cope with the failure inherent in baseball. If the teasing of a teammate could affect Williams, the logic went, how would he handle a long batting slump? If Williams had played in Minnesota or Kansas City, there might be a grace period of three or four years, but in New York, failures were examined daily by the media and the fans, and above all, by Steinbrenner. How would Williams react to that? He was called up in 1991 and hit just eight homers in his first 581 at-bats—a slow rate of development, particularly in the Yankees' organization, where even the best prospects usually got only weeks to establish themselves.

Brad Ausmus played with Williams in Class AAA Columbus and recalled Williams quietly playing his guitar in the corner of the clubhouse. Ausmus liked Williams but heard the doubts about his toughness. His quiet demeanor, Ausmus thought, was probably being interpreted as a lack of desire. Syd Thrift, one of Steinbrenner's many general managers before Gene Michael took over the team in 1990, once even suggested to Williams that he should charge the mound. Williams listened, stifling an urge to laugh. "He wanted me to be intimidating," Williams recalled, still greatly amused more than a decade later by the suggestion. "There was always the sense that I wasn't tough. The most important part for me was not to change my demeanor because they wanted me to be different. I consider myself a pretty intense guy; I just don't have to show it."

Brian Butterfield, the Yankees' first-base coach in the last two years of Showalter's tenure as manager, was sure Williams was much more resilient than most thought, mentally and physically. He had seen Williams run into fences, chasing deep fly balls—utterly fearless, Butterfield thought. Before the Yankees began a series in Cleveland, the players were told that when Indians second baseman Carlos Baerga fielded grounders with a runner at first base, he liked to tag the runner going by before throwing to first. Don't let him do this, the players were told, and that night, Williams was on first when Baerga fielded a grounder. Sure enough, Baerga stepped forward to tag Williams. "And Bernie just plants him," Butterfield recalled. "Levels him. After that, whenever Baerga had a chance to tag a runner, he always gave it up to the shortstop, instead." Once in 1994, the Yankees were involved in a tense game with Oakland, and it seemed there might be a fight. Butterfield and Williams moved down the dugout runway, toward the field. "We'll fill this place full of uppercuts," Williams said. This guy is a warrior, Butterfield thought, and there was never any question in his mind that Williams would succeed, in New York or anywhere else.

Michael declined to trade Williams for Montreal's Larry Walker in 1994, fighting Steinbrenner to keep the 25-year-old switch-hitter. Club executives struggled to define his value, but his progress remained slow and steady. He hit 18 homers in 1995, his fifth season in the majors. He had enough service time to qualify for arbitration, and he was beginning to make big money. But he wasn't putting up big power numbers, certainly not Albert Belle–type numbers. The Yankees offered Williams a four-year, $24 million contract in 1996, and agent Scott Boras rejected this proposal; to the Yankees, the agent was asking for money commensurate with the standout Williams might become, rather than what he was: "a good player," as Yankees GM Bob Watson said, "but not a great player." The Yankees arranged a trade with Detroit, tentatively agreeing to swap him for two pitching prospects. But then they called off the deal and offered a five-year, $37.5 million proposal, which Boras also rejected. "This is star money for a nonstar player," Watson said. Williams, always easily wounded, internalized the implicit criticism. "I'm sure it hurt," David Cone would say later. "I'm sure all the contract squabbles hurt, regardless of what any ballplayer says. There's a need to feel wanted, a need for some sort of validation."

In the fall of 1998, Williams became a free agent, and Boras hinted to the Yankees that they would need to offer a package of close to $100 million, for a salary of more than $12 million annually—not just star money, but superstar money. And club officials just didn't think of Williams as a superstar. He had never hit more than 30 homers, and he missed 15 to 30 games with injuries each season. The executives began to have doubts about whether Williams wanted to remain with the team, because he had seemed aloof during the postseason. After beating San Diego in the World Series, the Yankees were honored at City Hall, and the fans were chanting for Williams to stay. Williams bent forward to speak into the microphone and said, "You've got to talk to this guy here," gesturing toward Steinbrenner, as if the decision were solely in the hands of the owner.

The Yankees offered Williams a five-year, $60 million contract, take it or leave it, knowing Boras would reject the offer. And they bore in on Albert Belle.

Boston general manager Dan Duquette was leery of being used as a negotiating pawn, but as the Yankees' interest in Belle started to look genuine and it seemed Williams might, in fact, be willing to leave New York, Duquette began talking with Boras. Williams and Boras flew to Atlanta to meet with Duquette and his manager, Jimy Williams. The Red Sox offered a seven-year, $91.5 million package that was even more attractive to the center fielder than the $100 million proposal discussed by Arizona; the Diamondbacks' deal included a lot of deferrals, and Williams was accustomed to playing within the intense Northeast baseball corridor. The Yankees did not alter their $60 million offer. They wanted Belle, even if Bernie Williams signed with the rival Red Sox.

Boras arranged a meeting with Steinbrenner at the Yankees' complex in Tampa, and he encouraged Williams to speak his mind. "This is the time to tell them how you feel," Boras said.

They met in the square conference room, its walls covered in team colors, blue on the bottom half and off-white on top, adorned with framed pictures of Yankees' players. Steinbrenner sat at one end of a 14-

foot oblong table, and Williams sat directly to his right; Boras, Newman, and Cashman also were in the room.

Williams began talking, and his tone had an edge that surprised Steinbrenner. He mentioned how he knew the Yankees had not viewed him as an elite player, but now, Williams said, he had a $91.5 million offer from the Red Sox and a $100 million commitment from the Arizona Diamondbacks. Offers like that, Williams said, meant that he was pretty good.

Then Williams went on to say how much he loved playing for the Yankees, how much he wanted to remain a Yankee. "You'll always be a Yankee in my eyes," Steinbrenner responded affectionately. Later, Steinbrenner would recall, "I understood this was a young man who truly wanted to be a Yankee, and he didn't like the idea of going to another team."

Boras had walked into the room believing the Yankees would not increase their offer. But after Steinbrenner spoke, he thought there was a chance. "Bernie had never heard those things from George—his entire relationship with him, ever since he was a young kid, George wouldn't even know his name," said Boras. "George wouldn't say anything to him. This was the first time the Yankees' owner had accredited him with the type of affection and affirmation that he had always wanted."

Steinbrenner told Williams he would talk with the Yankees' other executives and review their offer, but the team was deep into negotiations with Belle. Williams waited in his hotel room that night, waited for Boras to call him with Steinbrenner's revised offer—and there was nothing. Finally, he called Cashman directly, and when Cashman told him the organization wouldn't budge, it dawned on Williams that his tenure with the Yankees was over. He sadly boarded a plane to Puerto Rico the next morning, resigned to the notion that he would sign with Boston. Waleska Williams saw her husband's eyes when he arrived in Puerto Rico and thought he was the saddest she had ever seen him.

Cashman closed in on a deal with Belle, the negotiations complicated by competition. Baltimore Orioles owner Peter Angelos, frightened by what Belle might bring to the Yankees' offense, had joined the bidding in the eleventh hour. But Belle told Cashman that if he offered a four-year, $52 million deal—which would give Belle the highest annual salary in baseball—he was ready to sign. "If you get me this, I'll be a Yankee,"

Belle said. Steinbrenner approved the terms, and Cashman was ecstatic; the negotiations were closed.

Cashman called Belle's agent 15 minutes later to tell him Steinbrenner had approved the $52 million, and Arn Tellem told him there was a problem: Belle wasn't going to sign with the Yankees, Tellem said, because of concerns about playing in baseball's media capital. He wanted to sign with Baltimore, where only three beat reporters followed the Orioles daily. Cashman exploded at Tellem. The Yankees had framed all of their postseason plans around signing Belle, who had led them to believe he couldn't wait to play in the Bronx, and now, at the last second, they were going to lose the bidding—to a division rival, no less. And Cashman knew that at that moment, Boras might well be completing Williams's deal with Boston. He phoned Steinbrenner with the bad news, knowing he'd look like a fool. The Boss was livid, believing that Cashman had misread the situation.

Boras, who had flown to Colorado that morning to meet with Rockies executives about pitcher Kevin Brown, was handed an urgent message: call George Steinbrenner ASAP. Their conversation lasted about 20 minutes, and in that time, Steinbrenner increased his offer to Williams from five years and $60 million to $87.5 million over seven years, an increase of almost 50 percent; Boras and Williams had won, and Steinbrenner was humiliated. As their lightning negotiation drew to a close, Boras raised the issue of awards bonuses, the hundred-thousand-dollar rewards for Gold Glove awards and such, and Steinbrenner, needing to feel as if he prevailed in some way, snapped that there would be no such bonuses in this contract. Boras called Williams to tell him, and Williams shouted happily. "This is it, man," he said. "Yeah, yeah, *yeah.*"

Once Cashman calmed down, he phoned Belle and thanked him for being honest at the conclusion of the contract talks. Cashman emerged as the biggest loser in the negotiations; he remained in Steinbrenner's doghouse for weeks over the final capitulation to Boras, but he realized almost immediately that the Yankees might have dodged a major mistake. If Belle had come to the Bronx with mixed feelings, on edge about the media and the fan reception, inevitably there would have been problems. On the other end of the phone, Belle listened but offered no apology. "I'm glad you made the decision you did, for both of us," Cashman said.

Belle may have made his decision against signing with the Yankees days before. A friend of his said that the slugger never had any intention of signing with the Yankees, and his qualified agreement with Cashman—If you get me this, I'll be a Yankee—was merely an attempt to drive up the bidding. Once Belle and Tellem got the go-ahead on the four-year, $52 million offer from the Yankees, they were better positioned to demand a five-year, $65 million offer from the Orioles: $13 million per year over five years.

Belle began feuding with the Baltimore media less than a month after joining the Orioles, and by the end of the 1999 season, he was booed in Camden Yards and responded with obscene gestures. What was thought to be a nagging hip problem in 2000 was eventually diagnosed as a degenerative condition, and Belle's career ended the following spring, with the Orioles still owing him about $40 million. Cashman may have misplayed the bidding, but he was right about Belle—the surly slugger had done the Yankees an extraordinary service in changing his mind. Once, on a rainy day in Detroit, Paul O'Neill sat in the dugout and idly speculated about what would have happened if Belle's disintegration had taken place in pinstripes and if Williams had signed with Boston. The Yankees might not have survived the Red Sox in the 1999 playoffs, causing a string of changes, from the front office through the lineup. It didn't matter that Belle may have used the Yankees in negotiations, Cashman thought. What mattered was that the Yankees succeeded with Williams and Baltimore floundered with Belle, and the episode, Cashman believed, was a major turning point in the history of the franchise.

"If I would have been general manager, I would have been pushing for [Belle], too," Bernie Williams said, years later. "He was arguably one of the best players in baseball. You need to separate the financial and the personal, because those guys"—the Yankees' executives—"they're all good people, good guys. But they have a job to do, to the best of their ability, and their job is to sign you for the least amount of money as possible. . . . It just seems like except for Jeter, every player who was raised in the organization had to go through the roof to get a deal."

Friends said Williams was keenly aware that with his huge contract, there would come greater expectations and responsibility. The performance of many players dipped after they signed long-term deals, and Williams was intent on proving that his effort and intensity and desire would not diminish: in 1999, the first season of his new contract, he played in a career-high 158 games, batting .342 with 25 homers and 115 RBIs.

Many hitters littered their minds with dog-eared pages of mental notes. From pitch to pitch they would think about scouting reports, what the pitcher liked to throw ahead in the count or behind in the count, what the pitcher threw the last time they faced each other: don't chase that high fastball, don't let your front shoulder fly open, don't be too aggressive, don't be too passive. Forget that you haven't gotten a hit in two days, forget the umpire's last call, forget that last strikeout, and remember, try to forget that there are 50,000 people watching.

Williams worked hard at clearing this kind of clutter from his mind when he hit, stepping out of the batter's box from pitch to pitch. He was bilingual, and when he was angry with himself, the words that rattled around his brain were in Spanish. He would chase all that away, reducing his mental traffic to a few English-language mantras.

Every time he came up to hit, he established a guide for himself by laying his bat across the front of the plate, the knob close to him. Using the barrel as a ruler, he noted where the knob rested in the dirt and drew a line straight back from that point, in the direction of the umpire. If he stepped over the line in striding toward the pitcher, he would know he was leaning too far forward and was vulnerable to the inside pitch. If he stepped parallel to the line, then he could reach pitches on both sides of the plate.

He would not be hurried in this process, stepping out of the batter's box, looking down. The pitcher and catcher and umpire would be waiting for him, but Williams would not be rushed. Glenallen Hill, a teammate of Williams in 2000, thought he could always tell when Williams was going to do something well, because he would pause just a little longer between pitches. "That's when you know he knows exactly what he wants to do," Hill said.

Williams would play his guitar in the same way, sitting at his locker and rambling through medleys after workouts or before games, nodding his head slightly in time while looking at the floor. If someone approached, Williams would see the feet and quickly glance up, then refocus and continue to play. Visitors would wait for him to finish, to reach a comfortable break—maybe 30 seconds, maybe three minutes, maybe five minutes. The music, Williams said, helped him clear his mind.

There was a rhythm to his at-bats and his swing. He would draw his front foot back before stepping forward to swing, like a dancer's toe tap. O'Neill thought Williams's balance at the plate was extraordinary; he never allowed his center of gravity to stray or lag as he swung his bat. Some hitters would try to accelerate their bat and because their bodies lurched forward, they would actually slow down their bat. The path of his swing was classic, hitting coach Gary Denbo noted: Williams kept the bat in the hitting zone longer and covered more of the strike zone than most hitters, a motion that could be honed and maintained only through rigorous practice.

Joe Oliver, a longtime major league catcher, was in the habit of watching hitters, trying to read their intent from pitch to pitch, and he found Williams to be an enigma. "He's not like some guys when they come up to the plate, where they're digging in and they're ready to lift and separate," Oliver said, standing and demonstrating how a hitter would try to drive the ball. "He's very smooth. I didn't know how to pitch him a lot of times. You would never know what his approach was going to be, and it confuses a lot of pitchers and catchers."

Williams didn't try to anticipate what Curt Schilling or any other pitcher would throw; he wanted only to read and react from pitch to pitch. If the ball was thrown outside, he wanted to be able to reach out and slam it to the opposite field; if it was low and inside, he wanted to be able to golf the ball into the stands. He would step out from pitch to pitch, removing the clutter from his mind. He would not be rushed.

Damian Miller, the Arizona catcher, set his target over the outside corner after calling for a slider, and Williams swung over Schilling's breaking ball; strike 1. Schilling spun another slider, low, and Williams took it. Schilling threw two more off-speed pitches; Williams fouled off one of those, the count reaching 2 balls and 2 strikes.

Williams stepped out of the batter's box, staring at Schilling, blinking. He stepped back in.

Miller called for an outside fastball, the first fastball of the at-bat, before settling in a squat behind the outside corner. Schilling missed his target, his hummer zipping inside at 97 mph, but Williams didn't react, and he took strike 3, ending the Yankees' half of the fourth inning. Williams flipped his bat away, disgusted.

CHAPTER 10

AN EXCRUCIATING NOISE often jarred Mary Cashman out of her sleep; she once described it to a friend as sounding as if her husband was "chewing on marbles." Brian Cashman's teeth-grinding intensified whenever the Yankees were going through a difficult stretch or were playing in the postseason. Cashman was a chronic worrier, anyway; then something would go wrong with the team, and in the middle of the night, his upper and lower jaws would grate like ice in a blender. Dentists advised him that a mouth guard might reduce the volume of his grinding and save his teeth, but he fretted that the guard would leave him perpetually cotton mouthed, a common side effect. Anyway, he figured the problem would stop as soon as he changed jobs—and Steinbrenner's general managers tended to come and go like pizza deliverymen.

But the 2001 season was Cashman's fourth as the Yankees' GM. Four years of success and irate phone calls from Steinbrenner, four years of teeth-grinding, four years of the team's unrelenting mandate: Win now; win today; win every day; win every year. The finish line kept moving to the horizon, and the only true acknowledgment Cashman might get would come in the World Series. And even if the Yankees won, the euphoria lasted only a few days. Then there would be more meetings, more discussions, the pressure ratcheted up for the season scheduled to start five months later. Steinbrenner hated to lose, but he distrusted success, convincing himself that it would make his employees soft, so when the Yankees won he pushed even harder, calling for days of meetings. Cashman came to believe his job was like that of Sisyphus, the Greek mythology figure who was charged with eternally pushing a heavy rock uphill. But Steinbrenner was not the hill in the analogy, Cashman once said through a small smile. "He'd be the cactus behind you at the bottom," Cashman said. "The reason it's such a high-demanding job is because of him. He's got more energy than everybody in this organization combined. It's his organization and he sets the pace."

And the pace was frantic. Every team in baseball closed its offices for the week between Christmas and New Year's Day—except for the Yankees. Maybe the employees could go home, maybe not; it depended on how the Boss felt. During one of Cashman's negotiations, he had it written into his contract that he could take that week off. He spent part of his days working, anyway, of course: because the Yankees had the resources to get any player available for trade or as a free agent, Cashman had to be aware of any market fluctuation.

Most teams went through a natural cycle with their own accomplished players. First, they retained the players at relatively low salaries in their first three years in the majors. Then they negotiated with them through their arbitration-eligible years—their fourth, fifth, and sixth seasons. At some point, the decision was made whether to trade the player before he reached free agency and got too expensive, or sign him to a long-term deal. These were hard choices made within budget constraints. The Seattle Mariners hung on to superstar shortstop Alex Rodriguez through the 2000 season, his last year before becoming eligible for free agency, knowing that keeping him would help the team that year. But they also understood that Rodriguez would probably sign elsewhere after the season, and indeed, he agreed to a 10-year, $252 million deal to play for Texas. For the Mariners, it was the loss of their most valuable investment. The Yankees would not lose any of their treasured assets during the championship run; they had the money to keep all of their best players. Bernie Williams received his $87.5 million deal after the 1998 season; Mariano Rivera would get a four-year, $40 million contract; Jeter a 10-year, $189 million deal. But the Yankees' financial clout went far beyond holding on to their own stars; during the season, they had the cash to add players from other teams.

There was an assumption among players on the Yankees—and players with other teams—that the Yankees would make notable upgrades during the season. Some teams, like the Yankees, Red Sox, and Mets, increased their budgets during the season and made deals. Other teams did not, in spite of practical competitive requirements. "The payroll coming out of spring training, that was just the entry fee," said Phil Garner, who managed in Milwaukee and Detroit. "The next question for the contenders was, Are you willing to add another 10 percent onto your payroll during the season?"

Teams like the Brewers would stand pat through June and July, unwilling to add payroll, which dampened morale. "What began to happen at the end of my run in Milwaukee is players starting to say, 'I'm not buying your bullshit anymore. We can't make moves to put us over the hump,'" Garner said. "If you give players excuses, they'll take it. If you overplay the large-market versus small-market dynamic, they'll buy into it."

The Toronto Blue Jays traded for David Cone during the 1992 season and won the World Series, and almost every team that won a league championship in the decade that followed made an important midseason acquisition. Milwaukee vied with Toronto for the AL East title in the summer of '92, and Garner begged club executives to make a bid for Cone to help the Brewers' pitching and to keep Cone away from other teams in the division. But the Brewers stood pat. "Not only that," Garner said, "they took our advance scout away from me, to save $3,000."

General managers with other teams would break from spring training already pressed against their budgets' ceilings, and even if the team was playing well, many owners were fixed to their bottom line, telling their GMs they could add an expensive player only if they offset the cost through other moves. But the Yankees did not have a hard-and-fast budget, and Steinbrenner's willingness—his desire—to spend gave Cashman flexibility other GMs did not have. As San Diego GM Kevin Towers noted, "Cash has cash."

Gene Michael, Bob Watson, and Cashman used the cash as a significant bargaining chip. When the Yankees traded for Detroit slugger Cecil Fielder in the summer of 1996, they added $1 million in the deal. For the rights to Hideki Irabu, they would pay $3 million to San Diego. The Twins got $3 million in the deal for Chuck Knoblauch. The Yankees would tack on a little extra money for San Diego, a few hundred thousand dollars, to complete a trade for Sterling Hitchcock in the summer of 2001—a pittance for the Yankees, but a possible deal-breaker for the Padres.

The Yankees' money served them like an air bag, deployed when they made mistakes. Steinbrenner's willingness to absorb the cost of the team's personnel blunders and move on, Showalter believed, was crucial to the championships. The Yankees signed free agent Kenny Rogers to a four-year, $20 million contract before the 1996 season, despite concerns that Rogers did not have the psyche to pitch in New York. After two frustrating seasons, the Yankees would ship Rogers off to Oakland, in the deal that brought them Scott Brosius, and include $5 million to help pay the remainder of Rogers's salary. Third baseman Charlie Hayes became a clubhouse problem for Torre in '97, and because Hayes had another year on his contract, the Yankees dealt him to San Francisco along with $1.8 million to pay his entire salary.

Steinbrenner wanted Cashman to be aggressive, constantly hitting him with suggestions accompanied by warnings: *What about Jose Canseco? Well, he better not wind up with the Red Sox.* Cashman sorted through the possibilities carefully. His first obligation was to make the Yankees' major league team good enough to win a championship each season, but he was fully cognizant of the long-term effects of trades in which the Yankees gave away their best prospects; Steinbrenner had run the team into the ground doing just that in the 1980s. So when Cashman considered trade possibilities, he weighed the immediate benefits of trades against the broader ramifications. In his first couple of seasons as general manager, Cashman stood pat.

Before the midseason trade deadline in 1998, for example, Seattle took offers for Randy Johnson. Cashman believed his own pitching staff, which had set a record pace of 61-20 in the first half of the season, was

THE LAST NIGHT OF THE YANKEE DYNASTY

good enough to win the World Series, but Cleveland—the team that had knocked the Yankees out of the playoffs the previous year—was also talking with the Mariners about Johnson. Seattle wanted Pettitte, Ramiro Mendoza, and others in return for the All-Star left-hander, and Cashman didn't want to surrender that kind of talent. Cashman felt the Yankees would, in the end, pay double for Johnson, who was eligible to become a free agent after the season; after giving up young and cheap players to trade for Johnson, they would then attempt to sign him to a contract that would undoubtedly scrape the top of the market.

Cashman liked Johnson but didn't want him at that price. But he also didn't want the Indians to get him cheaply, so he kept calling Seattle GM Woody Woodward, making unacceptable offers but giving Woodward a chance to drive up the price. Just before the deadline, Seattle traded Johnson to the Houston Astros—out of the American League. Cashman had won the battle, though for the rest of the year, he hoped privately for the Astros' demise, because he was loath to see Johnson appear on the mound against the Yankees in the World Series.

Cashman and the Yankees took the same careful approach before the 1999 trade deadline, hanging on to Pettitte and making a minor deal to reacquire catcher Jim Leyritz, who had hit the most important home run of the 1996 World Series, a pivotal three-run blast off Atlanta reliever Mark Wohlers in Game 4. In the 1999 World Series, Leyritz hit a meaningless home run against the Braves, and Steinbrenner rewarded him with a new contract for 2000, even when the Yankees didn't really need him. The bomb against the Braves in '99, Leyritz joked to a friend, was his $1 million home run.

The Yankees had won championships in Cashman's first two years as GM, and he'd mostly hung on to the team's best prospects, his only mistake a swap of Class AAA third baseman Mike Lowell to Florida in return for three young pitchers; Lowell would develop into a star, while the pitchers never developed for the Yankees.

By then, working for Steinbrenner had begun to take a toll on Cashman. In February 1999, the Yankees had lost arbitration cases to Jeter and Rivera, the awards coming in at a total of $3.05 million more than the team's proposals. Steinbrenner, livid, hammered Cashman, who had turned down prehearing settlements in both cases. His title didn't change, but he was in Steinbrenner's crosshairs much of that season— the Yankees' version of purgatory, a place where almost all of the club's high-ranking executives intermittently resided. Cashman would make phone calls and gather information, as he had in '98, but friends said that Steinbrenner constantly belittled him and, more important, turned to what the owner called "my people," rather than the GM, for information.

In Bob Watson's last days as general manager, he had joked that Steinbrenner's "people" were voices running around in the owner's head. In truth, Steinbrenner listened to a range of opinions, including many from outside the Yankees' baseball offices, from Clyde King, a former pitcher who had briefly managed the Yankees in 1982, to Al Rosen, once a team president for Steinbrenner, to agent Tom Reich. Arthur Richman, a former public relations director for the Mets, happened to have Stein-brenner's ear in the fall of 1995, and it was Richman who encouraged Steinbrenner to hire Torre.

Steinbrenner's people would sometimes disagree with Cashman and the team's other executives, and Steinbrenner would present these opin-ions—usually without the names or credentials of his sources—as evi-dence that the executives were screwing up: *My people tell me this Soriano kid can't play*. It was a management style that led to debate and discussion, but some of Steinbrenner's subordinates didn't think his goal was to foster thought as much as it was to humiliate. "You'd try to figure out who was giving him advice, to understand what his thought process was," one executive said, "but it was a waste of time. Brian was going to get blindsided, no matter what he did."

Cashman may have been better equipped than others to understand Steinbrenner and how the Yankees made decisions because, unlike Wat-son and most of his other predecessors, he was an insider. His father, John Cashman, operated a Florida horse farm and knew Steinbrenner through a mutual friend, and Brian Cashman first joined the Yankees as an 18-year-old summer intern in 1986. He compiled reports from the club's minor league affiliates in the daytime hours and sometimes worked with the Yankee Stadium security detail during games, aiding in the ejection of unruly, imbibing fans. He signed on full-time after graduating from Catholic University in 1989, and in 1992 became an assistant general manager, plunging into a range of administrative responsibilities that brought him into contact with the Yankees' clan in Tampa. Steinbrenner had once introduced him to other executives, telling them they would work for Cashman someday. But Cashman never thought of the general manager's job as a goal, he said, and there were days—when he overheard Steinbrenner castigating then GM Woody Woodward, for instance—that Cashman was sure he wouldn't want the position even if it was offered.

On a February morning in 1998, however, Watson walked into Cashman's office and said he'd decided to quit his job, and that he had recommended Cashman as his replacement. "And I think you're going to be offered the job later today," Watson said. "You've got a lot to think about, buddy."

Cashman met with Steinbrenner that afternoon, and he later liked to raise his voice several octaves to imitate his squeaky, tentative response to the Boss's offer: "I'm your man." Cashman was 30 years old, the second-youngest GM ever in baseball at that time—Randy Smith had been 29 when he took over the Padres in 1993—and he was excited and overwhelmed, feeling as if he'd just been handed something important, some irreplaceable jewel. "I didn't want to mess anything up," he said. "This is a very important franchise for people all over the world, and I didn't want to mess that up. I didn't want someone to have to come in after me and clean up a big mess." Cashman told Steinbrenner he initially wanted only a one-year deal, so he could prove himself to the owner.

Cashman was, in many respects, a perfect general manager for Steinbrenner because he had been trained within the organization, knew Steinbrenner's expectations, and could at least attempt to anticipate what Steinbrenner might want. He also had no track record and therefore no assumption of how much influence he should have or how he should be treated. Other experienced general managers had taken jobs with Steinbrenner and been appalled by the way he talked down to them and had lasted only months.

Cashman fit smoothly into the Yankees' chain of command because he needed the others. He had never formally worked as a scout, so he had to rely on Gene Michael and Lin Garrett and Gordon Blakeley, who ran the various scouting departments. He didn't have experience overseeing the farm system, as Mark Newman did. But Cashman had working relationships with each of the club executives, and he understood how the distance between the team's offices in Tampa and New York could become a problem.

Steinbrenner spent most of his time in Tampa, while the general manager was based in New York, and for years there had been little communication between the two branches. One of the executives in Tampa might lobby Steinbrenner directly, undercutting the others; some of the Yankees officials were deeply suspicious of Billy Connors, Steinbrenner's pitching advisor, in this regard. The dynamic promoted rifts and created turf wars. Steinbrenner tended to wear down his Tampa executives with his constant stalking around, being dissatisfied; diverting blame and constructing operational moats—*Make sure the Boss knows the mistake isn't yours*—became prime job responsibilities. During Michael's tenure as general manager, one of the Tampa-based executives required the Yankees' minor league managers and coaches to report any contact with the GM, as if such conversations were the equivalent of diplomatic relations. Bob Watson served as general manager for 27 months and had a good working relationship with Torre, but made little progress in bridging the void between the offices in New York and Tampa. Agents shopping free agent players preferred to deal directly with Steinbrenner; even if he didn't negotiate contracts, he at least knew which of his executives was currently empowered.

But for several years, Cashman nurtured an alliance of the factions. He and Newman and the others would talk and work toward a consensus they could present to Steinbrenner. "Having Brian up there has been very good for everybody, very good," Steinbrenner said at one point. "There is no jealousy, I won't allow that to happen. Cashman is doing an outstanding job, but without the other parts of the organization, he would be just another guy, and without each other, the others would be just another guy."

Cashman provided context to the trade talks through his conversations with scouts, agents, rival executives, and players. He was better at gathering information, San Diego GM Kevin Towers thought, than anyone else in the game. He always knew who was available for trade and why and which teams were interested, and who had an off-field problem that could affect his play. He felt it was important to know about deals between other teams as they were being developed, before they came down. This was a way for Cashman to check his own diligence in intelligence gathering: if he didn't know about a trade ahead of time, he figured he hadn't made the right phone calls. He spent much of his day on the phone, both at the office and at home. "The phone or the pager, constantly," said John Cashman. "The house phone, the cell phone."

There were no pictures hanging in Cashman's Yankee Stadium office, no shots of him shaking hands with a U.S. president or grinning under a rain of Champagne. Windows that opened to the stadium were built into one wall in his office, and two of the other three walls were covered with tiles containing the names of every player on every 40-man roster in the major leagues, with age, service time, and salary listed in small black lettering. The fourth wall was covered with the names of each player in the Yankees' organization. Piles of records rested on his desk and around his desk. When Cashman was growing up, his father said, his bedroom was cluttered, but he still was absolutely organized in what he did.

Data was collected, processed, stored, applied. Cashman detailed each of his many conversations with agents and general managers in computer files, the talks dating back to the days when he was an assistant GM. Seattle general manager Pat Gillick and Atlanta GM John Schuerholz were known for their extraordinary memories; Gillick had a veritable phone directory stored in his head. Cashman preferred to write everything down, so he could check the chronology of trade discussions and force himself to think through discussions.

Physically, he seemed cast for the role of a cerebral general manager: after seven weeks in Florida for spring training, his pale white complexion would hardly have changed; college buddies called him Powder. He was about five feet seven, with the bulk once gained through weight lifting now gone; he looked almost frail, especially with a suit coat draped over him. Cashman had trouble keeping pounds on his body because there was the small problem of remembering to eat between phone calls.

He was well liked by rival executives, who saw him as genial and humble. But Gene Michael thought that Cashman, in his heart, believed he could outwork anybody, make better arguments than anybody. "You'd have to have an ego just to be in the trenches like he is," said John Cashman. "If you didn't, you'd get run over. He's feisty, I know that. He'll fight verbally with anybody."

He would have to. After the costly arbitration losses to Jeter and Rivera, Steinbrenner effectively jettisoned Cashman from his inner circle for parts of the 1999 season, and other Yankees' officials were aware of serious, shouting arguments between the two men. John Cashman thought there was a period in 1999 and 2000 when his son was almost burned out, tired, ranting and raving. But Cashman had regained some peace of mind during the 2000 season, friends felt, maintaining his work ethic while distancing himself emotionally from the daily exchanges with Steinbrenner.

He stopped personalizing every setback, Mary Cashman thought, every criticism. He drew conclusions and moved on, and in 2000, his work and Steinbrenner's money turned the team around in midseason.

Still, Cashman jousted constantly with Steinbrenner in 2000. The Yankees turned down Anaheim's offer of slugging outfielder Jim Edmonds for Alfonso Soriano during spring training that year, and Edmonds was dealt to St. Louis, where he put up big numbers. Steinbrenner was enraged, especially because the Yankees' offense, dominant in 1998, was beginning to slow. Tino Martinez struggled much of the season, Brosius's average dipped to .230, and O'Neill's production was gradually regressing. On June 23, the Yankees were 36-32, in third place behind Boston and Toronto, and for the first time in Cashman's tenure as GM, the team had weaknesses—in its rotation depth, everyday lineup, and bench. With the Yankees' payroll nearing $100 million, Steinbrenner was furious that his money wasn't buying better performance.

The Chicago Cubs were considering trading slugger Sammy Sosa, a player of the type Steinbrenner loved: an established superstar with gaudy statistics. But Sosa wanted a contract extension that might cost the Yankees anywhere from $15 million to $20 million annually, at a time when they were about to face the huge price tag on Jeter; plus, the Cubs wanted five top-flight prospects in return. The cost in salary and prospects was far too great, as far as Steinbrenner's subordinates were concerned, and there was an underlying question about whether Sosa, who was often accompanied by an entourage of attendants, would fit in with the other Yankees in personality and playing style. The Yankees arranged a conditional trade for Detroit outfielder Juan Gonzalez instead, but Gonzalez vetoed the deal, wary of playing in New York. Houston's Moises Alou turned down a possible trade as well.

The day after Gonzalez rejected the trade, Cashman called the Cleveland Indians to find out how he could get a '99 championship ring to Gary Tuck, the former Yankees catching instructor who had taken a job with the Indians. Mark Shapiro, the assistant GM for Cleveland, answered the question and then mentioned that David Justice was available in a trade. The veteran outfielder was having a good season, hitting for power; he was earning $7 million that year and had two more years remaining on his contract at the same salary. The Indians wanted Justice's deal off their books and weren't asking for significant prospects in return. Cashman thought Justice was an ideal solution to the Yankees' lack of a big bat: his salary was locked in, and the organization wouldn't have to sacrifice its best prospects. Gene Michael fully endorsed the trade, believing that Justice was exceptionally tough-minded: he had played in the postseason almost every year in his career for Atlanta and for the Indians, hitting a crucial home run in the 1995 World Series. A deal was quickly arranged—Justice for Ledee and minor league pitchers Zach Day and Jake Westbrook.

In the weeks that followed, Cashman purposefully added seven other veterans—infielders Jose Vizcaino and Luis Sojo, pitchers Denny Neagle and Dwight Gooden (the latter at Steinbrenner's insistence), and outfielders Glenallen Hill and Luis Polonia—who would each make notable contributions. Former All-Star Jose Canseco fell into Cashman's lap when he was surprisingly awarded to the Yankees on a waiver claim.

(The Yankees had no practical use for Canseco, and Torre wasn't exactly thrilled about the acquisition. "I'm a little stunned," he said, momentarily forgetting, perhaps, that other managers would have been thrilled to have Torre's roster problems.)

Justice transformed the offense that summer, hitting .305 with 20 homers, 60 RBIs, and 39 walks in 78 games, and he played much better defensively than expected, smoothly tracking down long flies and cutting off balls hit into the left-center-field gap. During the playoffs, he again ignited the team. With the Yankees trailing Seattle 1–0 in Game 2 of the AL Championship Series after being shut out in Game 1, Justice led off the eighth inning against reliever Arthur Rhodes. Justice whacked a double against the fence in left-center field, then scored the tying run when Bernie Williams singled—the Yankees' first run after 16 consecutive scoreless innings. That run relieved a building tension, Torre thought; the Yankees went on to score six more runs in the inning.

The team won two of three in Seattle and came home for Game 6 with a chance to set up the city's first Subway Series since 1956—the Mets had finished off St. Louis in the NL Championship Series the night before. But the Yankees, who had struggled through the season and barely survived Oakland in the Division Series, trailed the Mariners in the seventh inning, 4–3, the tension in Yankee Stadium rising once more. Justice came to bat with runners at first and third, one out, Rhodes on the mound.

Part of the reason the Yankees wanted Justice was that although he was left-handed, he was adept at hitting left-handed pitchers, like Rhodes. With the count 2 balls and 1 strike, Justice checked his swing, and when the Mariners appealed to third base umpire Mark Hirschbeck, the ump flattened his hands: no swing. Seattle manager Lou Piniella screamed from the Seattle dugout; the call had brought the count to 3 balls and 1 strike, and now Justice knew that Rhodes would have to throw a fastball. Rhodes fired his next pitch. Justice timed the fastball perfectly and destroyed the ball, the thick sound of perfect contact unmistakable. Knowing he had hit a home run, a monster shot to right field, he turned toward first base and pumped his arm, and later, his voice choked up as he described the feeling of rounding second base and looking up to see the stands shaking, the fans going wild. "I wish you all could've experienced that feeling," Justice told reporters.

The Yankees finished off the Mariners, their success possible, Piniella thought, only because they had augmented their roster during the season. "I think if they would've stood pat it would've been the wrong decision," Piniella said. "You give an organization like New York the credit for recognizing that and going out and doing the things in volume that they did."

Cashman made more deals the next year without a similar impact, adding pitchers Jay Witasick, Mark Wohlers, and Sterling Hitchcock, and utilitymen Enrique Wilson and Randy Velarde. The 2001 season was the last on Cashman's contract, and he was getting fed up. His days at Yankee Stadium lasted 15 hours, and even when the team played road games and he could go home at night, Steinbrenner's presence in his life was constant. He called during games and after games and late at night, complaining that the Yankees weren't good enough, warning Cashman that he was responsible for the mess. Steinbrenner sometimes ordered him to fly to Tampa immediately or to join the team on the road, with little or no explanation. And sometimes, when Cashman or another executive rushed to Florida for a command performance, Steinbrenner would ask why he was there.

The passion that Cashman had when he first took the job in 1998 slowly bled out of him, and in this, he was like a lot of the men and women employed by the Yankees. He wanted to work in baseball, and the Yankees represented the pinnacle of the business, the most competitive organization with the most resources and the greatest history of success. Like the others, he accepted the fact that working for Steinbrenner meant long days, family functions missed or canceled, and many weekends and evenings when the Yankees would come before children and spouse. This was Steinbrenner's third decade as owner and his reputation was established; it was buyer beware, in a sense, because staff members took their jobs having heard all the horror stories. But many of the employees had not fully anticipated how joyless the organization could be in spite of its remarkable record. Some left the team simply to make their personal lives more tenable. But leaving the Yankees was like stepping off the top of a professional pyramid, and many employees stayed and were miserable much of the time.

Cashman would have opportunities with other teams after the 2001 World Series. The Toronto Blue Jays and the Orioles were interested in talking to him about running their baseball operations. And it seemed possible that he would emerge as a candidate for general manager of the Boston Red Sox, once ownership changed there. There were days when Mary Cashman was certain her husband intended to leave the Yankees. They talked about other cities, about how the move would affect their three-year-old daughter. Mary Cashman had grown up in Westchester County and had always wanted to stay close to home, but she told Brian she'd go wherever he wanted. "If you want to do it, then do it now," she said.

San Diego general manager Kevin Towers would call Cashman and hear the weariness in his friend's voice, knowing how much stress he bore each day. "You hear people talk all the time about how great it would be to have the Yankees' money," said Towers. "To me, I think it's almost more difficult when you have that much more money, because expectations are through the roof. Anything less than a World Series title and people think you've done a bad job."

But Brian Cashman agreed to a three-year extension, for 2002 and beyond, signing for more money—more than $1 million per season, which was the highest GM salary in baseball at the time—and more pressure. "I didn't know what he was going to do," said his father. "I was hoping he wouldn't leave. He would've always regretted it, I think. It's the only job he's had. He's a Yankee, period. Probably in the long term it's going to work to his benefit, because he will have seen it all. I'm not saying it isn't difficult at times. You always wish he'd have more time to enjoy himself."

Cashman would watch the World Series against the Diamondbacks anxiously, counting the strikes left in the game—something he always did—keeping track of how many outs the Yankees needed to finish off another team. He counted down from 27 outs through Game 7 of the 2001 World Series, sitting next to Mary in the stands; she did not share his habit of calculating outs and strikes.

The Yankees needed 18 more outs to finish Game 7 as Clemens took the mound for the bottom of the fourth. But Schilling was dominating the Yankees, throwing only 46 pitches through his first four innings, and Clemens was laboring. He required 62 pitches to get through the first three innings—high-stress innings, because he had to work with runners on base for eight of the first 14 batters he faced. At that rate, Clemens would never reach the seventh inning.

Danny Bautista flied out to open the bottom of the fourth; despite his difficulties, Clemens had retired the leadoff batter in every inning. Mark Grace singled to left, but Miller swung and missed a fastball, fouled off a splitter for strike two, and then waved helplessly at a 95 mph fastball, a three-pitch strikeout. Schilling came to bat with two outs, and Clemens quickly reached a two-strike count, then blew a 97 mph fastball past the other pitcher for his eighth strikeout. Clemens strolled to the dugout stoically, glancing over his left shoulder at the scoreboard. Through four complete innings of Game 7, neither team had mustered a single run.

CHAPTER 11

BASEBALL HAD filled David Cone's autumns for most of a decade, but he was out of the playoffs in 2001, his first October away from the Yankees since 1994. So he and Lynn Cone, his wife, went to Stowe, Vermont, during the World Series to see fall's last fading colors, driving along two-lane roads covered with curled brown leaves. At the end of their days, though, they made time for baseball. Some players didn't like watching the postseason games on television because as bystanders they found the pace excruciatingly slow. Others abstained because of the frustration they felt at not participating. But Cone's allegiance to his old teammates was still strong, and he watched every inning. He was not part of the group attempting to win a fourth consecutive championship, but he felt a part of it.

The Cones returned home to Connecticut, and on November 4, their day was planned around Game 7. They ordered takeout from Lamonaco's, a pizzeria in North Branford, picked up plates of fish and pasta, and settled in front of the television. Cone watched baseball in the same way he had competed, concentrating on each pitch, outwardly calm but intense—like Torre in the dugout, Lynn thought. She sometimes tried to make a point or ask a question, but Cone, completely focused, would gently shush her until there was a pause in the game.

Lynn rooted for the Diamondbacks, seeing the same soul in the Arizona players that had been evident in the Yankees for so many years but was now disintegrating, she thought. Her husband, of course, wanted success for Tino Martinez, Paul O'Neill, Mariano Rivera, and Mel Stottlemyre and others. His separation from the Yankees the previous winter had stripped away some sentiment, but his friends playing on the field in Arizona were adding onto a legacy he helped to construct. Cone had pitched 5½ seasons for the Yankees and won 64 regular-season games and six more in the postseason, including a pivotal Game 3 in the 1996 World Series against Atlanta. But he wielded far-ranging influence on the team, and not just on the days he pitched, for Cone was a natural politician, navigating the competing factions—the players, the management, the reporters who covered the sport—and swaying each group deftly. He could manipulate without engendering real resentment or suspicion; he could argue without offending; he could drive an agenda without sounding like a zealot. "He had a way of talking and making you understand," said catcher Jorge Posada. "During the championship years, we never really had a problem in the clubhouse, and part of that was because veteran guys talked to the younger guys, and there was no miscommunication. And David Cone was a big part of that."

Cone, Bernie Williams thought, was the voice of the Yankees' players in his years with the team, his public words often representing their collective will. That a starting pitcher would serve in this capacity was unusual; on most teams, the de facto spokesman was a position player. Within the clubhouse culture, position players were commonly viewed as the natural leaders—the alpha group—because they were on the field every day. A starting pitcher, on the other hand, might appear in 35 or 36 games over the course of an entire season. On most teams, pitchers were to be seen and not heard. When the Orioles slumped early one season, pitcher Mike Mussina spoke bluntly to reporters about how the team needed to play better and play harder, and the next day, Baltimore shortstop Cal Ripken summoned Mussina to the infield during batting practice and very firmly addressed his comments. The message was clear:

keep that kind of thing in-house, and if anybody is going to say it, it shouldn't be you.

Don Mattingly had served the role of de facto spokesman for the Yankees for years, but he retired after the 1995 season, leaving a void that was evident the next spring. Paul O'Neill did not like dealing with reporters daily, especially when he or the team was playing well, because he thought that commenting on success was bad luck. Bernie Williams was naturally reticent and tended to escape the clubhouse quickly after games. Derek Jeter was only a rookie, and Tino Martinez and Joe Girardi were new to the team. Cone recognized all this and thought there was a need for someone to make himself available to reporters, and he knew this was especially true in New York, where the media drum beat relentlessly. From his experience of six seasons with the Mets, Cone understood that every beat reporter and columnist was responsible for daily stories, regardless of whether the players spoke to them or not. Cone thought it was desirable, then, that the players' perspective be reflected in the papers, and more than any other player, he recognized the value of spin. He liked talking with reporters, had known many of them for years, and embraced the chance to relieve his teammates of pressure, understanding how his words could shape the next day's stories. The reluctance of other players to talk to reporters baffled him because, as he noted, you could answer any question any way you wanted.

Cone routinely acknowledged his own mistakes or a general failing of the team because he had learned that this tactic often defused an issue, particularly in New York, where failure was dissected in the newspapers, on radio, and on television. If you hung a slider for a home run with a count of no balls and two strikes, there was no point in trying to defend the selection. Just admit the lapse in judgment and move on, and reporters and fans would move on, as well. If Cone pitched well and lost, he accepted full responsibility for the defeat. He knew that if he blamed an infielder's defensive lapse or a lack of run support, he would only create more headlines—CONE BLASTS JETER—and spotlight a teammate's mistake. He had enough confidence in his own ability to take responsibility for a loss, even when he wasn't responsible. In this way Cone controlled reporters, presenting the preferred message, and in time nearly all his teammates routinely accepted responsibility for their mistakes.

He was probably quoted more than any other Yankee during the dynasty, and most pitchers would have been resented for this by other players, who would have seen them as attention seekers. But Cone's teammates realized he was trying to help everyone and acknowledged his skill with the media. During a day of possible crisis or before a big game, Cone would linger in front of his locker, a magnet for reporters. He might talk for 15 minutes, a half hour, longer, and by speaking, he relieved teammates of that responsibility. "He put everyone else on the team first when he did that," Girardi said. In the spring training after Cone left the team, reliever Mike Stanton began lingering at his locker—which happened to be Cone's old locker—and making himself available to reporters when there were important developments. In an insatiable media market, Stanton realized, Cone's role had been important to the team, and somebody needed to step into his shoes. Stanton sometimes asked reporters if he had answered a question the way Cone might have, his curiosity sincere.

Cone had not always controlled the press, of course. His career was covered with media scars. While pitching for the Mets in the 1988 playoffs, Cone agreed to cooperate with the *Daily News* and provide his name and thoughts to a column ghostwritten by beat reporter Bob Klapisch, and under Cone's byline appeared taunting words for the Dodgers and a belittling of reliever Jay Howell: "Seeing Howell and his curveball reminded us of a high school pitcher." The Dodgers, inflamed by Cone's printed remarks, beat him in his next game and went on to win the series, and years later, Davey Johnson—the manager of the Mets in that era—would say his greatest regret of that season was "David Cone's literary career."

In his days with the Mets, Cone was named in lurid sex scandals (though never charged with any crime) that made banner headlines in the tabloids, and later, during the protracted labor war of 1994–95, he had been an outspoken and visible representative for the union, once joining a contingent of players who met with President Bill Clinton. Fans castigated Cone and other notable union leaders after the strike ended. Despite those experiences, however, Cone never fled from reporters.

His locker was the closest to Torre's office, and the manager would talk to Cone about some of his decisions, about the mood of the players, or what might be said during a team meeting. Cashman occasionally sought Cone's thoughts about possible acquisitions. Some players, like O'Neill, were uncomfortable offering opinions, feeling it was not their place to pass judgment on other players. But Cone was frank. Before the 1999 season, the Yankees were considering a veteran American League reliever as a possible trade target, and Cone told Cashman that the pitcher was a good guy but lacked heart, an assessment that ended the inquiry. The other Yankees knew of only some of these conversations, but Cone had such credibility with his teammates that he was not viewed as a kiss-ass or suspected of bad-mouthing them. "Everything he did, he did for the good of the team," Andy Pettitte said. "There was never any doubt about that."

He also would counsel teammates, sometimes directly, sometimes subtly. In Joe Girardi's first days with the Yankees, he hit some weak ground balls, and because he was replacing an established .300 hitter in Mike Stanley, there was immediate backlash from some fans and members of the media. WFAN, the city's 24-hour sports station, kept rerunning a radio clip of Girardi grounding the ball to the pitcher, and this became the catalyst for early call-in complaints: *This guy has never hit for power, the Yankees have a huge hole in their lineup.* Girardi mentioned to Cone how much it bothered him. Call WFAN, Cone suggested, and all you have to do is give them one interview: make fun of yourself, acknowledge your low average, show them you don't take yourself too seriously. If you do this, Cone said, it'll all end. Girardi thought about it overnight and followed the advice the next day, receiving an immediate response. The angry calls faded away, and Girardi relaxed and began to hit; the broadcasters gave him a chance. He would leave the Yankees with three World Series rings. Time and again, he would thank Cone for his suggestion.

Chuck Knoblauch would listen to Cone during the playoffs of 1998, after making a pivotal and ugly mistake. In the 12th inning of Game 2, the Yankees were tied 1–1 with the Cleveland Indians. With pinch-runner Enrique Wilson at first, Travis Fryman bunted. Knoblauch had moved over from his position at second base to cover first, but the throw from Tino Martinez hit Fryman and rolled past Knoblauch. Rather than retrieve the ball and stop Wilson from advancing around the bases, Knoblauch tried to point out to umpires that Fryman had interfered on the play. As fans and teammates screamed for him to get the ball resting on the ground, Knoblauch stood and motioned to the spot of the supposed violation. Wilson careened around the bases and scored before Knoblauch finally regained his senses. The Yankees lost the game, and afterward, an army of reporters gathered at Knoblauch's locker, waiting for an explanation. Knoblauch politely but firmly said that he had done nothing wrong.

After the Yankees boarded their charter to Cleveland, Cone headed to the back of the plane, where Knoblauch sat. Some teammates found Knoblauch's intensity impenetrable and left him alone, but Cone and Knoblauch had a collegial relationship, their lockers adjacent in the Yankees' clubhouse, and Cone thought Knoblauch needed some advice. "I got you beat," Cone said, and went on to recount an incident from early in his career with the Mets. Pitching against the Braves in 1990, Cone had run to cover first base on a close play, his foot hitting the base, and when umpire Charlie Williams called the runner safe, Cone immediately charged Williams to argue, going face-to-face. But Cone failed to ask for a time-out, and as he complained, Atlanta runners circled the bases behind him. By the time Mets first baseman Gregg Jefferies grabbed Cone to alert him, two runners had circled the bases and Cone had assured himself a permanent place in baseball's legacy of blunders. On any given summer day, his mistake was probably being replayed between innings in some ballpark. Knoblauch and Cone sipped beer and chatted, and as Knoblauch became more relaxed, Cone made his point. "You know, there's nothing wrong with admitting you made a mistake," he said. "If you're perceived to be in denial, it's only going to get worse. That's just the way the media is." The next day, Knoblauch entered a roomful of reporters, climbed behind a microphone, and admitted he had blown the play, defusing the issue.

When the players met each September to discuss the disbursing of the pool of money made during the playoffs and World Series, the shares voting usually went according to Cone's recommendations, even when he proposed sacrifice. Almost all of the members of the Yankees' clubhouse community received full shares, from trainers Gene Monahan and Steve Donohue to the clubhouse operators, Rob and Lou Cucuzza, and batting practice pitchers Charlie Wonsowicz and Mike Borzello. The batboys were given money, in addition to the pool of players' tips gathered at the end of the season, generally receiving $2,000 or $3,000.

The Yankees' minor league coaches were not so well cared for. They were paid salaries for their work during the season, but in the off-season, they were expected to live in the Tampa area and be available to work full days at the complex on Himes Avenue, hitting grounders and throwing batting practice, for no extra compensation. Once spring training began, the coaches who worked with the major leaguers were not given daily meal money; there was no need, they were told, because they lived at home. These coaches had no leverage, and they were sure that if they protested, they would risk losing their jobs. When the Yankees met to vote on postseason shares in 1998, Cone, Girardi, Jeter, and Chili Davis talked about this situation. These guys work hard for us, they said, and it would mean a lot to them if we showed them some appreciation. A full postseason share was allotted to the coaches, to be split among them— about $30,000 apiece for those chosen. "The money allowed us to pay off some bills and get ahead of the game for a change," said Gary Denbo, a hitting instructor. "It made us feel more of a part of the championship season." The gesture, club vice president Mark Newman thought, resonated throughout the organization, connecting the big leaguers to the lowest levels of the team. The impact of something like that, Newman believed, was hard to estimate.

But Cone's pitching and the way he competed accounted for the bulk of his credibility with teammates. His games often played out like action movies, with Cone in the starring role, scraping through one crisis or another, improvising and usually succeeding. As a young pitcher he had had a powerful arm, and his instinct was to prevent the hitter from making contact, to go for the strikeout every time. Cone fell behind in the ball-strike counts constantly, not because of control trouble, but because of stubbornness. If the hitter expected a fastball, if the situation demanded a fastball—bases loaded, full count, nobody out—well, then, fuck it, Cone would throw a splitter. He would not surrender.

Pitchers constantly tinkered with new pitches while playing catch or throwing in the bullpen, testing a changeup or breaking ball, refining it for weeks or months before having the courage to throw it in a game. But Cone seemed to invent pitches in the middle of games, sometimes deciding in the middle of his windup to throw sidearm or change speeds, relying on his understanding of how to grip a baseball and his own feel for the moment.

Mets manager Bobby Valentine thought Cone released the ball from more angles than even the notoriously funky-throwing Orlando Hernandez and was more unpredictable, too. Cone had played Wiffle ball as a kid growing up in Kansas City, making the plastic ball break in different directions by throwing from different angles and with different grips, and he pitched in the major leagues the same way.

His face would transform when he was on the mound, his complexion reddening deeply from intensity or from anger and embarrassment when the game was going poorly. Neck muscles emerged, worry lines erupted on his forehead, veins popped up. Main Vein, he had been called as an adolescent. In the last years of his career, Cone talked each spring training about becoming more efficient, about trying to get more ground balls and reducing his pitch count. It was a theory he would never apply, however—he would have had to concede contact to the hitters.

Cone averaged 18 or 19 pitches per inning, five or six more than the most efficient pitchers; over the course of a season of 200 innings, this meant Cone would throw about 1,000 more pitches than many other pitchers. Based on the average number of pitches he threw inning to inning, Cone probably totaled about 110,000 pitches in his career—an accumulation of about 10,500 tons of force on his shoulder, according to an estimate by Yale physics professor Robert Adair; it was a toll increased by his obstinate style. In one game against the San Francisco Giants in 1992, Cone threw 166 pitches, 40 more than he probably should have. Arm trouble was probably inevitable.

In 1996, he developed a potentially fatal aneurysm, a frightening ailment that could have killed him, and was forced to sit out most of the season. There was much uncertainty about whether he would recover enough to help the team when he came back in September. But in his first game back, Cone threw seven innings against Oakland without allowing a hit. It was as if he could reach deep within himself to draw from some unseen reservoir of will, Joe Girardi thought.

With the Yankees down two games in the 1996 World Series, Joe Torre picked Cone to throw Game 3, in Atlanta—theoretically because warmer weather would help Cone's circulation and because Torre guessed that Game 3 would swing the Series. "Let's not get embarrassed," Steinbrenner told Torre, fretting about his team getting swept, and Torre replied the Yankees would be fine: they had Cone going in Game 3.

Cone shut out the Braves through the first five innings, the Yankees piecing together a couple of runs, but Atlanta loaded the bases with one out in the sixth. Torre wondered if Cone might be tiring, and with left-handed hitters Fred McGriff and Ryan Klesko due to bat, he went to the mound. He had the option of summoning left-handed Graeme Lloyd, but he wanted to hear from Cone first.

Cone's summation of his condition was almost preordained. In any given situation, his arm could be throbbing, he might have allowed a series of hits, but he was always certain he could get the next hitter and extricate himself from trouble. It was his nature to say he was OK, but this trouble was in Game 3 of the World Series and the Yankees would probably be swept if Atlanta took the lead. "This is very important," Torre said, staring into Cone's eyes. "I need the truth from you. How do you feel?"

"I'm OK," said Cone. "I lost the feel for my slider a little bit there, but I'm OK. I'll get this guy for you."

"I've got to know the truth, so don't bullshit me," Torre said.

Torre would manage Cone for five years, seeking his counsel, relying

on Cone's clubhouse radar and leadership. Torre would sometimes won-
der, however, if Cone was being completely honest with him about how
he felt, and truth was, he would never really know. All he could do was
ask the question and trust his instinct. This is what he did, standing on
the mound in the sixth inning of Game 3 of the 1996 World Series. "I
can get him," Cone said. "I can get out of this inning."

"Let's go get them," Torre said, before turning and heading back to the
dugout.

McGriff popped up; two outs. Cone walked Klesko, forcing home a
run to cut the Yankees' lead to 2–1. Better to do this, Cone thought, than
to give in to Klesko and throw a pitch he could drive. Javy Lopez popped
out, and the Yankees went on to win the game. Years after the fact, Torre
talked about how that victory, and Cone's effort, had turned the World
Series, the first of the Yankees' recent championships.

Cone's shoulder would break down at the end of the 1997 season, and
after pitching badly in the playoff series to Cleveland, he had surgery
and began his off-season throwing program early, on a cruise ship. He
went 15-3 in the first four months of the 1998 season, but his shoulder
ached badly. There was a moment each morning, when he first moved
his right arm, when Cone would listen to the crackling and popping in
his shoulder and get a sense of how his pain would be that day. He
stopped throwing in the bullpen between starts, saving his arm for the
day he pitched. Cone played catch on some of his days off between his
starts, slowly lofting the ball without extending his arm—as if he was
throwing a pie, Girardi said. Before one game that season, Girardi had
gone to the bullpen to catch while Cone warmed up, and after a couple
of pitches, Cone ordered Girardi to leave. He was struggling to get loose,
and he did not want Girardi to see him in a compromised state. Every
game Cone pitched late that year, Girardi recalled, Cone's challenge was
to find an arm slot from which he could throw comfortably; sometimes it
was three-quarters motion, sometimes lower. If Cone dropped down to
throw his sidearm slider—his Laredo, he called it—in the early innings,
Stottlemyre was relieved. Cone must be feeling reasonably well, Stottlemyre thought, if he could change his arm angles.

Cone always said he was OK, but his teammates knew otherwise.

"His shoulder was killing him the whole year," said Mike Stanton. "Sometimes you didn't know if he was going to make his next start. He wouldn't be able to throw for three days, and then he'd go out there and toe the rubber. The whole year was absolutely amazing in how he forgot the pain and got by. That's got nothing to do with anything except will, courage, and competitiveness." Cone picked up his 20th victory on the next-to-last day of the regular season and fell into Girardi's embrace, weeping.

Cone needed as much rest as possible, and he had a good five days off before pitching against Texas in Game 3 of the '98 Division Series. After winning that game, he had four days off before pitching well in a no-decision against Cleveland in Game 2 of the ALCS. But his shoulder was giving out on him, its strength diminished by swelling. He started Game 6 against the Indians and quickly took a 6–0 lead, but he allowed five runs in the fifth inning and had to be relieved in the sixth. The Yankees held on to finish off the Indians, but it was apparent Cone did not have much left in his arm.

Setting his rotation for the World Series against the Padres, Torre decided to use Cone in Game 3 in San Diego, where the warmer climate might give him a better feel for his breaking pitches. Cone decided to get an injection of cortisone to reduce the inflammation in his shoulder and also took a shot of painkiller. As he walked through the clubhouse, his arm wrapped heavily, he saw Steinbrenner in the hitters' meeting, where Yankees hitting coach Chris Chambliss was briefing the players about San Diego pitcher Sterling Hitchcock, the room tense. "What the fuck are you doing in there?" Cone shouted at Steinbrenner. "Don't screw things up!" The other players looked at Cone in shock, and Steinbrenner glared angrily and growled, "You better be ready," before the owner and players realized Cone was teasing him. The players burst into laughter, and the meeting broke up.

Cone started the game, but his pitches were all benign, his fastball floating through the strike zone. Time and again, a Padres hitter would take a tremendous cut and smash a foul straight back, a sign the hitter had timed the pitch almost perfectly. Cone was like a gunfighter with an empty pistol.

He varied the speeds of his pitches just a little; if he could not overwhelm the San Diego batters, he could at least try to affect their timing. He flipped a pitch over the middle to Tony Gwynn, the Padres' batting champion, and Gwynn flied out. Cone would remember Gwynn returning to the dugout, shaking his head. "I would never say he had nothing," Gwynn said, years later. "But I had some pitches to hit, and I think some other guys had some pitches to hit." Incredibly, through five innings, the Padres did not have a hit. Cone varied his arm angles and the vertical planes and speed of his pitches, and lasted into the sixth inning; the Yankees won, the 124th of the 125 games they won in the regular season and postseason in 1998. Late in Cone's career, he wondered what the '98 season might have taken out of him. But he had no regrets. He had won 20 games for perhaps the greatest team in baseball history.

Cone pitched a perfect game against Montreal the next July, spinning his slider past the young Expos, who had never seen him pitch. Chris Widger, the Montreal catcher and the 25th out in the game, read accounts of the game and resented the implication that Cone had merely exploited a group of inexperienced hitters. Cone would have dominated anybody that day, Widger thought, because his fastball and slider worked so well together.

That game would become a benchmark for Cone, for reasons he never could have imagined that July day. He would make 42 more regular-season starts for the Yankees and accumulate only six more victories, allowing 266 hits in 226 innings, with a 6.17 ERA. But in the midst of that ignominy, he dominated Atlanta in the 1999 World Series, and Cashman and Michael argued with Steinbrenner that while Cone's arm did have miles on it, he still was a formidable pitcher and one of the linchpins of the championships. None of them thought the Yankees should give Cone a long-term deal, but they wanted to keep him. In the end, Cone signed a one-year, $12 million contract, the largest one-year deal at the time. But although he returned to the team for 2000, his slider did not, and his fastball—now diminished to 86–88 mph— was not good enough to succeed on its own.

He beat Cleveland on April 28 and would not win again until 104 days later. He bottomed out in Minnesota on July 27, his 14th consecutive start without a victory, his confidence all but drained. The first five batters of that game reached base against Cone, whose body sagged hopelessly. He had no weapons to fight with, however, and as he labored inning after inning, bullpen coach Tony Cloninger kept his hand on the phone resting near his feet, preparing for the relief call that had to come.

Cone beat Oakland on August 10, his first victory in more than three months, but in September he dislocated his shoulder while diving to catch a bunt, ending any chance he would regain a spot in the rotation for the playoffs. For the first time with the Yankees, he felt irrelevant, his credibility diminished. Roger Clemens received a $30.9 million contract extension, and Cone thought: let Clemens deal with reporters.

Torre used Cone as a reliever against Seattle in the Championship Series, and when Denny Neagle—a newcomer who had fallen out of favor with his manager and teammates—pitched poorly against Seattle, Cone nearly started Game 4 of the World Series in his place. But Neagle started, and Mike Piazza crushed a monstrous foul ball in his first at-bat before striking out. Two innings later, Piazza launched a two-run homer, cutting the Yankees' lead to 3–2. With Piazza due to hit again in the fifth, Cone began warming up. Neagle retired Timo Perez and Edgardo Alfonzo to start the inning. But suddenly Torre was walking slowly toward the mound, and Neagle stared in disbelief. Nobody on base and just one more out needed to qualify for a World Series victory, and Torre was going to take the ball from his hand. Neagle stomped to the dugout, anger filling his face, as Cone trotted in from the bullpen. Torre had decided he wanted a right-hander to face the right-handed Piazza, especially after the long foul ball and the home run. But what it had come down to, of course, was that Torre trusted David Cone in a way he would never trust Neagle.

Piazza popped up weakly to second base to end the inning, and Cone was removed for a pinch-hitter in the top of the sixth inning. He returned to the clubhouse and found Neagle raging about Torre's decision and threatening to rip the manager to reporters after the game. Take the high road, Cone advised Neagle, who was about to become a free agent. You'll be better off in the long run. Neagle muted his postgame comments and signed a $51 million deal with Colorado.

Piazza would be the last hitter Cone would face in a Yankees uniform.

His earned run average had hovered near seven runs per game, and during that summer, he had heard how Steinbrenner perpetually blistered Brian Cashman and Gene Michael with rants about his massive salary and miserable performance. He had won only four games during the regular season and pitched to just one batter during the World Series against the Mets, and in the weeks after the victory parade, the Yankees lured free agent Mike Mussina. At the same time, they offered Cone a deal just over the minimum salary, without any promises that he would make the team as the No. 5 starter the next season. To Cone, it was a mixed message: we want you, but not really. He signed with the Boston Red Sox, instead, a decision that made complete sense to some of his former teammates, who understood his competitiveness. If Cone wasn't going to pitch for the Yankees, then he would do everything he could to beat their asses. "That's the natural reaction," Paul O'Neill said, "and that's probably the way it's always been."

When the Red Sox played in New York that May, Main Vein went into Yankee Stadium wearing his game face, ignoring the cheering fans as he walked to the mound for the first inning. He struck out leadoff batter Chuck Knoblauch without changing expression and might have gone through the whole game with the stone face if not for Derek Jeter, who stepped into the batter's box and grinned broadly at his former teammate.

A small smile ambushed Cone before he fought it off and went back to work, allowing a double. No matter what uniform Cone wore, no matter where he was, his connection with Jeter and the others would never fray. They shared something extraordinary, even while he sat in Connecticut eating takeout as his friends played Arizona in Game 7 across the country. He empathized with O'Neill and Martinez and Stottlemyre, still feeling a part of what they were trying to accomplish.

But Curt Schilling was controlling Cone's old teammates in the top of the fifth inning. Tino Martinez flied out to lead off the fifth inning at the end of an 11-pitch at-bat, and Jorge Posada struck out for the second out.

Home plate umpire Steve Rippley thought both starting pitchers were throwing exceptionally, each relaxed and yet totally focused. Calling this game was a dream for him: this was the first time since 1997 that a Game 7 was needed to decide the World Series, and the 47-year-old Rippley had longed his entire career to call balls and strikes in a game with this much at stake; his internal butterflies and sense of anticipation were no different for him, he assumed, than for the players. He took some pride in the fact that his chest protector actually had been behind home plate in three of the seven games: he had worked Games 1 and 7, and when there was a problem with Ed Rapuano's chest protector before Game 4, Rapuano had borrowed his. In his right hand, Rippley held the same ball-strike indicator he'd been using since attending umpiring school some three decades earlier, the frame and inner wheels held together with duct tape, clicking it to track the outs that were coming rapidly. Shane Spencer popped to second to end the top of the fifth, and now Schilling had retired 13 batters in a row.

Roger Clemens, facing the top of the Arizona lineup, fell behind Tony Womack, 3 balls and 1 strike. Arizona manager Bob Brenly stood at the front corner of the dugout, chewing gum manically; the Diamondbacks had threatened constantly but hadn't scored a run. Looking for a walk, Womack took the next pitch—a strike—then hit a grounder to Alfonso Soriano, for the first out.

Craig Counsell chopped a high bouncer over the mound, and Clemens leapt—and couldn't reach the ball. But Jeter rushed in from shortstop, cut across the infield, bent down at a dead run, and gloved and flipped to first base, an out; by the time Jeter slowed to a stop at the end of the play, gingerly putting on the brakes because of nagging leg injuries, he was near first base.

Luis Gonzalez, the next batter, reached first when Soriano fumbled his grounder, but Clemens overpowered Matt Williams, getting strike 1 with a 96 mph fastball and then throwing an arcing splitter, which Williams bounced into the dirt, a roller for the third out. The Yankees and Diamondbacks were still scoreless through five innings, the pitchers in control.

CHAPTER 12

THE BALANCE of power in the American League East seemed to be at stake after the 1995 season, when David Cone became a free agent. The Yankees were gaining strength but still not fully reestablished, the Boston Red Sox were a playoff team lacking depth, and Baltimore Orioles owner Peter Angelos was intent on turning his club into a powerhouse. The Orioles signed All-Star second baseman Roberto Alomar, and Angelos negotiated to the brink of a deal with Cone, after Steinbrenner stonewalled the pitcher.

Cone haggled over the last details of salary deferral with Angelos, and when the Orioles' owner hung up the phone to make some final calculations, Steinbrenner—realizing he was about to lose a star pitcher to a division rival—called Cone and capitulated. The next time Angelos spoke to Cone, the pitcher had an agreement with the Yankees, and in the years that followed, Angelos would speak regretfully about allowing him to get off the line. If only he had put Cone on hold, Steinbrenner never would have had the chance, in those days before call-waiting. The Yankees did some things well, Angelos thought, and they were lucky bastards, too.

But this was another case of the Yankees outmaneuvering a division rival, something they did too easily, too often. During the run of championships, the Yankees' greatest good fortune may well have been in sharing a division with rivals infected by crippling dysfunction. Yankees officials viewed the Baltimore Orioles, the Boston Red Sox, and the Toronto Blue Jays with fear and fascination: they were dangerous franchises, with high payrolls and formidable potential for developing revenue streams, but they never consistently challenged the Yankees.

Before the Yankees rose to prominence, Toronto dominated the American League East for the better part of a decade, winning five division titles. SkyDome, the first baseball park with a retractable roof, opened in 1989, and the Blue Jays soon became the first team in history to draw four million fans in any season. But the players' strike of 1994–95, slugger Joe Carter thought, deeply offended the sensibilities of Canadian fans, and many did not return to SkyDome. The Blue Jays abdicated their throne, shedding most of the stars of their championship years, and would struggle to be competitive for the next decade, playing at a level closer to the expansion Tampa Bay Devil Rays. (Nonetheless, Steinbrenner obsessed about the Devil Rays. Because he lived in the Tampa area, he wanted the Yankees to dominate the Rays, even in spring training. In an effort to placate him, Torre stacked his starting lineup in exhibition games against Tampa Bay with his stars, rather than using half of them, the usual system.)

The Orioles were a cash machine, thriving because of the popularity of their home field. Oriole Park at Camden Yards opened in 1992, the first of the parks designed to capitalize on the fans' longing for nostalgia. Camden Yards was unlike any of the sterile dual-sport facilities, and very similar to old parks like Brooklyn's Ebbets Field—the seats crammed closely around the playing surface, the outfield fences filled with nooks and crannies, the whole park open, so fans could see the Baltimore skyline. The Orioles had struggled to draw fans in Memorial Stadium, but Camden Yards was consistently packed. In the stadium's second year, the team was sold for an unprecedented $173 million to a group headed by Peter Angelos.

Angelos had grown up working in his father's tavern in East Balti-

more, then built himself into one of the preeminent lawyers in the country, his breakthrough coming when he represented workers in asbestos cases. Angelos was ambitious and competitive, and by the time he turned 70, his personal fortune was said to be in the hundreds of millions of dollars. His firm, the Law Offices of Peter G. Angelos, had 10 branches in five states, with about 75 lawyers—and one partner. It was not his instinct to trust any part of his fate to others.

In the decade before Angelos bought the franchise, the Orioles had been a terrible team, their payroll limited by the financial problems of owner Eli Jacobs, and Angelos wasted no time restocking the Orioles. Roland Hemond, the team's general manager, went deep into negotiations with San Francisco first baseman Will Clark. But before approving the deal with Clark, Angelos insisted that the first baseman submit to a physical examination. Most teams did not do this when pursuing high-profile free agents like Clark, but in Angelos's legal experience these exams had often proved fruitful. A doctor warned Angelos that Clark's body was deteriorating and he might not hold up, and the Orioles pursued Rafael Palmeiro instead. Palmeiro would go on to hit 182 home runs over the next five seasons, while Clark was never again the impact player he had been earlier in his career. Angelos's judgment turned out to be better than that of his general manager, and for a man who did not easily place faith in others, it was the first reason to distrust his executives.

The Orioles had a couple of terrible signings over the next two years. They gave overweight pitcher Sid Fernandez a three-year, $9 million deal, and catcher Chris Hoiles a five-year, $17.5 million contract even after doctors warned Hemond and Angelos that Hoiles's right shoulder was arthritic. When Baltimore went 71-73 in 1995, Angelos fired Hemond and hired Pat Gillick, who was regarded as the best general manager in baseball after he built the Blue Jays into a championship franchise. Angelos and Gillick worked well at the outset, with Gillick signing Alomar, gritty third baseman B. J. Surhoff, and closer Randy Myers.

But after opening the 1996 season with a burst of victories, the Orioles allowed the urgency of their day-to-day play to ebb, and manager

Davey Johnson began seeing flaws in their clubhouse culture. Some club officials, coaches, and new players found the team to be essentially leaderless, despite the presence of Cal Ripken Jr. As Ripken approached and then bested Lou Gehrig's consecutive-game record, he had an unsurpassed presence in the Orioles' clubhouse and around the league. But he would never explicitly endorse the decisions of Johnson or any other manager; rather, he tended to isolate himself, cloaking himself in his own daily preparation, and club officials became frustrated when he did not use his status to prod malingering teammates. Ripken ran hard to first base every time he hit the ball and played with consistent intensity, yet the Orioles came to be known as one of the dog teams in the American League. Scouts laughed disgustedly about how little attention the players seemed to pay to the game details—situational hitting and defensive fundamentals—that were often the difference between wins and losses. One of the chronic offenders was center fielder Brady Anderson, who often failed to run out grounders and fly balls, sometimes not reaching first base. Although Anderson and Ripken were close friends and Ripken was generally viewed as the only person in the organization with the power to change Anderson's habits, he didn't intercede. A friend of Ripken's thought his passivity was rooted in an ulterior motive: the lazier the other Orioles appeared, the more his hustle would stand out.

Most of the club officials did not trust Ripken, believing he was devoted solely to his own agenda. Two months into the 1995 season, Phil Regan, then the Orioles' manager, summoned catcher Chris Hoiles into his office to ask him about his pitch selection, and Hoiles responded that he hadn't called the pitches in question; Ripken had called them from shortstop, as he often did. Regan was dumbfounded: until that moment, he had no idea that his shortstop was overseeing the most fundamental communication in the game. Regan lasted only one season, and after Davey Johnson took over the next season, he tried shifting Ripken from shortstop to third base and inserting top prospect Manny Alexander at shortstop, but this lasted only a week. Alexander, quiet and benign, would say that Ripken refused to speak to him for more than a month, and years later remained deeply angry with Ripken for not help-

ing him. When Alexander was traded to the Mets in 1997, he demanded a new uniform after he was assigned No. 8—Ripken's number.

After the Yankees swept four games from the Orioles in Camden Yards in the first series after the All-Star break in 1996, Gillick decided it was time to break up the aging team. He arranged trades for veterans Bobby Bonilla and David Wells, hoping to create a stockpile of young players and begin changing the clubhouse culture. Angelos vetoed the trades, however, appalled by the notion the Orioles might field unproven minor leaguers in the last two months of the season. Angelos clearly remembered the fan backlash that resulted from the San Diego Padres' fire sale of players in 1993, and he thought the Orioles had a covenant with season-ticket holders to field a competitive team at all times. To the surprise of Gillick—and Angelos, as well—the Orioles went on a hot streak and eventually won a wildcard berth, Baltimore's first postseason appearance in 13 seasons. But the cost was the working trust between Angelos and Gillick: once again, the owner had vetoed a decision by his general manager and ultimately been vindicated. For Angelos, it was another example of how baseball professionals were fallible and unprepared to run a multimillion-dollar company.

Rather than delegate authority to Gillick, Angelos continued to insist that he approve decisions, just as he had in his law practice, where he closely monitored the full caseload. The arrangement created a bottleneck for the Orioles' front office; some matters that could have been disposed of quickly would remain unresolved for weeks. When Hemond was general manager, he would sometimes wait for hours in the law office to speak with the owner. Gillick was more efficient, arranging his appointments so he might have to wait only 30 minutes or an hour for Angelos's schedule to clear. Angelos referred to his baseball executives as the Pros, but often, he would delay, rather than defer. "Sometimes it was frustrating in trying to get things done," said Kevin Malone, the assistant GM for the Orioles. "He meant well. But I don't think he trusted Pat or myself or his baseball people enough. Without a shadow of doubt, he wanted to win—desperately. He wanted championships for the Orioles." Angelos hired Frank Wren as his general manager before the 1999 season, gave him some freedom to negotiate a deal with pitcher Mike Timlin—and was stunned when Wren gave Timlin a four-year deal, rather than the three years Angelos had approved. Wren lasted only one year, eroding Angelos's already meager capacity to trust.

Between his responsibilities to the team and his law practice, Angelos was spread thin, and after the wildcard berth in 1996 and a division title in '97, the Orioles collapsed, despite an enormous payroll that ranked in the top three in baseball from 1996 to 1999. They finished 79-83 in 1998, and Angelos signed Albert Belle, who was a disaster, subtly gesturing obscenely at fans while standing in the outfield. Attendance declined steadily, and Ripken, who was worth more to the team as a drawing card than as a player, retired. The Orioles' struggles were nothing like the baseball joyride Angelos had envisioned. "I can't say I've enjoyed this," Angelos would say. "It has been hard, because this is my hometown, because I do care about the Orioles' place in the community. Sometimes the criticism is hard to take, but I have to swallow my tongue. This is not the courtroom. I can't build my case point by point and deliver it." Baltimore never finished closer than 13½ games to the Yankees from 1998 to 2001, and before they would rebound, Angelos would have to learn to trust others, it seemed.

A NATIVE SON had taken over the Boston Red Sox, as well. Dan Duquette developed his executive skills as general manager of the Montreal Expos in the early 1990s, thriving in the small market and building a formidable roster. Kevin Malone, his scouting director in Montreal, thought Duquette may well have been the brightest executive in baseball. He was well educated, having attended Amherst, and he wrote and spoke with a vocabulary much more impressive than that of his peers, Malone thought, and he had a knack for identifying talent. Duquette was offered the job of general manager with the Red Sox in the winter of 1994, and as a product of western Massachusetts and a rabid Red Sox fan, he found it irresistible. Anyone who brought a championship to Boston fans would be immortalized in the Red Sox Nation.

But while Duquette had talent for evaluating players, he tended to be

insular and intent on control, and these habits were quickly exposed in Boston. Duquette had grown up reading baseball in the Boston papers and understood the unquenchable thirst for news about the Red Sox. Yet he immediately established hard off-season ground rules for reporters: he would limit his contact with reporters to one conference call a week and would refuse calls from almost all individual writers. That meant that if Tony Massarotti of the *Boston Herald* or Gordon Edes of the *Globe* needed to check on a trade rumor, he could not speak with Duquette privately. The situation was unworkable for the reporters because no experienced journalist would ever ask questions about fresh news he or she had uncovered on a conference call with competing writers listening. "He didn't get it," said one reporter. "The guy was the most prominent representative for the Red Sox, and what he didn't understand was that when he wouldn't talk to reporters, he was refusing to acknowledge their readers, as well." Duquette once tried to explain his high-handedness, saying that if you wanted to talk to the governor, you couldn't simply pick up the phone and call him—an egocentric remark that did little to alleviate the tension.

General managers with other teams became incensed with Duquette, too; he would often fail to return their phone calls, and if they did hear back from the Red Sox, sometimes it was assistant general manager Mike Port who called—days later. You might have an idea for a trade that could benefit both your team and the Red Sox, one general manager recalled, and you wouldn't get a chance to bounce it off anyone. By failing to put himself in position to listen to offers, Duquette was, in effect, limiting the talent pool from which he could draw players.

While Duquette was involved in negotiations with the agents for Roger Clemens after the 1996 season, Pat Gillick needed to speak to him about an unrelated matter. He tried calling and was put off repeatedly by Duquette's secretary: *I am sorry, but Mr. Duquette is in a meeting. Would you like his voice mail?* Mr. Duquette always seemed to be in a meeting. So Gillick called again, adopted a southern accent, and identified himself as Randy Hendricks, Clemens's Texas-based agent. Duquette immediately picked up the phone.

He and Gillick laughed about the ruse, but executives with other teams came to believe Duquette lacked some basic social wiring. On those rare occasions he did return phone calls to speak with executives with other teams, he would often remain silent, and the person on the other end of the line would feel compelled to fill in the conversation. San Diego general manager Kevin Towers grew weary of this, believing he was revealing information while Duquette contributed nothing, and so he decided to wait out Duquette in one conversation. The two men were working through speakerphones, and when Towers stopped talking, there was nothing but silence for a minute. Two minutes. Five minutes. Ten minutes. "Kevin, are you there?" Duquette asked. "Yeah, I'm here," Towers replied, feeling as if he had finally succeeded in wearing down Duquette. But others didn't get even this little bit of satisfaction.

At one function, a high-ranking executive with another team sat directly across the table from Duquette. The executive kept looking over, waiting to make eye contact so he could formally introduce himself, although the executive was very well known and Duquette certainly knew who he was. But Duquette furtively avoided his eyes, glancing elsewhere. This went on, the two men separated only by condiment dispensers and coffee cups, and the executive, fascinated and curious, decided to wait for Duquette to introduce himself. How long, the executive wondered, would the general manager of the Boston Red Sox continue to avert his eyes instead of making simple conversation? The dinner ended hours later without the two men ever speaking.

Duquette never seemed to grasp that it might help him to hear the opinions of his own employees or why it might be important to them to be heard. He would ask coaches or scouts to join a teleconference, but when one of them raised another pressing issue, perhaps about a struggling player, Duquette often cut off the discussion: "We're not here to talk about that." Some of his own managers and coaches found him distant, unapproachable, even untrustworthy: when Ken Macha, one of Boston's minor league managers, had discipline problems with young outfielder Michael Coleman, Duquette supported Coleman, and when volatile center fielder Carl Everett became a disciplinary problem for manager Jimy Williams, Duquette publicly defended Everett, undercutting his own manager.

Paul O'Neill, the right fielder. His daily fight for success was the Yankees' fight. (Barton Silverman/*New York Times*)

Gene Michael took over as general manager in 1990, Buck Showalter as manager in 1992; each made lasting changes that paved the way for a dynasty. (Barton Silverman/*New York Times*)

Brian Cashman became general manager in 1998 and, like other club employees, paid the cost of greatness. (Barton Silverman/*New York Times*)

Joe Torre closely monitored the collective psyche of his players with
what one called "social genius." (Chang W. Lee/*New York Times*) ·

Bernie Williams's gentle persona led some to question his toughness and his value to the organization.
(AP/Wide World Photos)

Ranging far beyond the ordinary bounds of his position, shortstop Derek Jeter (*foreground*) laterals the ball to Jorge Posada as Oakland's Jeremy Giambi nears home in the 2001 playoffs. "You're not going to see that play ever again," said teammate Luis Sojo. (Barton Silverman/*New York Times*)

Derek Jeter will be the foundation of a championship team, a scout predicted when Jeter was in high school. (J. Paul Burnett/*New York Times*)

Pitching coach Mel Stottlemyre (*left*), Joe Torre, and bench coach Don Zimmer (*right*) became inseparable, both in the dugout and off the field. (Barton Silverman/*New York Times*)

Tino Martinez greets Jorge Posada at home plate, wearing what teammates knew as his Mad Face. (Chang W. Lee/*New York Times*)

George Steinbrenner wept with joy after the Yankees won their championships. His employees knew the euphoria would quickly end. (AP/Wide World Photos)

David Wells celebrates the last out of his perfect game, May 17, 1998. He mustered many moments of infamy as well. (Barton Silverman/*New York Times*)

Teammates lift David Cone after his perfect game on July 18, 1999; throughout the season, in more subtle ways, Cone lifted them. (Barton Silverman/*New York Times*)

Darryl Strawberry seemed to hold his life together when he was with the Yankees. Away from the team, he was unable to fend off his demons. (Jon Adams/*New York Times*)

His fastball was mediocre and his mood swings frustrated teammates—but in big games, Orlando Hernandez was dominant. (J. Paul Burnett/*New York Times*)

Chuck Knoblauch came to the Yankees as a borderline Hall of Fame candidate. By the time he left, his career had been ruined by a mysterious neurosis that destroyed his ability to make even simple throws. (Chang W. Lee/*New York Times*)

Third baseman Scott Brosius reaches home plate after slugging a homer in Game 3 of the 1998 World Series. He would play in the World Series in each of his four years with the Yankees. (Chang W. Lee/*New York Times*)

Roger Clemens (*right*) was a despised rival before he came to the Yankees; Andy Pettitte was an earnest product of the farm system.
(AP/Wide World Photos)

Game 2 of the 2000 World Series: the barrel of Mike Piazza's bat tumbles toward Roger Clemens. A moment in time.
(Vincent Laforet/
New York Times)

George Steinbrenner would frantically watch his team in the postseason, convinced disaster was looming. (AP/Wide World Photos)

Mariano Rivera dominated hitters with one vicious pitch, even when they knew it was coming, and many believed he was the primary reason for the Yankees' postseason dominance. (Vincent Laforet/*New York Times*)

The superior pitching that had given the Yankees an advantage in earlier postseasons was now matched by Arizona's Curt Schilling (*left*) and Randy Johnson. (Reuters/Colin Braley)

As Rivera's pitch snaps his bat, Luis Gonzalez ekes out the blooper that ends the Yankee dynasty. (Reuters/Colin Braley)

Paul O'Neill and his son Aaron at Yankee Stadium, on the day O'Neill cleared out his locker for the last time. (Jeff Zelevansky/*New York Times*)

Most of the Red Sox players viewed Duquette as a corporate pencil pusher, a geek, someone who was more attuned to statistics than people. The Red Sox won the division in 1995, fielding a gritty team that was respected within the league. But Duquette remade that team, filling his lineup with slow-footed hitters. Kevin Mitchell and Jose Canseco, two sluggers who were terrible on defense, were both projected as outfielders for 1996, an experiment that was quickly abandoned amid failure. Roger Clemens would leave the team as a free agent after that season, signing with the Toronto Blue Jays, as Duquette stated—infamously—that Clemens was in the twilight of his career. Clemens would win three more Cy Young Awards with the Blue Jays and Yankees, while Duquette sparred constantly with the Red Sox players and managers.

His lack of personal charm made it all but impossible for him to fully exploit the formidable resources of the Red Sox. But Duquette would make the trade that would transform the Red Sox from a mediocre power into an intermittent threat to the Yankees.

He was still with the Expos when he first dealt for Pedro Martinez, swapping second baseman Delino DeShields to the Dodgers for the young right-handed pitcher. Martinez had gone 10-5 for Los Angeles in 1993, but while his talent was highly regarded, there were concerns about his durability. He weighed only 170 pounds, stood 5 feet 11, and like his older brother, Ramon—a star pitcher for the Dodgers—threw with a slingshot delivery that placed exceptional torque on his shoulder.

But Martinez thrived with the Expos, winning the Cy Young Award in 1997 and pricing himself out of Montreal in the process; the Expos determined they would trade him, just as they had traded so many other rising stars in the previous decade. Jim Beattie, the Montreal GM, turned down an offer from the Yankees and agreed to deal Martinez to Boston for pitching prospects Carl Pavano and Tony Armas Jr.

Martinez gave the Red Sox instant credibility because on any day that he pitched, Boston was arguably the best team in baseball. In his first three years in the American League, Martinez would go 60-17, compiling an earned run average of 2.25, allowing only 476 hits in 664 innings, with 848 strikeouts. The Yankees had seen some opposing star pitchers come into Yankee Stadium and pitch as if they believed they would inevitably be beaten. But it was clear that Martinez was not in awe of the Yankees. Rather, he treated the Yankees with the same disdain he treated all hitters.

The Red Sox won a wildcard berth in Martinez's first season with the team, and they had even greater depth the next season, in 1999. Shortstop Nomar Garciaparra was perhaps the best contact hitter in baseball, attacking pitches aggressively and yet still managing to consistently drive the ball with the barrel of his bat, and catcher Jason Varitek was developing into a leader. The Red Sox won eight of 12 games from the Yankees in '99, and in a game in Yankee Stadium on September 10, Martinez threw a one-hitter and struck out 17, the most strikeouts any pitcher has ever compiled against the Yankees. He whiffed every batter he faced at least one time, including pinch-hitter Darryl Strawberry, finishing his first and last strikeouts with 97 mph fastballs. There was very little talk in the Yankees' dugout during that game, no conversation between hitters about adjustments that might be tried; there was nothing to be done. Most major league pitchers mastered one or two pitches, but Martinez had three extraordinary weapons.

His fastball tailed away from left-handed hitters and into the hands of right-handed batters, exploding through the strike zone. Hitters found his changeup—a pitch he learned from Dodgers minor league coach Guy Conti in 1991—virtually indistinguishable from his fastball, because he threw both from the same angle, with the same arm speed. He just sort of slings the ball, Bernie Williams thought, like a rubber band. "His arm and motion is just so free and easy," said Scott Brosius. "He has that real easy cheese, that easy fastball. He's not an intimidating guy as far as size. He's not like Randy Johnson, or like Kerry Wood, who's got all those body parts coming at you. Pedro is nice and loose and—wap!—he's on you."

Martinez learned the grip on his curveball from Ramon, and he refined it to the point where he could throw it for strikes at any time. There was virtually no way for a hitter to consistently attack Martinez; you always had to be wary of his fastball, Brosius thought, because of its velocity and accuracy. Martinez was usually ahead in the count, and even if the hitter got the advantage in the count, Martinez would still throw tough pitches—bastard pitches, as the players called them.

The one hit the Yankees managed against Martinez that night was something of a fluke. The career of designated hitter Chili Davis was winding down, and because he had lost bat speed, Davis would often anticipate fastballs, starting his swing earlier to give himself a chance to catch up. Martinez threw a changeup and Davis was out in front of the pitch, but when the ball sailed over the middle of the plate, Davis drove it into the right-field stands. There would be no more accidental offense. Martinez struck out the side in three separate innings, including the seventh, when he whiffed Jeter, O'Neill, and Williams. "We didn't get beat by the Red Sox," said O'Neill. "We got beat by Pedro Martinez."

All of those years of growing up smaller than his peers and his siblings prompted Martinez to pitch as if he had a chip on his shoulder, one veteran scout believed, and his competitive instinct and stubbornness made the Red Sox a dangerous playoff team against the Yankees. He could start two games in a seven-game series, and perhaps relieve in a third game, if needed. Some of the teams that played the Yankees in these championship Octobers appeared intimidated by them, the Texas Rangers being the most notable example. But Boston had Martinez in the '99 AL Championship Series against the Yankees, and he seemed to instill confidence in his teammates.

Boston's history of postseason failure stretched back 81 years, as every Red Sox fan—and Yankees fan—knew. Martinez represented their best chance. "You can feel the energy he brings with each pitch," said Joe Kerrigan, Boston's pitching coach. "Somebody could walk in off the street and not know anything about baseball, and they would know this guy is good at what he does, just because of the passion he shows for each pitch, the intensity."

Martinez pitched six innings of scoreless relief as the Red Sox eliminated Cleveland in the Division Series, an appearance that set him up to pitch Game 3 of the Championship Series against the Yankees and Clemens in Fenway Park. This schedule meant that if the series extended to a seventh game, he would pitch in Yankee Stadium, a possibility the Yankees did not want to consider because of Martinez's dominance. Aided by an umpire's blown call in Game 1, the Yankees won the first two games of the series at home. On a sunny Saturday in Fenway Park, Martinez renewed the hope of the Red Sox, shutting out the Yankees for seven innings in Game 3, while Clemens—hated now by Boston fans, who booed him throughout his pregame warm-ups and every time he appeared on the field—was pounded, bothered by a bad back.

But the Yankees would win the next two games, eliminating the Red Sox, who had made 10 errors in five games. Of all the teams the Yankees had faced in the playoffs, Joe Torre would say, the Red Sox had been the most formidable. With Martinez, they were a different team, but the outcome was the same: the Yankees finding a way to win, the Red Sox reverting to their habitual postseason bumbling. The Curse of the Bambino remained intact.

It would be years before the Red Sox would seriously challenge the Yankees again, and the losing frustrated Martinez, who became increasingly demonstrative as he aged—staring down hitters, taunting them with his eyes, glaring at the Yankees if they tried stepping out of the batter's box to disrupt his timing. At one point, the Yankees would win five consecutive games started by Martinez. "I don't believe in damn curses," he said, after finally beating the Yankees in the summer of 2001. "Wake up the damn Bambino and have him face me. Maybe I'll drill him in the ass."

But by late in 2000, there were indications that Martinez's pitching shoulder was beginning to give out, his small body unable to fully sustain his violent delivery; he made only 18 starts in 2001, when the Red Sox finished 13½ games out of first. The Yankees had a stranglehold on the AL East because of their own play but also because of the sleeping giants in their division.

CHAPTER 13

FOR ALL of the Yankees' veterans, a rookie with crude skills was perhaps their most dangerous hitter against Curt Schilling in Game 7. Alfonso Soriano would open the top of the sixth inning, having been exploited by experienced pitchers all season. Since he would swing at any pitch within two time zones of home plate, he rarely drew walks, and no matter what the pitcher had thrown last, Soriano would always assume—would hope—that the next pitch was going to be a fastball. Early in the season, Jamie Moyer of Seattle threw him seven consecutive changeups in one at-bat, as Soriano kept anticipating fastballs. He eventually struck out, of course, one of the 125 strikeouts he accumulated that year.

But Soriano had the quickest hands in the Yankees' lineup, and though tall and relatively skinny, he had unusual strength in his wrists and forearms. His lithe and powerful body, at age 25, reminded Yankees broadcaster Jim Kaat of a young Henry Aaron, when Aaron was with the Milwaukee Braves. Swinging the largest bat on the team, a maple club that weighed 34 ounces and measured 35 inches, he had compiled 55 extra-base hits in his rookie season. Some of the older Yankees hitters, injured or weary, could be overwhelmed by the blistering fastballs of

Schilling, Randy Johnson, and other hard throwers, but Soriano could hit any fastball at any time, usually driving the ball when he made contact. He had been an important wildcard in the Yankees' sputtering offense this postseason, hitting .400 against the Mariners in the Championship Series, beating Seattle with an opposite-field two-run homer at the end of Game 4, and, in the 12th inning of World Series Game 5, supplying the RBI single that finished Arizona. Schilling was throwing very hard and dominating the Yankees, and Soriano could be easy to control for a star pitcher who had great accuracy. But there was an element of danger in this matchup for Schilling, the snake charmer confronting the cobra: if he made a mistake, Soriano could hurt him.

Soriano was the Yankees' first fully established position player to come through the team's minor leagues since Jeter and Jorge Posada, but he was not really a product of the farm system. He had first played professionally in Japan before becoming one of a large number of international amateur free agents signed by the Yankees during their championship run, a practice that allowed them to exercise their extraordinary financial power over other teams. The Yankees spent tens of millions to wade in this pool of talent, while other teams could not or would not pay the price of entry.

All teams invested in teenagers from the Dominican Republic and other Latin American countries, mostly for bonuses of a few thousand dollars. When elite international amateurs became available—most notably, the wave of Cuban defectors—most teams, leery of the costs and the risks, did not bother to participate in the bidding. In 1996, the Oakland Athletics dispatched scout J. P. Ricciardi to check on Livan Hernandez, a right-handed pitcher who defected from Cuba, and he reported back that Hernandez appeared to be a very good talent. Ricciardi's bosses asked the scout how much he would offer Hernandez, and he replied that Hernandez was worth $200,000. The Athletics' executives told Ricciardi to just come home; don't bother. If Hernandez could get a $200,000 offer from low-budget Oakland, some other team would surely dangle much more. (The Marlins, who intermittently dipped into the elite international pool, would sign Hernandez to a four-year, $4.5 million contract.)

It was after the onset of Nomomania in 1995 that the Yankees began pouring money into the signing of top international prospects. Hideo Nomo had been a star pitcher in Japan, but most executives in Major League Baseball believed that professional baseball there was equivalent to AA minor league ball in North America. Because of this skepticism and the restrictive free agency rules in Japan, few players had even attempted the move. But Nomo changed all that.

No major league hitter in the U.S. had seen a delivery like that of Nomo, whose flexibility made him something of a circus act. He raised his hands high above his head, stretching his arms backward—doctors with other teams believed his shoulders were double-jointed—and perched on his right leg, like a flamingo. Then he would twist to his right, swiveling on his right knee until his head and shoulders faced center field. Fully coiled, he would turn to his left and launch his body at the hitter, who had to try to ignore the many distractions in the delivery and focus on that place where he thought Nomo would release the baseball. Nomo relied heavily on two pitches, the fastball and split-fingered fastball, and as his pitches hurtled toward the plate, hitters had extraordinary difficulty distinguishing between them. If they looked for the splitter, Nomo's 93 mph fastball might blow by them, and if they anticipated a fastball, they often realized in midswing that the pitch was about to bounce in the dirt.

In his rookie season for the Dodgers, Nomo had 236 strikeouts in 191 innings, compiling an earned run average of 2.54, and Steinbrenner was livid, demanding to know why his own executives hadn't made a deal for him. He had realized a bit behind the curve that the acquisition of international free agents could be the simplest of transactions: because the Dodgers were not required to trade any of their own players to Japan, they landed an All-Star pitcher without compromising their own farm system. All that was required was cash, something both the Dodgers and the Yankees had in abundance.

Steinbrenner became infatuated with international free agents; he wanted his own Japanese pitcher. A year later, the Yankees paid $350,000 for the rights to Katsuhiro Maeda, a 25-year-old pitcher, and gave him a $1.5 million contract. Maeda had just 25 career appearances for the Seibu Lions, but Steinbrenner thought he could be the Yankees' answer to Nomo. Maeda would languish in the minor leagues, however, never pitching an inning in the majors for the Yankees.

In 1997, the San Diego Padres acquired the rights to Hideki Irabu, one of the hardest-throwing pitchers in his homeland, from Chiba Lotte, a team from the Japanese Pacific League. Steinbrenner became obsessed with acquiring the pitcher; he had seen Nomomania and thought that if the Yankees could get Irabu, the pitcher would become a marketing sensation for the team. Irabu, who had been compared by former manager Jim Fregosi to a young Roger Clemens, suddenly made it clear to the Padres that he would come to the U.S. only to play for the Yankees. Though they could never prove it, San Diego executives were convinced that the fix was in: they were sure the Yankees had used their financial muscle through back channels to sway Irabu. Ultimately, however, the Padres felt they had no choice; even if they waited for Irabu to capitulate, he'd probably be unhappy, anyway. The Padres swapped Irabu and three minor leaguers for $3 million and two prospects, outfielder Ruben Rivera and pitcher Rafael Medina. Steinbrenner gave Irabu a $12.8 million contract.

But while Nomo had some natural appeal because of his delivery, Irabu was a morose and erratic pitcher who seemed to derive little joy from his profession. He would have days when nobody could hit him, when his fastball reached almost 100 mph and his diving splitter made batters look foolish. He once dominated Atlanta in an exhibition game, embarrassing a lineup that included most of the Braves' regulars and striking out seven of the 12 batters he faced. Twice Irabu was named American League pitcher of the month, but still he appeared unhappy, unable to sustain self-esteem. His mother was Japanese, and his biological father had been an American serviceman; growing up, Irabu was larger than most of his peers, with a darker complexion, and it was thought he endured a difficult childhood. He rarely extended himself to his Yankee teammates and struggled to stay in condition. Surrounded by players who loved what they did—Jeter, Girardi, Clemens, Posada—he looked like he was moving in slow motion; he often neglected to cover first base, a mistake for which he was admonished repeatedly. In the spring of 1999, Irabu was in better shape and throwing more consistently, and it appeared that he was turning the corner. But in the last inning of the last exhibition game in Tampa, he once again left first base uncovered, and Steinbrenner stormed into the clubhouse, telling reporters that he was a "fat, pussy toad."

Irabu and his interpreter, George Rose, asked to meet with Mel Stottlemyre and Don Zimmer, who was filling in as manager while Torre was treated for prostate cancer. "His confidence is shot," Rose told the coaches. "He doesn't think he can pitch here anymore. He doesn't want to pitch." The Yankees were scheduled to fly to California that evening, but Irabu insisted he didn't want to remain with the team, so the Yankees left without him. He was coaxed to California, eventually, and finished the season, before being pawned off to the Montreal Expos; the Yankees, as usual, would pick up the tab. While with the Expos, Irabu was slated to pitch in a minor league game to rehabilitate an injury, but he arrived at the park appearing inebriated and was suspended. His final record in the U.S. was 34-35 with a 5.15 ERA.

Most of the elite international free agents signed by the Yankees would turn out to be busts: Jackson Melian, outfielder from Venezuela, $1.6 million in salary and signing bonus; Ricardo Aramboles and Edison Reynoso, $1.2 million and $900,000 respectively, pitchers from the Dominican Republic; Wily Mo Pena, outfielder from the Dominican Republic, $3.7 million; Adrian Hernandez, a pitcher who defected from Cuba, $4 million; all disappointments or worse.

In the spring of 2001, the Yankees signed another player from Cuba, third baseman Andy Morales, for $4.5 million. Morales had gained notice two years before when he hit a home run against the Orioles in Camden Yards as the Cuban national team beat Baltimore, waving his arms as he rounded the bases. It was better for the Yankees' scouts, as they tried to serve Steinbrenner, to sign a player and be wrong in their evaluation than to miss on an emerging star altogether, as they had with Nomo. So they were typically aggressive and overbid on international free agents, like Morales. But within a week after Morales reported to the Yankees' camp, staff members and players were sure a serious mistake had been made. Morales looked awful, with a slow bat and little power. The Yankees would cut him in midseason, on the flimsy but legally necessary pretext that Morales was actually three years older than he claimed.

They also invested heavily in Drew Henson, even though he announced before the 1998 draft that he intended to play quarterback at the University of Michigan. The Yankees picked Henson in the third round and gave him a $2 million signing bonus, without any assurance that he would eventually commit to professional baseball; it was the type of gamble other teams could not afford to take. The Yankees would trade and then reacquire Henson, and give him a six-year, $17 million contract. Within 18 months, it was apparent that he was a bust, and eventually he would return to football after receiving nearly $10 million from the Yankees.

After churning out Jeter, Williams, Rivera, Pettitte, Posada, and others in the early and mid-1990s, the Yankees' farm system became thin, its draft classes weak. A typical case was Ryan Bradley, who dominated hitters in the minors in 1998 and jumped all the way from Class A to the majors that summer. Because he tended to land with his front foot turned inward, he was asked to adjust his landing position, and Bradley, who was pigeon-toed, was never comfortable with his mechanics again, developing irreparable control problems. Afterward, the consensus in the organization was that Bradley had been rushed in '98. None of the players drafted in the first round by the Yankees from 1996 to 2001 advanced to play for them in the Bronx, and they were unable to sign one of their No. 1 draft picks in 1998, a pitcher who opted instead to go to college—Mark Prior, who eventually signed with the Cubs and ranked among the game's most dominant pitchers. Executives with other teams thought that the Yankees' inability to sign Prior would turn out to be a seminal moment in this generation, like the Dodgers losing Roberto Clemente to Pittsburgh a half-century before.

The Yankees also traded several prospects in midseason deals sparked by the team's win-now mantra. With the farm system suffering, the elite foreign free agents and Henson helped fill the need for tradable commodities. Henson was swapped in a five-player deal for Denny Neagle in

2000, and to get him back, the Yankees traded Wily Mo Pena to the Reds. Aramboles was traded to Cincinnati for reliever Mark Wohlers in the summer of 2001. Where the Yankees failed to develop their own assets, they bought others on the international market, in which few teams consistently competed with them. If, for example, another team "bid $1.2 million on a guy like Soriano, or $3.4 million for Orlando Hernandez, you would have had to rob Peter to pay Paul to come up with it," said John Hart, the former Cleveland general manager. "At the end of the day, you wind up spending that money somewhere else, and maybe it's not as valuable. But the tolerance for risk is much more narrow with other teams." The Yankees, Hart thought, had so much money that they could sweep their mistakes under the rug.

Twice, however, the Yankees' big-money international investments paid off in a big way. The Detroit Tigers made an offer of $300,000 to Orlando Hernandez, a defector from Cuba, in the spring of 1998. The Cleveland Indians bid a little over $3 million. The Yankees would get the right-hander for $6.6 million—a waste of money, in the estimation of scouts with other teams, who pegged him as a middle reliever or, at best, a No. 4 starter.

Hernandez had escaped from his homeland on the early morning after Christmas of 1997 on a boat that, in the first newspaper reports about "El Duque," was described as something close to a waterlogged shingle. In time, *Washington Post* reporter Steve Fainaru learned that the craft that carried Hernandez to freedom was actually 30 feet long with a 480-horsepower engine. The 10-hour journey had been tense, though, the risks and ramifications real; Hernandez had left two young children and his parents in Cuba. After he and his fellow defectors landed on a beach, Fainaru and Ray Sanchez wrote in their book, *The Duke of Havana*, they gathered all identification papers and burned them. Free of oppressive documents, Hernandez claimed to be 29, telling anyone who asked that his mother had told him he was born in 1969. But some scouts dug up programs from an international tournament a decade earlier that indicated El Duque's birth year was actually 1965 (which was later confirmed during Hernandez's divorce proceeding). In the midst of the contract negotiations, Brian Cashman joked that if the Yankees signed him, then he was 29 years old, but if the Indians signed him, El Duque might as well have wooden teeth. At the initial press conference with the Yankees, Hernandez declined to elaborate on details of his defection; his agent, Joe Cubas, serving as interpreter, said the memories were too painful for Hernandez to discuss. In fact, Cubas was in the process of trying to sell the movie rights to those excruciating remembrances to Disney.

Hernandez's enthusiasm, at least, seemed absolutely genuine. Baseball had been the center of his existence since he was a boy, and after his brother Livan defected in 1995, the Cuban government had given El Duque a lifetime suspension from competition. Now, in signing with the Yankees, baseball was part of his life again, and in his first days, Hernandez bounced joyously through mundane drills that bored the other pitchers. In one workout, minor league pitching coach Oscar Acosta stood at home plate and chopped a series of grounders to a pitcher stationed on the mound as the other pitchers stood in a long line and watched, lounging and chatting. As Hernandez began his turn, he eagerly spread his feet and hands, poised for Acosta to challenge him. With another coach flipping balls over the plate, Acosta began smashing grounders. As they came harder and harder, faster and faster, Hernandez jabbed at the bounders with his glove, never pausing, even when a ball ricocheted off some part of his body. He looked like a hockey goalie, and the other pitchers began responding to El Duque's energy, shouting with each catch. The drill ended, and Hernandez, serious and single-minded, quickly collected the baseballs around him, piling them into his glove, like a child gathering Easter eggs.

Torre and Stottlemyre and club executives stood at the back of the bullpen to watch Hernandez throw for the first time, and right away, some staff members were leery of his complicated delivery. After accepting a sign from the catcher, Hernandez made a quarter-turn to his right, drew his left knee upward, and cocked his head downward, so that his knee and cheek nearly collided (and sometimes did). In the midst of his delivery, he held the ball at his right hip, crammed into his glove, hidden from the hitter. The mechanics were self-taught, refined more than a decade earlier, after Hernandez saw Dwight Gooden pitch on television and decided to incorporate Gooden's high knee pump into his own delivery. There was charm to it; for Torre and Stottlemyre, it was easy to compare El Duque's motion to that of Luis Tiant, the Cuban-born pitcher who had dominated American League hitters two decades earlier with his whirling, twisting motion.

Hernandez moved fluidly, bouncing off the front of his toes as he stepped. He was a superior athlete, unquestionably. Stuart Hershon, the Yankees' team doctor, said that El Duque's flexibility reminded him of a professional dancer. A reporter once asked Hernandez how high he could lift his leg, and without stretching or warming up, he raised a foot to the nameplate above his locker—6½ feet. Darryl Strawberry, watching from a locker nearby, waited till Hernandez completed the interview and walked away, then stood and began lifting his foot toward the nameplate above his own locker, but stopped before he reached his waist; not even close. Slumping back into his seat, Strawberry shook his head incredulously.

With Torre and Stottlemyre standing behind him, Hernandez warmed up. As catcher Joe Girardi set his glove over the left corner of the plate, he whipped fastballs easily through that one slice of the strike zone, whap-whap-whap. Midway through his 10-minute session, Hernandez paused; turning his right hand inward and waggling his fingers, he motioned to Girardi to set up over the other side of the plate. Whump, whump, whump. Girardi's left hand barely moved as the fastballs thumped into his glove. "I can't wait to see him pitch, because that kid has got presence, I'll tell you that," Torre told Cashman.

El Duque's raw stuff wasn't much to look at in a bullpen workout: his fastball was short, as players and coaches would say—90 mph at best— and didn't have the downward movement that distinguished Ramiro Mendoza's sinker. The initial concern among the Yankees' developmental staff was that Hernandez's delivery might have to be broken down and then rebuilt. There were too many moving parts; everything about it was overly complicated. Then there was the matter of holding baserunners; he certainly had to change his motion dramatically with runners on base, they presumed, and the changes probably would greatly diminish the quality of his stuff. Hernandez appeared to be an abstract work in an organization that valued steel-girder players.

But what they could have seen in a bullpen workout didn't reveal his extraordinary feel for reading hitters. He showed a knack for seeing weaknesses and doubt; a batter might look slightly unsure and off balance swinging at his slider, and as catcher Jorge Posada pointed two fingers at his own eyes—Did you see that?—Hernandez already would be nodding vigorously: Yes, yes, we'll throw him another slider in an important situation. He often recognized the hitters' most subtle adjustments, changes that other pitchers didn't see—the hitter moving forward in the box a fraction of an inch, or leaning forward to anticipate a pitch on the outside corner. Teammates could not recall an instance in which Hernandez complimented an opposing hitter; rather, he referred to them by their weaknesses.

At his best, Hernandez could throw four different pitches for strikes—fastball, slider, curve, and changeup—making him completely unpredictable. And he threw his slider from the same angle as his fastball, and with a tight spin, two features that made it more difficult for hitters to distinguish between the pitches. In the vernacular of scouts, Hernandez pitched backward, throwing changeups when he might be expected to throw fastballs, spinning sliders when he was behind in the count and pumping fastballs when he was ahead. David Cone played catch with Hernandez and was impressed by what he called "a dry spitter": most pitchers would anchor their fingertips onto the seams when they threw, using them like levers, but Hernandez could grip the ball on the smooth surface and still control it, still make it move.

Hernandez was promoted to pitch in June, after Cone was bitten on his pitching hand by his mother's Jack Russell terrier, Veronica. The plan was for him to make the one emergency start and return to the minors, but he pitched exceptionally against Tampa Bay, and there was such fan response that Steinbrenner insisted that he stay in the rotation, with Mendoza moving to the bullpen. Hernandez would compile a 12-4 record in only four months, and he would go 29-13 in his first two regular seasons.

A few weeks after El Duque's debut, the Yankees were in Atlanta, and as the national anthem began, Luis Sojo beckoned Hernandez to the front of the dugout, reminding him of the club rule that all players stand in a line for "The Star-Spangled Banner." Hernandez, cursing, told Sojo he couldn't tell him what to do. Sojo was taken aback; he had only been trying to help the new pitcher. After the anthem finished, Sojo retorted in Spanish—*Fuck you*—and they came close to throwing punches.

His teammates knew Hernandez could be emotional, from his first exciting days with the club to his tearful thankfulness after he made his first start for the Yankees. But the exchange with Sojo was perhaps the first they'd seen of his dark moods. The players empathized with Hernandez, recognizing that his separation from his children, his parents, and other family and friends probably tore at him. It must be horrible, Cone thought, to know that you could never return to your homeland. Cone was not enamored of Kansas City, but it was a part of him, it was where his family was from, and he could never imagine being in exile from that place. If Hernandez erupted or complained or stalked through the clubhouse wordlessly, the other players attributed it to his adjustment to a new society.

But his unpredictable disposition remained long after his children and his mother emigrated from Cuba. Posada, who was El Duque's catcher every fifth day, regarded him as a brother and would sometimes engage him in screaming arguments during games as a means of pushing him. But others on the team who were not required to interact with Hernandez got fed up with his shifting moods. He might be cheerful and smiling at four o'clock, angry and petulant a couple of hours later, and his teammates rarely understood why; by his third season with the Yankees, they didn't care.

He was suspicious, paranoid, stubborn. He and some Spanish-speaking teammates talked within earshot of reporters about how to pitch to a particular opponent, and Hernandez hissed to the others for silence, lest they reveal their secrets. His teammates tried to convince him that the journalists probably didn't understand Spanish, and even if they did, it probably wouldn't matter, but El Duque would have none of it and walked away.

Hernandez often went through an elaborate set of decoy gestures on the mound when there was a runner at second base, a countermeasure to the rampant sign-stealing he fretted about. In fact, most base-runners were oblivious, and if anyone was actually thrown off the scent by Hernandez's gestures, a glance at the faces of the Yankees' infielders would have revealed the hoax. Jeter could barely contain his laughter, and he would smile at Brosius, who would grin back. "His signs," Jeter once said, chuckling. In a game against Oakland in 1999, Hernandez had motioned to the infielders and to Posada with his hands, then stomped on the mound. What had it all meant? "You'll have to ask him," Posada replied, shaking his head.

There were two regular-season games in 2001 in which many of his teammates believed Hernandez gave up and stopped competing on the mound—at Toronto in April and in a home game with the Orioles at the end of the season. In both cases, the first innings went badly for Hernandez; he had been upset with the calls of the home plate umpire and seemed to suddenly detach himself from the competition. In the game against the Blue Jays, he refused to throw any breaking balls; in the game against Baltimore, he shook off all suggestions for fastballs.

But like David Wells—albeit with different physical packaging—Hernandez would shelve his moods and concentrate wholly when he pitched in October. He was among the best postseason pitchers of the modern era, winning his first eight decisions in the playoffs and World Series. The Yankees won each of the first 10 games he pitched in the postseason, including his first, Game 4 of the 1998 AL Championship Series.

The team had won 114 games in the regular season and swept Texas in the Division Series, but after they lost two of the first three games in the Championship Series to Cleveland, their incredible season was in jeopardy of going down the drain. Torre had slotted Hernandez as his No. 4 starter because Wells, Pettitte, and Cone all had strong track records. By the time of his Game 4 start against the Indians, Hernandez had not pitched in 15 days. Sojo and the others had no idea how Hernandez would respond to this kind of pressure, but on the afternoon of

Game 4, Sojo had bumped into El Duque and thought he seemed relaxed and confident. "He looked like he was going to kick someone's ass," Sojo said.

For the first five innings, he shut out the Indians. Then, with the Yankees leading 3–0 in the sixth, two Cleveland base-runners reached base, and Hernandez struck out sluggers Manny Ramirez and Jim Thome, finishing off Thome by throwing a changeup—a grip he had learned only that summer—on a full count. This was not his first exposure to postseason pressure: he had pitched in national team games in Cuba, where, he said, there was much more at stake than wins and losses. When you've pitched in those games, Hernandez once explained, you can pitch anywhere. He acknowledged he felt pressure when he pitched in a big game. "What I don't have," he said, "is fear."

FOR $3.1 MILLION, about half of what they had paid for Hernandez, the Yankees signed Alfonso Soriano in September 1998. Born and raised in the Dominican Republic, Soriano had taken an unusually circuitous route to professional ball in North America.

Soriano signed with the Hiroshima Carp when he was 19 years old. There was only one other person in the Carp organization who spoke Spanish, Soriano's native language, but the man had only a rudimentary vocabulary and his conversations with Soriano were always the same: they talked about the weather and baseball, while Soriano stared at the clock and visualized what his mother and his friends were doing back home, at that moment. His first stay in Japan lasted three months, and he was desperately lonely; he was able to call his family twice, for 15 minutes, conversations that merely whetted his longing for home.

But Soriano believed he had to take advantage of this opportunity, and he went through the regimented Japanese training without complaint. This was a common trait in Dominican youngsters, Sojo later said. Many of the young players from Sojo's native Venezuela came from middle-class backgrounds, he noted, and were better educated. But Soriano's compatriots were surrounded by poverty that clarified their choices.

Even Dominicans playing for minor league salaries in the States realized relative wealth after U.S. dollars were exchanged.

Some of the Dominicans who ascended to the majors had slept on dirt floors as children, but Soriano thought of himself as middle class. His father, who lived apart from his mother, made a good living as an engineer and hoped Alfonso would do the same. Whenever Alfonso was around, he encouraged him to study and discouraged him from playing baseball; Alfonso had once gone to live with his father but returned after only a couple of weeks, weary from too many hours spent staring into textbooks. The boy was obedient and understood the need for an education, but he wanted to play baseball—to be a shortstop—and his mother would let him.

But nothing could have fully prepared him for the relentless training regimen in Japan. The four-a-day hitting sessions blistered his hands, and sometimes he hit with cloth wrapped around his knuckles. When he returned to the Dominican Republic after his second stay in Japan, his mother remarked how much his upper body had changed. Muscles covered his skinny frame, most noticeably on his forearms. By the end of his second season with the Carp, he had even learned Japanese.

After a long fight, Soriano would win his free agency from the Carp. Jean Afterman, general counsel in the office of Soriano's agent, Don Nomura, met Soriano and briefed him on his options, and she was impressed by his sophisticated questions. It was evident to Afterman that while Soriano was young and being manipulated, even threatened, by a franchise that might conceivably control his life for the next 10 years, he was extremely bright and tough. He did not merely nod as Afterman explained the complicated legalities, as some players might; he listened and followed up with his own thoughts.

Soriano won his free agency, signed with the Yankees, and hit a home run during a brief promotion at the end of the 1999 season. But he struggled intermittently in the minor leagues and looked very shaky defensively during spring training of 2000, one error seemingly leading to another. The Yankees were fully prepared to trade him in the right deal. He was part of almost every major trade discussion, and on the eve of spring training in 2001, Cashman was talking about dealing him to Seattle, if he could get reliever Jose Paniagua in return. Gary Denbo, a minor league hitting instructor, and Trey Hillman, Soriano's manager in Class AAA, argued strongly to keep him, insisting he was going to be a star. And from the outset of spring training, Soriano flourished, looking much more comfortable and confident, switching from shortstop to left field to second base, as Chuck Knoblauch's throwing problems finally overcame him.

The erratic prospect whom the Yankees had nearly traded continued to improve through that season, the playoffs, and his first World Series, becoming more dangerous. Batting against Schilling in the sixth inning of Game 7, he exuded confidence in the box, chomping on gum and waggling the bat as though he was sure he was going to hit the snot out of the next pitch. Schilling challenged Soriano with a fastball inside to start the top of the sixth, and Soriano fouled the pitch back. Once the count reached 2 balls and 2 strikes, catcher Damian Miller called for a pitch outside the strike zone, and Schilling nodded and threw a 95 mph fastball a foot outside; Soriano swung and missed badly, striking out.

Schilling would strike out the next hitter, Scott Brosius, and then Roger Clemens smacked a fly ball to right field, where Danny Bautista took several steps back and made the catch to end the inning. Clemens's fly ball was among the hardest-hit balls by the Yankees, who had sent only 18 batters to the plate in six innings, the minimum; Schilling already had eight strikeouts. The way the Yankees were struggling to hit, it seemed as if their only hope was that Schilling would tire and that Clemens could continue to match him, zero for zero, to prevent the Diamondbacks from scoring. "I couldn't let them do that; I was determined not to allow them to do that," Clemens recalled, months later. "We weren't scoring many runs."

Right away in the bottom of the sixth, there was trouble. Steve Finley smashed a line drive into center field to lead off, rounded first base, and then held. Finley was a threat to steal, particularly against Clemens, who was slow in his delivery to home plate. A bunt from the next hitter, Bautista, would probably push the potential go-ahead run to second base. But if Clemens could get this out, the rest of the inning might well fall into place: Mark Grace was on deck, and with one out and a runner on base, Clemens might work around Grace before attacking the No. 8 and No. 9 hitters, Damian Miller and Schilling. Arizona manager Bob Brenly, standing in the corner of the dugout, put on the sign for a bunt and then changed his mind, flashing another sign to take the bunt off. Bautista had started in place of Reggie Sanders in this game because he was blazing hot against the Yankees, six hits in nine at-bats. Brenly would give him a chance to swing the bat.

Posada pumped his fingers, giving Clemens the sign for a splitter, and Clemens agreed. He could get a double play with a splitter if it broke down correctly, and there was reason to rely on this pitch; for the first five innings, Clemens recalled later, his splitter had been "dancing all over the place."

Clemens had learned to throw his splitter 15 years before at a golf tournament where Mike Scott, the former Houston Astros star, showed him how to jam the ball deeply between the index and middle fingers on his right hand. It was crucial that his hand was dry so Clemens could re-lease the ball cleanly and it would tumble sharply downward as it neared the plate. If his hand was damp, the splitter would stay tacked to his fin-gers—baseball flypaper—and roll out of his hand, becoming a benign fastball. It was a humid night in Arizona, and a passing shower was fore-cast, but Clemens had managed to keep his hands dry—until he threw the splitter to Bautista. The pitch rolled over, "right into his zone," Clemens recalled, "and he smashed it into Death Valley."

Bautista's line drive touched down in left-center field, then skipped and rolled and bounced against the fence 413 feet away. Clemens turned, setting his right hand on his hip and tilting his body in disgust, grimacing angrily. Later, Schilling would watch the videotape of the game and see Clemens's face, and from his own experience he would recognize the helpless feeling: Clemens knew this could be the hit that beat the Yankees.

Finley was going to score, and Bautista rounded second base, racing for third. Jeter, positioned in short left-center field to relay the high throw from Bernie Williams, leaped to reach the ball. He rotated his hips in midair and landed with his feet set to throw, then whizzed the ball to Brosius. Bautista launched himself headfirst toward third—and

Brosius snapped down a tag on his hands millimeters from the bag. Bautista was out, a base-running mistake, but Arizona had a 1–0 lead and the fans in Bank One Ballpark were standing and roaring.

Clemens retired the next two hitters, Grace on a groundout, Miller with a strikeout. Jeter stood at shortstop and muttered in pain, sore from the nagging injuries he had accumulated during the postseason. He was scheduled to lead off the top of the seventh against Schilling, his body hurting, the Yankees hurting. But none of that mattered to Jeter, Tino Martinez thought. The greater the pressure, the more relaxed he would be.

CHAPTER 14

HAL NEWHOUSER had thought Derek Jeter would play in many World Series games. When Jeter was a teenager, Newhouser would sometimes drive the 3½ hours from his home in Bloomfield Hills, Michigan, to Kalamazoo Central High School, where Jeter played. "That kid is something special," Newhouser raved to his wife, Beryl. "He's got the softest hands I've ever seen." He talked about Jeter's family, too; the kid has a great support system, Newhouser would say.

Newhouser, the Michigan area scout for the Houston Astros, was 71 years old in the spring of 1992, Jeter's senior year at Kalamazoo Central. He had been a pitcher for the Detroit Tigers and had been named the American League Most Valuable Player in 1944 and 1945. Teammates called him Prince Hal because of his courtly manner; Beryl Newhouser could not remember ever seeing him with his shirttail hanging out or wearing anything tacky. Even in the mornings, Newhouser would come to the table with his hair combed. He had gone into scouting after retiring as a player in 1955, eventually moving up to become the regional supervisor for the Baltimore Orioles. Newhouser left baseball for 20 years, becoming a vice president of the Community Bank of Pontiac, but inevitably he went back, taking the job as an area scout, converting the third bedroom of the Newhousers' home into an office. His desk and files were neatly kept, and because his script was messy, he wrote out all of his reports in meticulous block type.

Michigan high school baseball was usually played in the frigid cold of spring. Newhouser would dress in corduroy pants, a sweater, a jacket, and a hat he could pull down over his ears and load a folding chair in the back of his car to make his scouting trips. "What more can you ask for than to see a ball game in spring?" he would ask Beryl cheerfully before heading off for his long drives—often to Kalamazoo in the spring of 1992 to see the young shortstop he thought would become a star.

Some scouts filled their evaluations with hyperbole, a way for them to lobby for the players they were scouting, but Newhouser was understated, balanced, direct. And what he told the Astros before the 1992 draft—in which Houston would have the first pick overall—was that Derek Jeter, the skinny shortstop from Kalamazoo Central, would be the anchor and foundation of a winning major league club. He's a special player and a special kid with great presence, Newhouser told his supervisor, Dan O'Brien.

Jeter's confidence had always been evident. The parents of his grade school friends saw it, his teachers saw it. Evelyn Lal watched Derek and her son, Shanti, play together—the two became friends in Mrs. Garzelloni's fourth-grade class at St. Augustine Cathedral School in Kalamazoo—and although Derek was quiet, she could see that he effortlessly fit in with any group of children and made the others feel comfortable. "He was one of those kids you just never forget," recalled Shirley Garzelloni, "and I would say that even if he wasn't playing baseball." There were kids who would complain about not having anything to do, she said, but "not with Derek. He was completely self-motivated, creative, never wasted any time." He was already certain about what he wanted from his life: in Chris Oosterbaan's eighth-grade writing class, he penned an essay about his dream of playing shortstop for the New York Yankees. When he was a junior in high school, his English-literature teacher, Sally Padley, asked each of her students to create a personal coat of arms, and Jeter's rendering included a baseball player in a Yankees uniform, swinging a bat. Padley taught her class in the last period of the day, a time when some student-athletes departed to prepare for games. "He absolutely never asked for any special consideration," Padley recalled. "He never asked out of class, never bragged about his baseball. . . . He just had an easy manner, no signs of conceit, and when he was helping people, he didn't make any of them feel less important."

His teachers, like Newhouser, thought Jeter's values came from his parents. Charles and Dorothy Jeter invested time in teacher-parent conferences, asking questions and listening to answers. At the beginning of each school year, Charles and Dorothy sat down with their two children—Sharlee, their daughter, was five years younger than Derek—and wrote out contracts, with clauses on grades, sports, extracurricular activities, and the possibility of bad behavior: "No. 6—Trouble At School. We Want To Know About It From You." Parents and children would sign together. Charles was black and from Alabama; Dorothy was white and from New Jersey. Derek Jeter grew up believing he had the best of both worlds, and his teachers thought he was completely at ease with kids from different racial and economic backgrounds.

Newhouser was taken by the aura that emanated from the teenager and strongly lobbied the Astros to draft Jeter. There were initial concerns that Jeter, who had been promised a scholarship at the University of Michigan, would hold out for a signing bonus of $1 million or more, a large sum at that time. "No one is worth $1 million," Newhouser told his supervisor. "But if one kid is worth that, it's this kid."

Newhouser got to know Jeter's family and wrote the young shortstop a letter, advising him to swing a bat as much as he could, to toughen his hands. Al Kaline bought a tee and a ball and swung at it all winter, Newhouser said in his letter. Look where it got him, the Hall of Fame.

Shortly before the draft, O'Brien talked to Newhouser and explained that the Astros would pass on Jeter and take Phil Nevin, a good offensive prospect from Cal State–Fullerton; Nevin had agreed to a $700,000 signing bonus. "It's an organizational decision," O'Brien told Newhouser. Four other players were drafted before Jeter: Cleveland picked pitcher Paul Shuey, Montreal took pitcher B. J. Wallace, Baltimore selected outfielder Jeffrey Hammonds, and Cincinnati took outfielder Chad Mottola fifth. The Yankees picked Jeter sixth. Newhouser was devastated. If he couldn't convince the Astros to take Jeter, he figured, then he could never convince them of anything. The former player who had happily driven hours and sat through cold weather to watch baseball quit his job and left the game he loved for good.

Newhouser passed away in 1998, but Jeter had long since vindicated him. The World Series against Arizona was Jeter's fifth, and by his 27th birthday he already had four championship rings and played with the presence and confidence that Newhouser had seen in him. No matter what the situation, he seemed completely relaxed. The Yankees would be in the midst of tense games, and from third base, Scott Brosius could hear Jeter reacting with muffled delight if the hitter took a particularly bad swing—*Yeesh, look at that!*—as if it was a game among friends. Jorge Posada would do something unusual behind home plate, fumble a pitch or something, and Jeter—a close friend of Posada's—would make eye contact with the other fielders and grin, and they would all laugh. Sometimes, when Jeter fielded a grounder awkwardly, not quite getting in front of a ball and barely avoiding an error, he would smile and look around at Tino Martinez and Brosius and Chuck Knoblauch, acknowledging that he had gotten lucky.

He carried on a series of rituals. Whenever Joe Torre went to the mound to make a pitching change, Jeter loped in from his position and slapped him on the chest with his glove. Playoffs, World Series, ugly blowout of the Yankees, it didn't matter; he'd always hit his manager. If a teammate scored a run, Jeter made a point of being the first out of the dugout to offer congratulations, a towel draped over his shoulder, something he'd done since he was in Little League. He had called off Brosius on a relatively simple pop-up one day, and Brosius turned to ask, "Are you going to let me catch any?" Later, as Brosius stood under a pop-up, Jeter circled close by and yelled loudly in his ear, just to mess with him, and from then on, whenever a pop-up went up on the left side of the infield, there was a friendly competition between Jeter and Brosius about who would catch the ball. The Bleacher Creatures who inhabited the right field stands at Yankee Stadium would do a roll call of the starting position players at the outset of each game, continuing to chant a player's name until he acknowledged them in some way, with the wave of a glove or hand. Before the tradition was fully established, Brosius had once stood stone-faced at his position, concentrating on the pitches being thrown, and Jeter shouted at him, "Are you going to wave?" Jeter began teasing Brosius that he had merely wanted the chant of his name to continue, a joke that would last through the long season. "He did a lot of little things like that," Brosius recalled. "You know he still thinks of it as a game."

Jeter had a knack for drawing in the personalities on the fringes of the team, mostly with humor. He had a long-standing friendship with Ramiro Mendoza, who was quiet and mostly kept to himself, and gave Hideki Irabu his nickname of Bu-Bu. Roger Clemens joined the Yankees with a history of drilling Jeter with fastballs, so Jeter and Knoblauch immediately played a practical joke on him, donning full catcher's gear to take batting practice. Jeter was liked and respected by teammates, the only serious blip being a run-in with Chad Curtis during the 1999 season.

Curtis was serious and strong willed, a 45th-round pick in the 1989 draft before he had driven himself to the major leagues. A religious man, he led the team's prayer group and Bible study. The large group of practicing Christians among the players cut a broad cross section of the Yankees' clubhouse—Andy Pettitte, Mike Stanton, Scott Brosius, Paul O'Neill, Mariano Rivera, Darryl Strawberry, and others. Among those who did not participate, there was no standing resentment or tension, but some other players were uncomfortable with Curtis, believing he was too overt with his religion; he had approached other players to discuss their faith, and for some, this crossed a line. Jeter had politely declined him once, and when Curtis went to him again, the shortstop felt offended. Chad can do what he wants, Jeter told a friend, and I'll do what I want to do. Jeter was single and laid-back and lived the life of a rich celebrity bachelor, while Curtis was older, private, and serious, married with children. They were very different in their outward manner on the field, as well: Curtis was uniformly intense and stone-faced, while Jeter laughed and smiled and joked with opponents who stopped at second base.

During a game in Seattle in 1999, Frankie Rodriguez, a demonstrative young pitcher, screamed from the Mariners' dugout at some of the players in the Yankees' dugout. Girardi, taking his position at home plate before an inning, told Rodriguez that if he wanted to fight, well then, come on over, and Rodriguez charged the catcher. The brawl ended relatively quickly, the other players separating Girardi and Rodriguez swiftly, Yankees and Mariners grabbing one another with the intent of containing the fight. Jeter and Alex Rodriguez, then a shortstop with Seattle, were friends, and as the players began drifting off the field, Jeter and Rodriguez joked with each other, both grinning broadly. Curtis saw this and thought it a terrible breach of an unwritten code: when your teammate is involved in a fight, it is not a good time to be laughing with someone on the other team. Curtis confronted Jeter in the dugout, and there were angry words between them. Curtis, as always, stood square to Jeter; if there had been punches, he would have been ready. Jeter, aware that television cameras were probably focused on their exchange, walked away. After the game, Curtis approached Jeter again at his locker, with the full complement of New York beat writers watching. With a wave of his hand, Jeter noted the presence of the reporters and told Curtis it was the wrong time and place. Curtis later apologized to Jeter for being indiscreet, but he stayed convinced that Jeter's conduct had been inappropriate. Other things that Jeter did grated on Curtis, such as swinging at the first pitch after the first two hitters in an inning made quick outs. Curtis had learned hard-line fundamentals, having broken into the majors when young players were expected to be deferential, and Jeter—always smiling, always joking around on the field as if he were playing Little League—offended his sensibilities. Jeter accepted Curtis's apology, but Curtis had crossed a line and Jeter spoke of him harshly, disdainfully. He viewed Curtis as a peer and thought Curtis had no right to judge him, certainly not in public. "I guess the best way to put it is, you asked if I'm worried about something that Chad Curtis said," Jeter told a reporter. "No, I'm not."

Years later, Curtis would decide there was nothing wrong with the way Jeter played the game; if anything, Curtis thought, his own approach—the approach he had been taught—was wrong. "When you come right down to it, what is really the difference between a three-pitch inning and a four-pitch inning?" Curtis said. "I do like the respect of the game that I was taught, especially when it came to mingling with players you were playing against. But Derek really approached the game with a fun attitude, and he played hard and he played to win. Some of that old-school stuff went a little too far." Curtis had seen Jeter's incredible play against Oakland in the first round of the 2001 playoffs, when Jeter ran to the first-base foul line to intercept an errant relay before flipping the ball to Jorge Posada for the out. Curtis realized that if he had been playing shortstop, there was no way he would have been in position to make the play; he was used to structure and discipline, and Jeter had roamed outside the diagrams, used his imagination, and as a result, made a play that probably was the difference between elimination and advancement to the World Series. There is not a greater champion in baseball than Derek Jeter, Curtis thought.

(Another of Jeter's very few run-ins with teammates was with Bernie Williams, before the Yankees played Game 6 in Arizona. Williams arrived late to Bank One Ballpark, and by the time he put on his uniform and made his way out to the field, his teammates already were taking batting practice. Jeter confronted Williams twice, first in the clubhouse, with teammates around, and then in the bathroom, shouting that on this day, at this moment, Game 6 should be the most important thing in Williams's life, and he shouldn't be anywhere else. Williams absorbed the criticism.)

Jeter mostly contained his own ego, never boasting, which distinguished him from some of his peers. After the 2000 World Series, Alex Rodriguez signed a $252 million contract with the Texas Rangers and then speculated in a radio interview that Jeter—a friend of his—would not get as much money when he signed, because he didn't hit for power and wasn't as good on defense. Months later, Rodriguez would snipe at Jeter again, in an interview published in *Esquire* magazine. Jeter was "blessed with great talent around him," said Rodriguez. "He's never had to lead. He can just go and play and have fun. He hits second—that's totally different than third or fourth in a lineup. You go into New York, you wanna stop Bernie and O'Neill. You never say, 'Don't let Derek beat you.' He's never your concern." Jeter talked to Rodriguez about his remarks but kept those conversations private out of respect for a friend. Both players were young, accomplished shortstops, and Rodriguez was, by most standards, the better player. But while Jeter was comfortable with himself, Rodriguez would always seem a little insecure and a little jealous of the Yankees' shortstop.

If someone else wanted to credit Jeter with greatness, he would accept with proper aw-shucks graciousness: Jimmy Stewart in pinstripes. But teammates knew that his competitive ego was immense. Jeter "doesn't just think he's going to kick your ass," Luis Sojo once said, "he knows it."

No matter what Jeter did in his first at-bat in a game, he would come back to the dugout with his confidence still running over. "This guy doesn't have anything," he would say. "He's going to get killed." It could have been Randy Johnson on the mound or a recent call-up from Class AAA, and Jeter might have looked great or terrible. It didn't matter: the opposing pitcher never had anything, or at least nothing insurmountable. Even if the pitcher got him out the first time, Jeter was certain he would get the pitcher the next time. Most of the Yankees—most players— would fight to maintain their wavering morale at one time or another, but Jeter's confidence was resolute and steady, like a flag waving over the team in even the worst of times. This kind of self-assuredness, Torre thought, was extremely rare. "He's absolutely sure of himself all the time, but not in a way that can be counterproductive. He's not arrogant; he's confident. He's sure he's going to do well."

The hubris was a necessity, really, to sustain his performance in the face of such extraordinary expectation and pressure. But if Jeter was the target of the mildest criticism, he bristled. As he accomplished more and gained more fame and celebrity—and became a larger target for critics—his competitive instinct occasionally overwhelmed modesty. Jeter labored through the first months of the 2001 season, playing below the standards he had established in the first years of his career. A sore arm was greatly inhibiting his defense and reducing his offense to mostly singles; just 21 of his 89 hits from April through June were extra-base hits. Meanwhile, Alex Rodriguez was leading the All-Star balloting, and if Jeter was going to make the team, he would have to be added by Torre as an at-large selection. But other shortstops, such as Cleveland's Omar

Vizquel and Oakland's Miguel Tejada, were playing better than Jeter. That didn't prevent ESPN from promoting its All-Star programming with repeated references to Jeter and other stars. "Are you comfortable with that?" a reporter asked Jeter, and the implication of the question—that he might not be worthy of All-Star status that summer—irked Jeter. The next day, the All-Star reserves were announced, and Torre had included Jeter, keeping four shortstops rather than the standard two or three. When the same reporter passed through the locker room, Jeter called out his name. "I guess that answers your question," Jeter said, a smile masking day-old defensiveness. When he celebrated crucial plays or big victories, he would bend his right elbow and make a fist—the same gesture that another hypercompetitive soul, Michael Jordan, had used in similar moments.

Jeter had struggled terribly in the minors after signing with the Yankees, hitting .202 for the Gulf Coast rookie league affiliate in 1992, committing a staggering 56 errors in Class A the next year. He would put in hours of extra work in his hitting and his fielding: like other Yankees prospects at this time, he was fortunate that the minor league system was loaded with hardworking and positive instructors. Many teams filled their minor league spots with jaded ex–major leaguers who were finishing out their working lives, but Jeter, Williams, Posada, and others were helped through their rough spots by the likes of Brian Butterfield, Gary Denbo, Trey Hillman, Rob Thomson, and Mark Newman.

Ricky Ledee and Jeter played in Tampa together in 1992, and Denbo recalled that when they performed badly, both of them would come out for early batting practice the next day. Jeter would work at his swing till he regained the feel he wanted and then walk away from the batting cage, confident he would get hits in the game that night. Ledee would remain, frustrated, still searching, still unsure. It was an early insight into one player absolutely certain he was destined for greatness, Denbo thought, and another no less dedicated but lacking a similar self-confidence.

By the 1995 season, Jeter had developed into a star prospect, and he would make the team in Torre's first spring training the next year, despite serious doubts about whether he could play consistently enough, particularly on defense. "My advisors tell me they don't think Jeter is ready to play," Steinbrenner told Torre late in spring training. "Well, it's too late for that now, folks," Torre replied, committed to Jeter despite his own reservations. But Jeter would hit a home run on Opening Day and make a great catch, and would also begin to endear himself to the Yankees' staff in extracurricular ways. During a game in 1996, Jeter was thrown out trying to steal third with two outs, a fundamental error, and Torre fumed in the dugout, muttering complaints to Zimmer next to him. After Jeter played the next half-inning of defense, he jogged off the field and planted himself next to his manager—Jeter always called him Mr. Torre—knowing that he was furious and had something to say. It was as if Jeter had violated the terms of an unwritten player-manager contract and was ready to accept his punishment. Torre was deeply impressed by Jeter's accountability, and like a parent, he was somewhat touched. "Get out of here," Torre said, grinning and pushing Jeter away.

Jeter batted .314 in his rookie season, and he hit over .300 most years in the first half of his career. His approach to hitting—like his attitude toward the game—had hardly changed from the days he played Little League: see the ball, hit the ball. If a pitch was thrown within the strike zone, he probably was going to swing, and if the ball was outside the strike zone, Jeter, always aggressive, might swing anyway. Experience taught him to anticipate where a pitcher might try to throw next, and the tilt of his body in the batter's box sometimes betrayed his thoughts.

But Jeter concerned himself much less than other good hitters with the identity of the pitch or even the pitcher, or how the ball-strike count might affect his options. Early in Jeter's career, Yankees outfielder Tim Raines thought he would eventually develop into a daunting power hitter, capable of 30 to 40 home runs a season; he had the raw strength, certainly. But Raines later decided Jeter was unlikely to be a standout power hitter because he was too impatient. If the count reaches 3 balls and 1 strike or 2-0, hitters can look for a pitch in one particular part of the strike zone; if the next pitch isn't in that zone, the hitter doesn't swing. But Jeter would never wait for the ball-strike count to ripen in his favor: he would swing at almost anything he could reach with his bat, particularly early in games. Paradoxically, Raines thought, Jeter just loved to hit too much to be a great hitter.

When Jeter was in his worst slumps, it was often because he fell into the habit of reflexively swinging at pitches thrown low and inside, out of the strike zone. But his greatness as a hitter, Torre thought, was that even when things were going badly and he was hacking at bad pitches, he found ways to get hits. He'd have a terrible day and still muster a single, or perhaps a pair of singles, slow rollers that crawled through the infield. Even when his mental form was at its worst, he would be rescued by his swing.

Jeter was right-handed, and his natural and unorthodox stroke allowed him to hit the ball to the opposite field consistently, as only a few hitters could do. It is far easier to teach someone to pull the ball, Denbo thought, than to show a hitter how to hit the ball to the opposite field. Unlike other strong opposite-field hitters, though, such as Wade Boggs or Tony Gwynn, Jeter did not routinely make contact with the ball on the thick part of his bat's barrel. He struck out often—he earned a minimum of 99 strikeouts in each of his first seven seasons and a high of 125 in 1997—and went through periods when most of his hits dribbled through the right side of the infield. But Jeter was a contact hitter, nonetheless, drawing his wrists and hands into his body so he could push almost any pitch, no matter its speed or placement—inside, outside, high, or low—to right field. Denbo occasionally saw Jeter pull his hands so far in that the base of his left hand brushed against his chest in the midst of his swing, and he would still manage to punch the ball to right field.

Near the end of the 1999 season, Tampa Bay pitcher Jeff Sparks busted a fastball inside to Jeter, a good pitch, and Jeter pulled his hands in and dropped a hit over the first baseman. The ball skipped off the foul line and bounced into the stands for a ground-rule double—Jeter's 100th RBI. In a rematch days later, Jeter again faced Sparks, and Sparks jammed him again, and again Jeter bounced the ball off the right-field foul line, in almost exactly the same spot. As Jeter stood at second base, Sparks walked behind the pitcher's mound, overcome by exasperation. "That's twice," he shouted at the Yankees' shortstop.

Jeter watched videotape constantly, before and during games, but he was less interested in his swing than in the pitch location. And he cared more about timing the pitches than about the particular strengths of the pitcher. As he stood in the on-deck circle, he would make eye contact with the Yankees' employee who sat in the stands and operated a radar gun. Jeter would guess how hard the pitcher was throwing—holding up two fingers if he thought the pitcher was throwing 92 mph, for example. Using this sign language, the radar gun operator might respond with three fingers if the pitcher was throwing 93 mph, and Jeter would nod.

Thus forewarned, Jeter would sometimes turn toward fans sitting in the front rows and ask them what he should do in his forthcoming at-bat. *Think I should hit a double? OK, sounds good.* Fans loved him for this sort of solicitousness; teenage girls shrieked each time his name was announced (a reaction that was often teasingly reproduced in the Yankees' clubhouse), and if a fan with a camera called to him from the stands, Jeter would turn just enough in the on-deck circle to facilitate a picture. Most of the Yankees were gracious in their fame but did not particularly enjoy this part of their baseball existence. Players like O'Neill, Cone, and Mussina probably would have preferred to be left alone once they walked off the field. Many felt uncomfortable because they could never fully satisfy all the requests made of them; as Yankees, there seemed to be somebody asking them for something all the time. But Jeter embraced and enjoyed his celebrity, appearing perfectly comfortable in those settings, making jokes with fans, putting them at ease. He did not make a point of veering into the large crowds that gathered in the lobbies of hotels where the Yankees stayed on the road, but when surrounded by fans Jeter didn't give the impression that he was inconvenienced.

He would become a major star, and mountains of fan letter requests piled in his locker. A columnist for *Sports Illustrated* once asked Jeter to let him open a heap of his mail. Among 261 pieces, the reporter found 141 requests for autographs, many from people who detailed dire personal circumstances—their own or those of someone they knew—which would seem less terrible if Jeter sent his signature. There were requests for him to make appearances at movie premieres, auctions, a Playboy

Mansion party, an Eagle Scout ceremony, a backyard barbecue, and birthday parties.

Jeter chose his endorsements carefully, aware of maintaining his glowing public image. He signed with Nike under a brand name developed by Michael Jordan and picked a favorite peanut butter and a sports drink, deals which increased his celebrity status. His name appeared regularly in the gossip pages of the *Post* and the *Daily News,* and when he dated pop singer Mariah Carey in 1998, one of the tabloids sent a writer to Tampa specifically to dig out information on the two. His fame surrounded his life in a way that fame had encircled Joe DiMaggio, a Yankees star of another generation.

Eventually, DiMaggio's celebrity seemed to strangle part of him. Spontaneity became almost impossible for him; all his associations and conversations were weighed against how they might affect his image. "Joe understood the bargain perfectly," Richard Ben Cramer wrote in his book about DiMaggio. "He understood the bargain with perfection. He could have our honor, our adulation, the glory of the Big Name. . . . He understood: we would give him anything—if he would be the hero we required."

As the prominent Yankee, Jeter existed in the same vortex as DiMaggio, as Mickey Mantle, as Reggie Jackson, and as he entered the second half of his career, it remained to be seen whether he would control his celebrity or vice versa. "People thought I liked it, but I didn't like it; I knew how to thrive within it," said Reggie Jackson. "I'm still uncomfortable with it. The more you come from an average background, like Jeter—from working parents, middle class—the less you understand it. It's always a battle. I got into my fifties before I understood it. I think the people around you are important. They're the ones who keep you grounded and make you think the right way. The players who go helter-skelter, who don't deal with it—it's the people they're around who don't help them. You need help, for grounding." Early in his career, Jeter believed his parents would serve as the auditors of his personality. He couldn't change and get away with it around Charles and Dorothy Jeter, he said.

• • •

JETER AND Jackson shared another trait: they were both masterful in postseason play. Jackson, who had starred so often in the playoffs and World Series that he was known as Mr. October, once told Jeter that when September rolled around, the writers and the fans would start talking to him about the postseason, reminding him of how well he had done in the past. Reggie, this is your time of year, they would tell him. You hear it so much, Jackson told Jeter, that maybe you start believing it; you start expecting to play well in the postseason. Jeter listened and thought that this explanation made sense in his own case.

His self-assuredness made him a transcendent postseason player, his performance spiking in the most crucial moments. Jeter found the postseason games to be more fun: the stakes were greater, more people were watching, and he loved playing in the spotlight; perhaps his concentration became more acute. He would generate a solid batting average, usually accumulating 200 hits and 100 runs; then the playoffs would begin and suddenly he would start bashing long balls all over the place. Jeter batted .333 or better in 10 of his first 14 postseason series; he seemed born to play in October, Torre once said.

In the crucial Game 4 of the 2000 World Series, he batted leadoff against Mets right-hander Bobby Jones, and as he walked to the plate to open the game, Knoblauch predicted to others that Jeter would hit a home run on the first pitch. When Jeter rocketed Jones's changeup into the left-field stands, Knoblauch bounced out of the dugout, shouting and pointing at teammates—*I told you, I told you.* Jeter hit a triple in his next at-bat and scored, increasing the Yankees' lead to three runs, the early dagger that would all but finish the Mets.

In Game 3 of the 2001 Division Series against Oakland, Jeter made the play that would probably serve as the benchmark of his career, in the way Willie Mays's over-the-shoulder, back-to-home-plate running catch in the 1954 World Series would always be remembered. The Yankees had a 1–0 lead in the seventh inning, with Oakland needing only one victory to finish off a Division Series sweep. With the Athletics' Jeremy Giambi at first base, Terrence Long pulled a double into the right-field corner. Giambi rambled around second, turned at third base, and aimed for home plate.

Jeter, stationed near the mound, saw Shane Spencer fire the ball from the right-field corner and realized that the throw would sail over both cutoff men—Soriano and first baseman Tino Martinez. When Martinez saw the ball sailing over his glove, his heart sank. Spencer saw his throw carry and cursed aloud.

But Jeter had sprinted toward the first-base line with one thought: Get the ball. Spencer's throw bounced along the baseline, 30 feet or so from home plate, without enough momentum to reach home before Giambi. Jeter grabbed the ball and flipped it sideways to the catcher—lateraled it, like a college quarterback pitching out to a running back. Giambi tried to go into home plate standing up instead of sliding, and Posada swept a tag against the runner's leg. Out. Inning over. It was as if Superman had swooped down and saved the Yankees, Brian Cashman thought. Oakland manager Art Howe wondered how, under any circumstances, a shortstop could end up in that place on the playing field. "You're not going to see that play ever again, a shortstop making that play behind first base, in foul territory," said Luis Sojo. The Yankees would survive Oakland to meet Arizona.

JOE TORRE'S contract was set to expire on October 31, 2001, at midnight—during Game 4, as it turned out. The World Series would have been over under normal circumstances, but the cancellations caused by September 11 had extended the season. Because Torre was still engaged in protracted negotiations with Steinbrenner, postseason play extended beyond his written obligation to the Yankees. Torre would continue to manage the team, of course, the technicality irrelevant under the circumstances. But as Jeter passed by in the dugout, he kept reminding his manager how many hours and minutes he had left as the Yankees' manager. *Eighteen minutes to go. . . . What are you going to do?* Torre laughed. It did not matter that the Yankees were involved in a tense World Series, fighting to continue their dynasty; Jeter seemed to extract every possible bit of enjoyment from the games he played, regardless of the circumstances. Other players would be fully focused, almost in a trance, and he would be making jokes. His behavior was possible, some teammates thought, only because Jeter was absolutely certain that the Yankees would find a way to win, and that if the pivotal opportunity fell into his hands, he would succeed. "It was amazing how relaxed he was," Martinez recalled. "He could be 0-for-4 that day, but if he needed a hit that fifth time, with men on base and the game on the line, he got it."

After Tino Martinez tied Game 4 with two outs in the bottom of the ninth, Jeter was scheduled to hit third in the bottom of the 10th inning. "It's over—this game is over this inning," Jeter told Martinez in the dugout. "Yep, it's over." And four minutes after Torre's contract expired, in the first World Series baseball in the month of November, Jeter lined a ball into the right-field seats to end the game, raising a fist as he rounded the bases, baseball's Mr. November.

In the seventh inning of Game 7, the Yankees needed Jeter to come through once more. He was in rough condition: his World Series average was .120, and he had a strained left hamstring, a bruised back from a tumble he'd taken into the third-base stands while making a catch in Game 5 of the Division Series, and a lingering problem in his right shoulder, which had bothered him all year. He probably would not have played if this had been a regular season game, but there was no chance he was coming out now. He was having too much fun.

Curt Schilling whipped a fastball across the outside corner. Steve Rippley, the home plate umpire, called a strike, and Jeter's head sagged slightly. Down a run, the Yankees needed to gain traction quickly.

In situations like this, the Yankees' players often focused on rescuing their teammates rather than on their own responsibilities. If Paul O'Neill struck out with the bases loaded and nobody out, Bernie Williams would follow and concentrate on picking up for O'Neill. If Chuck Knoblauch made an error to put runners in scoring position, Andy Pettitte would bear down and try to prevent the runners from crossing the plate, to pick up for Knoblauch. It was unselfish but also useful, Tim Raines believed: thinking about trying to help a teammate, rather than the mounting pressure on your own shoulders, eased your mental burden. Raines would fondly remember this as a fundamental element of the Yankees' success.

Roger Clemens had allowed the go-ahead run to the Diamondbacks in the sixth inning of Game 7, and somebody needed to pick up for him; Jeter had the first chance, leading off the seventh. With the count at 0-1, Schilling threw another fastball outside, and Jeter tilted his chin down— head on the ball—pulled his bat through the strike zone, and whacked a single to right field, dropping a line drive in front of Danny Bautista; Jeter limped to first base, the Yankees' first baserunner since O'Neill was thrown out trying to stretch a double in the first inning.

O'Neill was next and Torre had the option of asking for a bunt, but he had always let O'Neill swing away; the right fielder didn't have a sacrifice bunt in nine regular seasons with the Yankees. Torre knew Schilling would probably continue to be aggressive and throw strikes, so he sig- naled for a hit-and-run. Jeter broke from first as Schilling delivered his first pitch to O'Neill—a slider without bite. O'Neill extended his arms, reached down, and hit a soft liner toward center fielder Steve Finley, who rushed the ball. Jeter, racing toward second, slowed and stopped for an instant, thinking Finley might make the catch. But O'Neill's liner fell at Finley's feet, and he could only smother the short hop. The moment of indecision forced Jeter to hold at second, and he slapped his fist against his right thigh and swore aloud—"GOD-damn!"—believing he could have reached third. But the Yankees had runners at first and second with nobody out with Bernie Williams coming to bat, and Schilling's pitch count was climbing. Miguel Batista and Greg Swindell, a right-hander and a left-hander, began warming up in the Arizona bullpen.

Williams fouled off a high fastball. Schilling threw a slider—a hang- ing slider—and Williams, batting left-handed, turned his front shoulder, trying to pull the ball to the right side. But he could only foul off the pitch, and slapped at his bat in frustration; no balls and two strikes. Schilling had a chance to get the first out with a strikeout.

He stepped to the rubber, and the Yankee center fielder stepped out of the batter's box, fighting to control the tempo of the at-bat. Schilling set his right foot against the rubber, took the sign, and fired a fastball designed to put Williams away—the velocity ratcheted up, 97 mph, the ball thrown high, above the hitter's hands. Williams fouled off the pitch. Schilling tried a splitter, and Williams bounced a grounder toward first base, where Mark Grace fielded it and flipped it to second base. O'Neill, forced out, slid into shortstop Tony Womack with his right foot pointed skyward, trying to break up any double-play attempt; Womack held the ball.

One out, Williams at first, and Jeter at third, the tying run 90 feet from home plate. Opportunity, and the burden of the inning, had shifted to Tino Martinez, the next hitter.

CHAPTER 15

LUIS GONZALEZ and Tino Martinez had been high school teammates, batting second and third in the lineup at Jefferson High in Tampa, Florida, and before Game 7 of the 2001 World Series, the two former Dragons had wished each other luck near the batting cage. But Gonzalez smiled inwardly as the two old friends parted. *Tino's already got four championship rings,* Gonzalez thought, *and I'm wishing him luck.*

With 367 RBIs in the past three seasons, Gonzalez was the best hitter in the Arizona lineup, a star. But this was a distinction he came by relatively late in his career. In 1997, the summer that Gonzalez turned 30 years old—an age when most stars are well into the best seasons of their careers—he batted .258 with 10 homers for the Houston Astros. He was perhaps better known for his gregarious personality than for his run production, and while he was generally viewed as only an average player, he seemed to be the type of person, one baseball executive said, who would be wanted beyond the days when he was productive because of his professionalism and the way he treated teammates. He bounced to Detroit for 1998, signing as a free agent, but was traded after one season with the Tigers to Arizona for outfielder Karim Garcia—a fading prospect who had fewer than 400 at-bats in his career—and cash. Gonzalez was

33 years old the first time he hit 30 home runs in a season, in 2000; the next year, his offense erupted and he hit 57 homers.

Until then, his high school teammate had always been the better player. Martinez and Gonzalez met when they were six years old, played Little League together, and when they were teenagers, Gonzalez admired the work ethic of his friend. Tino Martinez's father and grandfather urged him to practice, to work at his baseball. A chain-link fence surrounded the Martinez home, and the boy hit balls off a tee into that fence, eventually pounding out a hole through his diligence. His father, Rene Martinez, had also played at Jefferson High—the school's field was named for him—and when Tino was struggling at the plate, he would ask, "Are you working hard enough? Are you hitting enough off the tee?"

Tino began lifting weights at 13, and he and Gonzalez hit and ran together and ate egg sandwiches at Burger King before games. They took turns in a batting cage at the home of Bucky Faedo, the Jefferson High cleanup hitter. Martinez drove Gonzalez to practices and games daily, but when they were scheduled to play on opposing teams in the Jefferson High Blue and Gold intrasquad game, Martinez did not pick up his friend, and Gonzalez scrambled to find another ride. "I can't believe you left me," Gonzalez said when he got to the field. "Let's go; it's time to play ball," Martinez responded.

Years later, his Yankee teammates noticed that before games, Martinez's expression would change, his eyes widening, his mouth tightening. He would get very serious, focused; it was obvious he was preparing himself to play, Jorge Posada recalled, and if you looked at Martinez you couldn't help but feel adrenaline yourself. Derek Jeter and Posada—two of Martinez's closest friends on the team—once mentioned this metamorphosis to third baseman Robin Ventura, who had played with Martinez on the U.S. national team in 1988, and Ventura nodded knowingly. "Tino's Mad Face," Ventura said, and Jeter and Posada laughed, agreeing that the description was perfect. Throughout the long seasons, Martinez wore the Mad Face daily.

Now, with Jeter on third base and Bernie Williams at first in the seventh inning, the Yankees down a run, Martinez stepped deliberately into the box, piercing Curt Schilling with his concentrated stare, tapping his bat on home plate. And at that moment, it began raining inside Bank One Ballpark.

The ballpark's retractable roof was open. Russ Amaral, the Diamondbacks' vice president for events services, had been checking the weather forecast throughout the game, ducking into the room that served as the operations center for Bank One Ballpark. The stacked panels that made up the roof could unfold in four minutes and 20 seconds in the event of a downpour, as long as the wind did not rise above 15 mph. But the weather looked fine on the computers Amaral watched in the operations room, which was located on one of the top levels of Bank One Ballpark, 175 feet above the playing surface and the left-field corner. The radar indicated the skies would be clear throughout the game, except for the chance of a passing shower, but it appeared just as likely the rain would miss the ballpark altogether. In any case, the showers would be brief, Amaral believed, and there was probably no reason to close the roof or alert the umpires.

The wind had started blowing as the Diamondbacks finished batting in the bottom of the sixth; Shane Spencer felt the change as he returned to the Yankees' dugout from left field. The slight breeze turned into gusts, blowing from right field toward home plate; it pushed at the face of Arizona catcher Damian Miller as he took his position, and it drove into home plate umpire Steve Rippley. Hot dog wrappers and empty soda cups swirled, and with Martinez at the plate, the chance for a passing shower reached 100 percent. Drops pelted the brim of his helmet, turning its surface shiny. "It was goofy," said Steve Finley, Arizona's center fielder. "We hadn't had a wind like that at all, plus it was raining."

Schilling had been using a splitter against Martinez: the Yankees' first baseman had seen 14 pitches while hitting in the second and fifth innings, and of those, 10 were splitters. Now Miller signaled for a slider and set his target low and away so that Schilling could spin the ball over the outside corner.

But Schilling's pitch came over the middle, and Martinez smashed it into right field, a base hit. Jeter jogged home with a limp, tying the score. Danny Bautista, the Arizona right fielder, moved toward the line to intercept Martinez's hit, playing the ball carefully; Williams slowed as he neared second base, glanced at third-base coach Willie Randolph, and stopped. Tim McCarver, the Fox broadcaster, would say later that Williams should have tried to reach third, especially with one out; from there he could have scored on a fly ball or deep grounder. But months later, Williams still believed differently: Martinez had hit the ball hard, reducing the time Williams had to get to third, and Bautista had a strong arm and made a good throw to the infield.

After Jeter crossed home plate, he stopped at the on-deck circle and tapped Posada, the next hitter, on the helmet, encouraging him: *Let's go, keep it going.* The Yankees were going to win this game, they were sure of it. They had always won these games. Martinez stood at first base, his Mad Face burning.

David Cone thought Martinez was the best possible teammate, considerate and supportive of other players. He was not naturally social in the way Jeter and Tim Raines and Luis Sojo were, but he was the sort of person, one clubhouse attendant said, who would walk over to your dinner table and greet your friends because he knew that might be important to you. Martinez rarely revealed much of himself to reporters or even to teammates. He would play six seasons with the Yankees, and in the end, some teammates felt they barely knew him. He would have been perfectly suited to the 1950s, a club official thought, as a man who felt uncomfortable expressing emotion and preferred to keep his feelings private yet still had many friends.

But Martinez had an unusual devotion to winning, and a subtle, almost clandestine manner of fostering success. When the reporters left the clubhouse after games, leaving the players to themselves, Posada said, "Tino was something else. The reporters didn't know. We knew." Cone and Sojo and others would recall how Martinez talked incessantly about upcoming games and series. "He always talked in terms of facets of the game—'We need to do this thing well to beat this team,'" Cone said. Martinez would identify a Yankee who could play a crucial role against the forthcoming opponent, someone whose performance could turn the series, and then go to that player and talk to him. If the Yankees were about to face Boston and there figured to be a late-inning matchup between right-handed reliever Jeff Nelson and Boston shortstop Nomar

Garciaparra—in any close game, this was a near certainty—Martinez might walk over to Nelson in the clubhouse or drop into the seat next to him on a team flight and begin encouraging his teammate. If Williams was slumping, Martinez might talk to him over lunch: *We need you to pick it up; you're going to be the key to this series, no matter what you've done or what kind of slump you are in, this team fears you.*

Martinez prepared himself to play, as well. Before games he and Cone would talk about reasons to dislike that day's opponents, a method of manufacturing a mental edge. They might focus on a rival's quote in the newspaper, translating benign remarks into inflammatory slights, or concentrate on an annoying mannerism. "If the opposing pitcher struck out one of our hitters," Cone said, "and pimped around the mound a little bit, we were all over him—'Who does this guy think he is?' 'Is he showing us up?' It could be something completely innocuous." It was an old-school way of competing, Cone thought, a method of tricking yourself into a competitive fury.

Martinez didn't cater to the media, but he understood its power. He realized opposing teams would be watching the Yankees' reactions on television after big wins or losses, and he tailored his remarks accordingly. After the Yankees lost the first two games of the World Series to Arizona, Martinez said, "We made sure we were upbeat in our TV interviews, and that we were saying, 'It's far from over.' We made sure that the team that was watching didn't see us hanging our heads or didn't see us grumbling.

"I used to tell Derek, 'Hey, watch my interview tonight, watch my interview.' And he'd say, 'Watch mine, wait till you see mine.' Everybody watches those interviews, and you can see what a team is going through. Like sometimes, when we were leading a series 2–0, and you saw the other team's interviews and saw their faces, you knew you had them. You could sense they were down, just like you could with their mannerisms on the field."

If a team's internal strife played out in headlines and stories and TV clips, the accumulated stress could wear on it, break it up, and Martinez and the other Yankees diligently guarded their palace secrets; very few of them complained about teammates to reporters, on or off the record.

Posada and Martinez went weeks without speaking at the end of the 1998 season—"an argument over something stupid, probably," Posada recalled—but their short feud would run its course and be resolved without any reporter knowing.

Occasionally, Martinez would address a lagging teammate—quietly, Cone remembered, cajoling but encouraging. "If a guy wasn't doing his job or dogging it a little bit, we could get on that guy face-to-face," Martinez said. "The guys were ready to play most of the time, but if it needed to be done—the few times—nobody had a problem on this team going to somebody else and telling them, 'Let's go. You need to do this and that.' And that player would understand. It didn't have to be a media thing; it didn't have to go through the writers. We handled all that inside, and it was a great thing we had going."

Martinez had replaced another player who worked at cultivating the clubhouse culture, Don Mattingly, who retired at age 34 the year before the Yankees began winning championships. Veterans like Paul O'Neill and Bernie Williams thought the general tolerance and mutual respect that were traits of the Yankees' championship teams could be traced back to Mattingly, who had treated teammates uniformly well, regardless of their age and prestige. In spring training of 1995, Mattingly finished a workout with the Yankees' best minor league prospect, the 20-year-old Jeter. Other players were participating in the Yankees' exhibition that day, and Mattingly and Jeter were alone on a back practice field, picking up their equipment to head back to the clubhouse. "Let's run it in," Mattingly said to Jeter. "You never know who's watching." And so the old star and the young player ran through an otherwise empty ballpark.

Hobbled by back trouble, Mattingly accumulated just seven homers and 49 RBIs during the regular season of 1995. Before the Yankees faced Seattle in the first and only playoff series of his career, he told Yankees manager Buck Showalter that he was going to go all out, not worry about his back, swing aggressively. He batted .417 with four doubles and a homer, and on the depressing flight back to New York after the Yankees lost, Showalter recalled, Mattingly's back was so bad that he couldn't sit down. "If I can't bring what the New York Yankees need for a first baseman," Mattingly told Showalter, "I'm not playing. I can't do that to them." He quickly informed the Yankees of his decision to quit.

A few weeks later, the Yankees would trade third baseman Russ Davis and pitcher Sterling Hitchcock to the Mariners for Martinez, then almost 28 years old, plus pitchers Jeff Nelson and Jim Mecir. Like many new Yankees, Martinez was booed at Yankee Stadium, but he hit 25 homers and drove in 117 runs in his first season in the Bronx and the fans were quickly converted. He would drive in at least 100 runs in five of his six seasons with the Yankees and accumulate 722 RBIs in the regular season and postseason, often batting fifth and protecting Williams. He was a high-ball hitter, unusual for a left-handed batter—lefties tend to feast on low pitches—a trait that might have resulted from years of swinging level at balls sitting on raised tees. Martinez also was adept at hitting against left-handed pitchers, so much so that he broke out of some slumps while facing lefties because of the requisite discipline: to hit a left-handed pitcher's breaking ball, he was forced to keep his front shoulder tucked in, and he glided directly at the pitcher in his swing, rather than pulling out too soon. He would often dump singles into left field or over the shortstop against left-handers, restoring good habits.

Martinez would become an adroit first baseman, even though he lacked some of the qualities most great first basemen possessed—natural quickness and sure hands. Most great first basemen were left-handed, and he threw right-handed. Many right-handers struggled with throws to second base, because the angle of their trajectory flirted with the path of the base-runner; some right-handed first basemen, afraid of hitting the runner, would just hold the ball, sometimes missing crucial outs. But Martinez had learned to step toward the catcher before throwing to create a better angle to second base. And for the rest of his career, each time he threw to second base—during infield practice, or when he was taking ground balls from a coach—he always imagined there was a runner moving toward second. This play became instinctive for him, which would be fortunate for pitchers like Rivera and Pettitte; their cut fastballs often resulted in choppers hit in the infield, which Martinez would field and whip to second for a force-out.

Martinez gained expertise in digging out low throws from other infielders, learning to gauge the most difficult short hops—those that skipped three or four feet in front of him. He was probably better defensively than any right-handed first baseman in baseball during his time with the Yankees, and his teammates, many of whom thought he was the best first baseman in the league, were shocked he did not win at least one Gold Glove. He didn't have the range or the butterscotch-smooth hands of someone like J. T. Snow; by comparison, Martinez could look robotic in his movement. But he made plays and had the full confidence of the other infielders. It would not be until after Martinez left the team, Scott Brosius thought, that his fielding would be appreciated. Clemens thought Martinez probably saved about 30 errors a year and joked that when Martinez departed, the Yankees would have to sign an NHL goalie to replace him.

While O'Neill's outbursts happened in the open, for all to see, Martinez's explosions were mostly internal and, teammates thought, perhaps even more combustible. Ricky Ledee had learned in the Yankees' minor league system that when a teammate made a tough out, smashing a line drive at someone, the proper response was to walk over in the dugout to tap the luckless soul and tell him to hang in there. In one of Ledee's first days in the major leagues, Martinez had made a hard out and Ledee started to approach him, but Luis Sojo stepped in with some advice: *Don't do that here; better stay away from Tino*. Ruben Rivera, a young outfielder, accidentally riled Martinez during a game by walking into the dugout just in time to see him throw his helmet and bat. "What are you looking at?" the first baseman screamed. He couldn't stand it when other players tried to make him feel better about his line-drive outs and deep fly balls, because to Martinez, there was nothing to be gained from those at-bats—not even satisfaction from hitting the ball hard. If he made a hard out in his last at-bat, Jeter would try to both console and gently tease him. "Way to swing it," Jeter would say. "What good does it do?" Martinez would snap back; for him, the bottom line was that a line-drive out would never be as good as a hit.

Martinez liked taking batting practice to hone his swing, whether he was hitting well or not, and like O'Neill, he wanted to hit more when he was struggling. Torre sometimes thought it would be better if they hit less and stopped grinding at themselves. There were days when they wanted more batting practice, but Torre would not only deny them the extra work but also cancel regular batting practice. There was no hard evidence that either philosophy was better, but Martinez would always feel better if he did more work.

He failed to drive in any runs in his first two playoffs series with the Yankees in 1996, and the World Series shifted to Atlanta, where the designated hitter rule was not in effect. Torre benched him for Games 3, 4, and 5, going instead with the hot bat of designated hitter Cecil Fielder, a late-season acquisition who had driven in 12 runs against Texas and Baltimore. After playing every day during the season without asking for a day off, Martinez was livid. But he suppressed his anger, believing it was best for the team, and returned to his locker to start readying himself to come off the bench. "I was disappointed I wasn't playing—I wanted to be out there," said Martinez. "It was our first World Series, and you didn't know if you'd get that opportunity again. But then, I also knew that we were in trouble. I was struggling, some of the other guys were struggling, and we needed a change."

Cone, who knew how hurt and angry Martinez was, watched him on the bench in Atlanta and noticed that he was always the first player to shake Fielder's hand. Martinez could console himself, Cone thought, with the knowledge that he would play if the World Series went back to New York. But Martinez also understood that if he complained to reporters about Torre's decision, he would be implying that he was better than Fielder, "and he had too much respect for Cecil to do that," Cone said. "He knew that if he went off in the papers, he'd come off as selfish or disrespectful to a teammate, and he didn't want to be perceived that way. I know it really hurt him, and yet he was as supportive as any teammate on that particular night, yelling and screaming on the bench, cheering, the first guy to greet anyone who did anything positive."

The Yankees won the World Series, and Martinez never loudly aired his disappointment, choosing to make peace. He sent Torre some cigars that Christmas, and they would work well together for another five seasons. But some players on the team thought there was a well-hidden tension between them. Torre was never a strong advocate of Martinez in the organizational meetings, particularly as his production declined. He suggested that Martinez's intensity sometimes made him unapproachable, difficult to be around, and in at least one instance—during the 2000 season—Torre gave his blessing to a proposed deal that would have sent Martinez to Atlanta, a trade that was ultimately killed.

But Martinez would look back and feel he was "pretty close to Joe. I didn't go in his office or anything—I never did that. I was ready to play every day. He knew it, and he knew I was happy if he put me in the lineup every day. That was the bottom line. I loved playing for him; he was the best manager I ever played for."

He loved playing in New York, too; it was as if Martinez and Yankee Stadium had the same blood type. He could relate to the maddened intensity of the crowd, the feel of the place, especially in October, when the players wore long sleeves and the fans wore sweaters, breathing clouds. Organists were an endangered species in other major league parks, but the distinct sound of Yankee Stadium was created by Eddie Layton's keyboard, ricocheting off the facades. Bob Sheppard, the team's public-address announcer in the Bronx since the first days of Mickey Mantle, intoned the player introductions in the King's English, the handshake before the punches. You haven't heard loud until you've heard Yankee Stadium in October, Joe Girardi would tell new teammates after he left the Yankees. "Never heard a place like this," Girardi said. "People are so emotional and passionate and intense. To me, it's the greatest place to play." If the Yankees got any kind of momentum going in Yankee Stadium, Martinez thought, the crowd would just take over and help to finish off the opposing team, reminding them of how far they had fallen, or how much history and talent they had to overcome.

Martinez drove in just five runs in his first six postseason series for the Yankees, struggling to get a big hit. In Game 1 of the 1998 World Series, he came to bat in the seventh inning, with the bases loaded; Knoblauch's three-run homer earlier in the inning had tied the score at 5–5. Veteran left-hander Mark Langston was pitching for the Padres, and with a count of 2 balls and 2 strikes, Langston threw a pitch right down the middle. Langston paused and glanced at home plate umpire Rich Garcia. For years to come, San Diego manager Bruce Bochy would endlessly, painfully speculate how that game, and that World Series, might have played out if Garcia had called the strike, retiring Martinez. But the count was full, Langston threw another pitch, and Martinez blasted a grand slam, and after he circled the bases, Martinez—his adrenaline overflowing—slammed teammates with high fives. Three years later, when Martinez would hit another World Series home run, tying Game 4 against Arizona with a two-out, two-run homer in the bottom of the ninth inning, the fans summoned him for a curtain call; Martinez stepped out of the dugout and thrust his helmet into the air.

But his home run and RBI totals declined steadily; he had hit 44 homers and driven in 141 runs in 1997, and in 2000 he hit 16 homers and accumulated 91 RBIs. The Yankees explored the possibility of trading him, and as the summer of 2001 played out, it became apparent that the management, concerned about the team's plummeting on-base percentage, would probably pursue Oakland slugger Jason Giambi. After the World Series with Arizona, though, Torre would change his mind; he wanted Tino back, he said.

Game 7 against the Diamondbacks, however, would be Martinez's last with the Yankees; these were his last innings, his last at-bats. He led off first base after hitting his seventh-inning single that tied the score at 1–1, his eyes wide as he glanced at the Arizona fielders, a last check of their positioning.

Posada, his left-handed swing now infected with a weary late-season loop, lifted a pop fly to medium left field for the second out of the inning. If Williams had been at third base, he might have tried to tag up and score the go-ahead run; Luis Gonzalez, the left fielder, had a poor throwing arm that other teams had challenged throughout the postseason. But Williams remained at second, as Gonzalez gloved Posada's fly ball.

Curt Schilling had thrown nearly 90 pitches and was scheduled to bat first in the bottom of the inning; it seemed the top of the seventh would be his last on the mound. With two outs and the possible lead runs on base, Schilling began throwing his fastballs as if to expend his remaining energy, hurling his body toward the plate, his effort spinning him to the side as he completed his release.

In 73 plate appearances against Schilling in the Series, the Yankees had tallied 25 strikeouts and just 10 hits; Schilling had simply overwhelmed most of them. But Shane Spencer, up next, felt confident against the Arizona star. Spencer was short and strong, his body like a tree stump; when he was promoted to the majors in 1998, he had hit 10 homers in his first 67 at-bats, including three grand slams. Now he was seeing the ball well as it came out of Schilling's hand and was taking powerful and quick swings. Earlier in the World Series, in the third inning of Game 4, Spencer had taken a close pitch from Schilling—a third strike, probably; Spencer probably should have been called out. But home plate umpire Ed Rapuano called it a ball, and Spencer mashed the next pitch for a home run, giving the Yankees a 1–0 lead. As Spencer rounded the bases, Rapuano—respected by the players for his honesty—leaned forward and muttered to Miller, the Arizona catcher, "Don't let that pitch beat me," an acknowledgment that he had made a mistake.

Spencer seemed to build off his success in that at-bat. He had driven a deep fly almost to the center field wall in his first at-bat of Game 7, and now, in the seventh inning, he swung aggressively at Schilling's first pitch, a chest-high 94 mph fastball; he timed the pitch perfectly but just missed, fouling it straight back.

Ahead in the count, Schilling fired another fastball, 95 mph, and Spencer started to swing and stopped, but accidentally fouled off the ball with the barrel of his bat. No balls, two strikes. Schilling, his hair fluttering in the wind around the brim of his cap, threw a splitter, and Spencer saw it all the way; his hands and bat were quick, and he felt the ball cave in on contact, soaring toward right-center. He'd crushed it, and taking his first steps out of the batter's box, Spencer knew he had just driven in the lead runs for the Yankees with an extra-base hit; a double, perhaps, or a triple. Miller thought Spencer's drive might scrape over the fence for a three-run homer. Steve Finley, playing center field, turned and sprinted toward right-center.

And then he began to slow. The wind Spencer had felt as he jogged off the field after the previous half inning—that crazy, goofy rainstorm—slammed into his long drive, holding it up. When Spencer had made contact, Finley thought he would probably reach the ball, though he might have to launch his body at the end of the play. But the drive died, and Finley closed on the ball with short, choppy steps, gloving it easily. Three outs. Spencer, rounding first base, tilted his head upward, disgust covering his face. He glanced again toward right-center, looking in vain for the goddamned unfathomable wind that murdered his game-winning hit. He couldn't believe it. Tie score.

CHAPTER 16

IN THE FALL of 2001, Darryl Strawberry was in the custody of the state of Florida, his life cycle still seemingly locked into the baseball calendar: his arrests and court appearances often came in early spring, as the Yankees were breaking camp and opening the regular season, or midway through the fall, when the team was in the playoffs and World Series. On October 21, 2000, the Yankees and Mets began New York's first Subway Series in 44 years, but Strawberry, who might have been at center stage, was assigned to a drug-treatment clinic in Tampa, with no baseball, no bright lights, no teammates. He was 38 years old, 335 home runs in his career, still powerful, and through addictions, incarcerations, and hearings, he had never lost the beautiful buggy-whip swing he'd had when the Mets picked him first in the 1980 draft. But as Game 1 stretched into extra innings, Strawberry walked out of the clinic and met a woman named Christine, with whom he smoked crack and took pills. Thirteen days later, he stood before circuit court judge Florence Foster. "The last couple of weeks of my life have been downhill," Strawberry told the judge. "I basically wanted to die. . . . Life hasn't been worth living for me, that's the honest truth. I am not afraid of death."

Some of his friends had worried that Strawberry would harm himself once he did not have baseball, which had provided the structure and peer group that forced him into daily accountability. "He's going to be faced with a lot of time where he's used to playing and used to coming to the field every day, and it's a situation where he doesn't have that," Derek Jeter said after Strawberry was suspended in the spring of 2000. "He's got to find something on his own to do as well."

Strawberry had come to the Yankees in 1995 for the first of his last chances, and for virtually all of his five seasons with the team he arrived early, doing everything he was supposed to do when he was at the ballpark. He was a fallen star by then, an addict who had squandered the $30 million he'd made in his career. He was living his life day to day. Pregame stretch at the same time every day, batting practice, fielding practice, group prayer with Christian teammates, and Alcoholics Anonymous meetings.

He was a model citizen with the Yankees, Torre would say often. When he first managed Strawberry in the summer of 1996, he had given him a clean slate, believing that whatever had happened in the past should not matter; he would judge the player on his conduct with the Yankees. Strawberry was never any trouble, he was reliable, even deeply considerate of teammates. During spring training in 1997, he approached Jeter, whose first season in the majors had been much like Strawberry's explosive 1983 debut with the Mets—instant fame at the age of 21, in New York. He talked about the wave of enticements that would come at Jeter, who listened and appreciated Strawberry's concern; Jeter would come to think of him as a big brother.

But Jeter was generously equipped for stardom, having grown up in a strong and stable two-parent home, with a finely calibrated internal compass. Strawberry, by his own admission, was completely unprepared to deal with everything that came his way when he played with the Mets. His childhood had been troubled and essentially fatherless, and when stardom engulfed him, he had no sense of limits, no inner equilibrium. When he joined the Yankees, Strawberry was nearing the end of his career and tried thinking of himself as a work in progress. If he could be a good father to his children, if he could be a good teammate and a good person, then everything that had occurred earlier in his life would make sense. "I can't say that I feel bad for the mistakes I made, because it was a part of the learning through my life," Strawberry said in February 1998. "If your outcome can be positive, people look at you in a different way. If it's more of a negative outcome, then I think people have a right to say negative things, because you have the opportunity to change."

Strawberry spent hours sitting in front of his locker in the clubhouse, arriving before most of his teammates and remaining late after games. The Yankees mattered to him; they were his safe house. Time had hardly diminished the scope of his smile, but slight sagging half-moons were forming under his eyes. He usually joked easily with teammates, teasing Paul O'Neill or Tim Raines, awing them in batting practice. "Physically, he's still very impressive," David Cone said. "He hits long home runs, and when he takes batting practice, everybody stops to watch."

He sometimes reminisced about his days with the Mets, about the craziness—Doc and Lenny and Davey Johnson, his infamous spring training fight with Keith Hernandez, when he'd taken a swing at the first baseman as they sat for a team photo. But Strawberry's voice tended to trail off into silence as he told those stories; he knew how it all turned out. There were moments when Strawberry would be surrounded by teammates in a packed clubhouse and appear completely alone, quiet and sad, a bat in his hands—as if he closed himself off from the outside world, a friend said.

Strawberry batted .352 that April, driving in 14 runs in 54 at-bats, running well, stealing bases, playing effectively in left field. It was his best baseball in a decade. His life and addictions seemed in full recovery, but because of the nature of his problems, he would forever be in a precarious state. And this was about the time Strawberry stopped attending his Alcoholics Anonymous meetings. "He got lazy," said a friend.

The Yankees would win 114 regular-season games in 1998, breaking the American League record of 111 established by the 1954 Cleveland Indians, and Strawberry, as much as any Yankee, epitomized the team's dominance. The lineup was so extraordinary that Strawberry often batted seventh, behind Bernie Williams and Tino Martinez and Chili Davis. He shared time in the outfield with Tim Raines and Chad Curtis. The role players for most teams were veterans who had fizzled as regulars and found spots as part-time players, or young players whose primary value to their team was their low salary. "But you'd look over at the Yankees' bench," Kansas City manager Tony Muser said, "and they had Darryl Strawberry sitting there." To Muser, it was almost absurd that a slugger so dangerous could serve as a part-time player. But the Yankees were that good in '98, from top to bottom: leadoff batter Chuck Knoblauch would score 117 runs, and No. 9 hitter Scott Brosius drove in 98.

Through his experience, Strawberry knew the strike zone, often taking pitches until he got ahead in the count, cornering the opposing pitcher and forcing him to throw fastballs. At six feet six, his biceps exploded out of his sleeves, the veins on his arms bulged, and he looked almost too big for the bats he held, as if he were swinging toothpicks. Strawberry would hit 24 homers in 295 at-bats in 1998, and though his knees were in bad shape and he had increasing trouble playing consecutive days in the outfield, he remained a respected threat.

The Yankees were 18-6 on May 2, 1998, and had begun to gather momentum when they played on a cold night in Kansas City. The wind was gusting from right field to left field and most fly balls were getting knocked down like badminton birdies. Strawberry was not in the lineup, but with the Yankees leading 8–6 in the ninth inning, Torre inserted him as a pinch-hitter for Girardi. Strawberry launched a home run through the wind—as if he'd hit a golf ball, Cone noted afterward—to straightaway center field, halfway up the grass embankment beyond the fence. Strawberry circled the bases with his head down, a slight smile on his face. His money and his youth were gone, his knees were almost shot, he could no longer play the outfield every day, and his sobriety would always be in jeopardy. It seemed quite possible he would spend the rest of his life pissing into small plastic cups for strangers. But he could still crush a baseball. When it seemed impossible, Strawberry had blasted a 435-foot exclamation point.

The Yankees had almost completely separated themselves from the rest of the American League by the time they played Baltimore at Yankee Stadium 17 days later, their record 28-9. They trailed 5–1 late in the game, but Bernie Williams mashed a three-run homer in the eighth inning off Armando Benitez, the Orioles' hard-throwing reliever, to give the Yankees a 7–5 lead. The park shook as Williams crossed home plate, and with his next pitch, Benitez drilled Tino Martinez in his upper back with a 97 mph fastball. If anyone was viewed as an enforcer on the Yankees, it was Strawberry, and he immediately stepped to the top step of the Yankees' dugout and shouted at Benitez, "FUCK YOU!" Benitez slowly removed his glove and waggled his fingers toward the Yankees' dugout: bring it on. Strawberry charged the mound, and the 10-minute brawl that followed was thought by some players to be the nastiest they had ever seen.

Strawberry stood at his locker afterward, his face dotted by a small mouse from a punch, and said he was fine. "I took a couple of knocks," he said, grinning. "It was like a hockey game."

The Yankees would go on to win their last six games before the All-Star break, and midway through the season, they were 61-20. Their games developed a sense of inevitability: they usually crushed their opponents early, but if the Yankees trailed, they would almost always make a late charge. They would outscore their opponents by 309 runs over the season, an average difference of almost two runs per game. The players began sensing what they were creating, this monster season unlike any other ever, and they started chasing the carrot of collective greatness. The Yankees, Joe Girardi thought, were playing with the emotion of a high school team.

After the All-Star break, the Yankees traveled to the West Coast, which had been a speed bump in past seasons. But they took two of three from Anaheim and two of three from Seattle, then began a four-game series in Oakland by crushing the Athletics in the opener, 14–1. In the first game of an August 4 doubleheader, Chuck Knoblauch led off with a home run, and the Yankees racked up five hits and seven walks in 4⅔ innings against Oakland starter Jay Witasick, going on to win 10–4. They had 27 hits, 24 runs, and six homers in the first 18 innings of the series, including a home run in each game by Strawberry. Kenny Rogers, their former teammate, finally slowed them down in the second game of a doubleheader, carrying a 5–1 lead into the ninth inning, and appearing to be in complete command.

Tino Martinez opened the ninth with a single off Rogers; Raines followed with another. Knoblauch and other Yankees shared a clear vision of what was going to happen. If the next hitter, Curtis, could reach base, then Strawberry would pinch-hit for Girardi with the bases loaded, as the potential tying run. "You better be loose, because you might hit," Jeter told Strawberry. "Well, if I do, you know what I'm going to do," Strawberry replied. "I'm going to try to go deep."

Billy Taylor relieved Rogers, and Curtis hit a surefire double-play grounder to third base, where Mike Blowers booted the ball. The bases were loaded, there was nobody out, and Strawberry was walking to the plate, a moment that seemed scripted. It was late, and most of those who remained from the crowd of 23,357 were Yankees fans, and they roared as Strawberry stepped into the batter's box. They were thinking grand slam. Everybody was thinking grand slam. "Oh, yeah," said Knoblauch. "You've got Darryl up there and you're down four runs."

Jeter yelled encouragement. With a count of 2 balls and 2 strikes, the left-handed-hitting Strawberry fouled a pitch to the left field side, which encouraged Torre; Strawberry was always at his best when he wasn't rushing his swing.

Taylor threw a fastball at the outside corner, and Strawberry flicked his bat, the contact making a distinct sound. "He's got it!" Jeter screamed, and as the Yankees' players tumbled out of their dugout as if they had just won a Little League championship, Strawberry rounded the bases, grinning. The Yankees would score five more runs in the inning for a 10–5 victory, and afterward, Torre was stunned. "They refuse to accept the fact they might lose," he said.

"They are by far the best team I will ever face," said Rogers.

The Yankees' players shared a postgame spread, filling plates with pasta and sitting at tables to watch the highlights of their doubleheader on ESPN. When Strawberry's grand slam was replayed, they all shouted in unison at the moment of contact: "Ooooooh!"

Strawberry enjoyed this immensely. He was respected again, liked by his teammates, part of something special. Strawberry would never make it all the way back to what he had been, but he was making the best of what he was.

There was something troubling him, however. He had begun having wrenching abdominal pains.

Strawberry didn't tell anyone about his increasing discomfort for almost two months because he just wanted to get through the season and the playoffs and World Series. He finally pulled aside team doctor Stuart Hershon on the eve of the playoffs. Initial blood tests showed nothing unusual, but a thought nagged at Hershon: Strawberry had been a boyhood friend of Eric Davis, who had already been treated for colon cancer; the doctor hoped there was not some unknown common denominator involved. Hershon had Strawberry go through a CAT scan, which revealed a tumor, and after a biopsy, Hershon told him he had colon cancer. Torre informed the players in a team meeting in Texas, and many of his teammates wept. They would call and visit Strawberry in the hospital during the postseason, after doctors removed 16 inches of his colon and 36 lymph nodes.

Steinbrenner gave him $2.5 million for the next season, an act perceived as virtual charity by other executives in the organization, in a deal structured so that he would be paid even if he was unable to play. Strawberry was going through chemotherapy, and no one had any idea if he would be able to play baseball again. But he returned for spring training, determined to be a part of the team at the beginning of the season. His chemo treatments hampered his workout program, and from day to day the Yankees were never sure of his availability. The team wasn't counting on him, and Strawberry felt hurt and betrayed. He began griping about being left out by the coaching staff, at a time when Torre was away from the team for his prostate cancer treatment. For the first time, Strawberry was a problem. "You kind of sense he was very depressed going through chemotherapy and that one of his goals was to make the team out of spring training," said Cone. "He seemed very deflated when that didn't happen."

When the Yankees flew to the West Coast to begin their season, Strawberry was left behind in Tampa to continue his workouts, and two weeks later, he was arrested for cocaine possession and solicitation of prostitution. Commissioner Bud Selig suspended him for 120 days, but

George Steinbrenner—who had once warned Strawberry that if he re-lapsed, the owner would become his worst enemy—kept him in the or-ganization. Baseball, it seemed, was his lifeline, and the Yankees were probably the only major league team that would give him a chance. Strawberry had four children from two marriages, debts, and responsi-bilities, a friend noted, but the daily fix of playing for the Yankees was the one thing that kept him from being consumed by his addictions. When he was with the team, Strawberry cared enough about obligations to teammates to stay clean. The structured existence of baseball enabled him to get through the day without seriously confronting his problems; baseball was a placebo for him. "He never had to hit rock bottom," said a member of the organization. "If he had hit rock bottom, he would've had to deal with his addiction head-on."

Strawberry rejoined the Yankees for the last month of the 1999 sea-son, and although he had not played in a major league game in almost a year, his swing was perhaps even more impressive than it had been in 1998. He faced Angels reliever Troy Percival in a game on September 4 and locked onto Percival's exceptional fastball, fouling it straight back, timing it well, before drawing a walk. When he was on the field, Straw-berry said, he never felt pressure. Off the field, that's where there was pressure.

He batted .327 in 24 games and slugged a three-run homer in the first round of the playoffs. Chad Curtis suggested that in deference to Straw-berry, Champagne sprayed by the players should be nonalcoholic, a practice the Yankees would maintain for the rest of the playoffs. When Boston fans taunted him during the American League Championship Series by chanting, "JUST SAY NO," Strawberry answered with a home run, the first run in a 9–2 victory in Game 4, which all but finished the Red Sox. Torre used him like a dagger in the first game of the World Se-ries, inserting him as a pinch-hitter against Greg Maddux in the eighth inning when Atlanta led 1–0, making sure that Strawberry would get a chance to hit against a right-hander. Maddux, worried about having his whole night wiped out with one bad pitch to Strawberry, walked him, setting up a four-run inning. In 13 months, Strawberry had had colon cancer surgery, been arrested, suspended, reinstated, and rejuvenated. After the Yankees swept the Braves in the World Series, he would ride in the victory parade down the Canyon of Heroes.

Strawberry went to the microphone at City Hall to speak. "These guys are very special to me," he said. "Without them, I don't know if I would have made it."

He began to thank Torre but was overcome, weeping. Torre stepped forward from his seat and put his hands on him, assuring him, and after a minute, Strawberry resumed, tears streaming down his face. "I'd just like to say to Joe, thanks for caring for me. And I love you guys."

Three months later, in the off-season, Strawberry failed a drug test and admitted to using cocaine. As Commissioner Selig considered a penalty, Strawberry showed up at the Yankees' camp for the first full-squad workout as if nothing had happened. "I came here today because this is where I feel I want to be," he said, his lower lip quivering.

He worked out and jogged with teammates, but just before he was supposed to take his first round of batting practice, Brian Cashman called him off the field; Selig had sent a directive telling him to stay away from the team until a decision was made. Those were Darryl Strawberry's last moments as a major league ballplayer. Within months, he was in a Florida drug treatment center, having violated the terms of his probation.

In the same weekend that the Yankees broke camp in 2001, Strawberry went on a drug spree, slipping away to a motel in Orlando to smoke crack after telling his probation officer he was going to attend an AA meeting. Most of what his former teammates knew of him was from the images they saw on television, time and again—Strawberry dressed in an orange jumpsuit again and standing in front of a judge. Maybe it was for the best, said a close friend. Maybe he had to be forced to find something other than baseball. His teammates, the game, maybe they were all just Strawberry's enablers.

Charlie Nobles, a Florida-based sportswriter for the *New York Times*, had covered many of his games during spring training and the regular seasons. As Strawberry's sobriety disintegrated, Nobles was assigned to cover his many court appearances. On the day Strawberry was finally sentenced to prison, he looked over and made eye contact with Nobles, who had known him before as a great player and who had seen him in those days of fame and glory. Strawberry smiled slightly, lifted his hand, and waved.

CHAPTER 17

THE SUNDAY of Game 7 was supposed to be a day off for Rudy Giuliani. His plan had been to play golf with his son in the morning and then, after taking his daughter to the pool, to go see Game 7 at Bank One Ballpark. As the Diamondbacks obliterated the Yankees in Game 6, Giuliani had heartened himself by thinking about the next morning; it was going to be his first day off since September 11. But late in the Game 6 blowout, Sunny Mindel, his communications director, approached Giuliani, accompanied by chief of staff Tony Carbonetti. "You have a phone call," Mindel said. "And you're going to have to take it on the hard line." Giuliani knew the news would be bad.

Spores of anthrax had been found in City Hall, in Carbonetti's office, adjacent to the mayor's office. New York officials would figure out almost immediately how the anthrax got there: a month before, Carbonetti had received a videotape of a White House ceremony from Tom Brokaw, the NBC anchor, and it sat in a package in one of the unmoved piles that rose like the Alps in Carbonetti's office. Anthrax had been sent to NBC in mid-September, and apparently a trace amount had traveled with the package shipped to Carbonetti. No one working in City Hall had exhibited anthrax symptoms, but it was a tense time and City Hall employees would be concerned, so Giuliani decided to fly back to New York overnight. His plane landed about 5:30 a.m., he attended a morning press conference for a visiting dignitary, and then, with the change of plans bringing him home, Giuliani played host for the start of the New York City Marathon. He then boarded another plane to Arizona for his third cross-country flight in 36 hours, racking up about 5,800 miles. There was never any question that he would return to see Game 7, to see his Yankees.

Giuliani had always been a Yankees fan despite growing up in Brooklyn a mile away from Ebbets Field, an area where it was impolitic to root for anyone but the Dodgers. When he was about five years old, a group of boys surrounded him and demanded that he turn over his Yankees cap. He refused, and they informed him he would be hung. The boys led him to a tree, bringing along a rope—probably just to scare him, Giuliani would say years later with a smile. His grandmother saw the confrontation from her window and yelled at the boys, who scattered, but there would be plenty of other scrapes: most of Giuliani's childhood bouts began because he loved the Yankees.

He played catcher in neighborhood games, so it naturally followed that Yogi Berra, the Yankees' catcher, was his favorite player. His mother had once taken him to Yankee Stadium while his father was at work, a journey that meant a long and inconvenient train ride. Why would you want to go all the way to the Bronx, his mother asked, when you could just walk to Ebbets Field? She didn't understand. He followed the Yankees with passionate scrutiny: after becoming mayor, Giuliani met former Yankees pitcher Bob Turley and told him he had not gotten credit for being the star of the 1958 World Series, for pitching in Games 5, 6, and 7, winning two and saving the other. Turley, proud and touched that Giuliani would remember, asked him to repeat those words to his son.

Giuliani continued to attend Yankees games, and as he ascended in city politics, advisors suggested it might be better for him to mute his ardor for the Yankees lest he offend voters who rooted for other teams, particularly the Mets. Maybe it would be better, they said, if you expressed equal appreciation for the Mets and the Yankees. But Giuliani thought New York baseball fans would never buy that. Mets fans, he believed, would respect him more if he maintained his allegiance, and so when the Yankees faced the Mets in interleague play and in the 2000 World Series, there was no question whom His Honor was rooting for.

When the Yankees eliminated Seattle in the American League Championship Series six weeks after the terrorist attacks, Giuliani was in the seats next to the Yankees' dugout, standing and clapping as the players celebrated, and Joe Torre walked over to Giuliani's box. They had become friends during the championship years, having much in common: both had grown up baseball-crazy and Italian in Brooklyn. The year after Torre was treated for prostate cancer, he would call Giuliani when the mayor was similarly diagnosed, and in the months that followed, each would wryly greet the other by asking about his urination. There was a kinship, and Torre wanted Giuliani to come on the field to join the players after they defeated Seattle.

"I can't do that," said Giuliani. "I'm not part of the team." Yes, you are, Torre responded, and when Giuliani walked out to the mass of players in the infield, they began reaching out to shake his hand, the Yankee Stadium crowd roaring.

For Game 7, Giuliani sat on the side of the visitors' dugout, good-naturedly making faces into the late innings at Arizona senator John McCain, a political ally who became a baseball rival during this Series.

Roger Clemens came out to work the bottom of the seventh, the score tied, his pitch count at 102 after six stressful innings. Bob Brenly had a difficult decision. Curt Schilling was due to lead off the bottom of the seventh, and Brenly had the option of inserting a pinch-hitter. Schilling appeared to be nearing the end of his outing, anyway, having accumulated 90 pitches and labored through the top of the seventh as the Yankees scored the tying run. Brenly had a full complement of rested relievers, plus one more rather well-established pitcher: before the game, Randy Johnson, who had pitched the night before, had assured Brenly he was ready to work again. All hands on deck in this game.

To Brenly, it made sense to win or lose this game with his best on the mound—Schilling or Johnson. Despite Johnson's confidence, Brenly did not know how long Johnson might be able to last, pitching on consecutive days; maybe an inning, maybe two. So Brenly decided to stick with

Schilling a little longer and let him bat leading off the bottom of the seventh. "Schill had been his own closer up to that point," Brenly recalled, months later. "He had been the horse, and as long as he was pitching effectively, he was the guy we wanted out there."

Schilling struck out on five pitches, the 10th strikeout for Clemens in the game, before Tony Womack grounded a single through the first-base hole, past a diving Soriano. Clemens pursed his lips and looked down, knowing that he was going to be replaced; he had thrown 114 pitches, and the next two hitters due to bat, Craig Counsell and Luis Gonzalez, were both left-handed. Because there was one out, Torre would have to do everything possible to keep the speedy Tony Womack—who had 28 steals during the regular season, 267 in his career—from swiping second base. Clemens, with his big leg kick and relatively slow delivery, had allowed 34 stolen bases during the season; he would be a poor deterrent in this situation.

Torre walked to the mound, reached for the ball, and slapped Clemens on the back; Tino Martinez patted him, as well, and the pitcher ambled off the mound, his teeth still gritted, until he paused and nodded at home plate umpire Steve Rippley, acknowledging him for calling a good game.

Torre summoned Mike Stanton, who was effective in holding runners. Most left-handers with deceptive pickoff moves were lithe and graceful, like veteran Kenny Rogers, who would lift his right leg and then pause for milliseconds, staring down the runner almost hypnotically, freezing him, before zipping the ball to first. But Stanton, though a gifted athlete and an excellent hitter, didn't look particularly athletic; he was squarely built, like a furnace, his arms appearing shorter than most pitchers'. His blocky body made his pickoff move look somewhat awkward, as if his legs and arms were being hurled in different directions. It was a dangerous though well-kept secret; Nick Johnson, a young first baseman with the Yankees, was occasionally fooled, edging off the bag before realizing suddenly that Stanton was throwing the ball to him. Stanton nailed four runners in 2000 and three in 2001, usually with his first throw, ambushing them before they realized that his funky move was tricky.

Counsell waited intently at the plate. He wanted to allow Womack some time to try stealing second base. Womack took his lead, the brim of his helmet pulled low; he bent forward slightly at the waist, his arms dangling.

Stanton took the sign without bothering to look at Womack, appearing relaxed, almost as if he had forgotten the runner at first base. He raised his hands, coming to a set position before beginning his motion. Still without looking directly at Womack, he drew up his right knee, and Womack took a half-step back toward first base, unsure—and Stanton fired the ball to first. Martinez slapped down the tag on Womack's elbow.

Too late. The Yankees' first baseman crow-hopped and grinned. Almost.

This was the part of the game the Yankees had dominated during the championship run, from the seventh inning onward, on the strength of Stanton and the other middle relievers Torre trusted, Jeff Nelson and Ramiro Mendoza and intermittently others. The Yankees outscored their opponents 99–46 after the sixth inning during the playoff and World Series games from 1996 to 2000. They had won eight games in extra innings, including Games 4 and 5 of this World Series against the Diamondbacks, and lost only one. In all of Torre's time as manager, the Yankees had allowed extra-inning runs in only one postseason game, a reflection of their brilliant and deep middle relief.

Mendoza, a right-hander with a hard-running sinker and fading changeup, rarely spoke and watched television in bulk. His nickname of El Brujo—the witch doctor—was suited perfectly to his personality, the mysterious pitcher whose sinker dove unnaturally. He was nothing if not placid, and although he preferred to start, Mendoza reacted with little more than a shrug of the shoulders when Torre shifted him back and forth from the rotation to the bullpen. Torre had used him against Boston in the Championship Series in 1999, and Mendoza—appearing absolutely relaxed, as though he were pushing the buttons of a remote control—had twice shut down Red Sox rallies.

Nelson was six feet eight, a crew cut underneath his cap, right-handed. He threw sidearm at the hitters, stepping to the right side of the mound as he threw, and because he was so tall and had such long arms, he looked as if he were releasing the ball somewhere near third base. Right-handed batters would often step back with their front foot and swing weakly at his sharp-breaking slider, and during the 2000 season, Nelson held right-handed hitters to a .157 average with 47 strikeouts and one homer in 159 at-bats.

Orlando Hernandez and David Wells ranked among the best postseason starters of all time, and Rivera was perhaps the best October closer, but Stanton's playoff and World Series performance had been no less remarkable. He had pitched in every postseason from 1991, and in 50 appearances, he had a cumulative ERA of 1.70, with a record of 5-1.

There was a junkyard edge to this group that was not evident in the starting pitchers or in Rivera. Before Clemens arrived, it usually was left to Nelson or Stanton or Graeme Lloyd to fight the beanball wars. If an opposing pitcher drilled O'Neill or Martinez or another of the Yankees' batters, Nelson would ask the bruised hitter if he thought it was deliberate, and if they wanted a particular batter taken down in retaliation.

"At times I've said: 'Hey, I'm going to go out there and drill someone. Do you want me to hit this guy?'" Nelson said. "If they say, 'No, no,' I say fine. If they say, 'Go drill someone,' I'm going to drill someone. I don't care about the manager; I don't care about the coach. Even if they told me not to, I'm going to go out there and do it. I'm going to protect my teammates."

In spring training of 1999, Cleveland pitcher Jaret Wright threw a neck-high fastball at Luis Sojo—in apparent retaliation for a couple of hit batsmen earlier—and when Sojo recoiled to protect his face, the pitch fractured his hand. Nelson felt it important to respond in kind and nailed one of the Indian batters later in the game. Martinez, who had played his entire career with Nelson, both of them breaking in with Seattle and coming to the Yankees in the same trade, said, "Jeff is definitely one guy who, if you need to send a message to another team, he's going to do it." Nelson was occasionally irked that the relievers had to take care of the dirty work, but neither he nor Stanton ever shirked the duty.

Stanton and Nelson had rescued the Yankees in the 2000 Division Series, after a profound weariness infected the team at the end of the regular season. The Yankees swept a three-game series in Fenway Park in early September, all but burying the Red Sox, but then stalled and spun into a death spiral. They lost 15 of their last 18 regular-season games, getting outscored 148–59. Privately, some of the veterans thought the team was tiring of the expectations placed upon them every year. The loss to Cleveland in the 1997 playoffs had propelled them through '98, but by the summer of 2000, they sometimes seemed bored with the regular season; their goals could be reached only in October, making the summer seem like drudgery. Torre occasionally warned his team about turning their maximum effort on and off like a light switch; there will come a time, he said once in 1998, that you won't be able to do that, and two years later, he turned out to be right. As the Yankees tried to pull out of their dive in the last days of the 2000 regular season, their play was saturated with panic. They were in serious trouble.

A Boston loss handed the Yankees the division title in the final weekend of the 2000 season, but that same night the Orioles pounded them, 13–2. The players quietly retreated to the clubhouse after that defeat, and Torre had to remind them they had reason to celebrate. The Yankees appeared listless, an easy target for another team in the playoffs, and Oakland beat them in Game 1 of the Division Series, 5–3, before Pettitte threw 7⅔ shutout innings the next night to even the series. They had a chance to close out Oakland in Yankee Stadium in Game 4, but Clemens was ripped in the first inning and they lost, 11–1. Forced to fly to the West Coast overnight to play in Oakland the next day, the veterans were exhausted—and angry, Stanton recalled, furious that they had failed to finish off the Athletics and that they had created an extra leg of travel for themselves.

But the Yankees had learned to use anger like that, to channel it. In a press conference just before the decisive Game 5, Oakland third baseman Eric Chavez cheerily remarked that he was pleased the Yankees' dynasty might be ending. "I mean, they've won enough times," Chavez said. "It's time for some other people to have some glory here."

Chavez, 22 years old, had made the comment offhandedly, not so much to dismiss the Yankees as to please the reporters in the room. Chavez didn't know, however, that his remarks were being broadcast live on the two massive scoreboards in Oakland's Network Associates Coliseum, his face filling the screens as the Yankees took batting practice before Game 5. Jeter and O'Neill and Williams stared upward, absorbing Chavez's words as they reverberated around the ballpark. "But, no, they've had a great run," he continued. "It's hard to stay No. 1. Everybody's gunning for you; everybody's trying to beat you. They're going to throw their best at you. They've done a phenomenal job as it is."

The Yankees looked at each other incredulously. "So he's dropping the past tense on us, is he?" Scott Brosius said, picking up his helmet and bat as he walked to the batting cage. "Did you see that? OK, we'll see how it goes." The Yankees had their artificial energizer, and Knoblauch, Jeter, and O'Neill all reached base to open the game, and with one out, Oakland center fielder Terrence Long misplayed a deep fly ball into a three-run double; the Yankees had a 6–0 lead before the Athletics batted in the first inning.

The Yankees' pitching staff had fragmented at the end of the 2000 season. Torre had only six healthy pitchers he used with confidence: Clemens, Orlando Hernandez, and Pettitte, and relievers Rivera, Nelson, and Stanton. Mendoza was hurt, and Torre was leery of relying on Denny Neagle, so he started Pettitte on three days' rest. But Pettitte was awful, surrendering 10 hits and five runs in 3⅔ innings. The Yankees' lead was cut to two runs; this was an emergency, and Torre took all necessary measures to stop the bleeding. Stanton took over in the fourth inning with two runners on base, retired Chavez on a groundout, and turned over a 7–5 lead to Nelson in the sixth, after six of the most crucial outs of the dynasty.

Nelson got four more, protecting the lead through the seventh, and El Duque, pressed into relief, got the first out in the eighth inning, before Rivera got the last five. Chavez fouled out to end the game. "I think it's fitting that the last out was from the guy who insinuated we were over the hill," Bernie Williams said afterward, as the tired Yankees drank Champagne in a subdued celebration, leaving four cases unopened. "It's my understanding we're not done yet."

"Who said we're old?" Stanton shouted. "We're just old enough." Except for the playoff defeat against Cleveland in '97, it was the only time the Yankees had been pushed to the brink of elimination, and they had survived.

Nelson became a free agent after the 2000 World Series, and the Yankees offered him a three-year, $9 million deal. He had begun his career with the Seattle Mariners, had built a home in the Seattle area, and the Mariners offered Nelson $10.5 million over three years. The Yankees informed him they would not adjust their offer.

Nelson generally thrived in his role as a setup man, but he was 34 years old and had some wear and tear in his pitching arm, and some members of the Yankees' front office and staff considered him a high-maintenance player. He was among the few Yankees who expressed his displeasure publicly; during the summer of 2000, he reacted angrily when Torre didn't pick him for the All-Star team, and on another occasion, he and the manager had a shouting match. He was the only Yankee able to nudge Torre into bad body language on the bench.

Nelson relied heavily on his slider, despite the fact that he threw his fastball in the low 90s. But sometimes, he threw more sliders than the coaching staff preferred and struggled with his control, and Torre's frustration would begin to seep out. The manager might push his cap high onto his forehead or grimace with exasperation or fold his arms and squeeze his own chest. Rivera and Stanton showed no outward emotion when they pitched, but Nelson would throw his hands in the air after a big inning-ending strikeout, slapping his glove with his pitching hand. In truth, his intermittent control problems and opinions were very mild by the standards of most major league teams. He never complained about his role and embraced his assignment as a specialist. He was always on time and was never afraid to take the ball. But compared to the other highly controlled Yankees, who suppressed any feelings of discontent, Nelson came off like a rebellious malcontent. The Yankees never increased their $9 million offer, deciding to look for other right-handed relievers to assume Nelson's role, a decision that ultimately added to the already enormous burden on Mariano Rivera in 2001.

The Yankees tried about a half-dozen right-handers as replacements, including midseason acquisitions Jay Witasick and Mark Wohlers, but Torre never developed real faith in any of them. With the bullpen thin, and Torre relying on fewer relievers in close games, Rivera pitched 80⅔ innings in 2001, more than in any season since 1996, when he was 26 years old.

Rivera pitched like a sprinter running 100 meters, going all out, pumping fastballs on virtually every delivery, and after a highly effective first barrage, he tended to tire. During the regular season in 2001, opposing batters hit just .200 against him in his first 15 pitches in each game, with a .224 on-base percentage and a .257 slugging percentage. Beyond the 15th pitch, however, the numbers worsened: a .232 batting average, a .282 on-base percentage, and a .317 slugging percentage. Hitting Rivera was always difficult, but he was somewhat more vulnerable in extended outings, and in 2001, he was required to pitch more. Without Nelson or a suitable replacement, Torre was basically trying to get through the postseason with a three-man bullpen: Rivera, Mendoza, and now, in the seventh inning of Game 7, Mike Stanton, who was closely watching Tony Womack at first base, trying to keep him from stealing second.

Stanton's initial pickoff move had surprised Womack, and when the pitcher threw over to first base a second time, Womack was again perplexed. Uncertain whether Stanton was going home or to first base, he edged tentatively toward first base before scrambling back to the bag. Womack finally relented, shortening his lead a bit, and when Stanton threw over to first base a third time, Womack got back easily.

The count reached 1 ball and 1 strike on Counsell, and Stanton began his motion, lifting his knee, driving toward the plate, his front foot landing—and Womack broke for second, a late jump; the hit-and-run play was on. But Counsell swung underneath Stanton's chest-high fastball, and Posada caught the pitch rising out of his crouch, with plenty of time to throw to second. But he pumped and tapped his glove. Womack was closing on second base, and Posada was running out of time.

Posada whipped the ball right to the bag, where Jeter swept a tag down on Womack's front leg an instant before his foot slammed into second base. Two outs. Jeter punched the air with his fist. Counsell, behind in the count, popped up a curveball to first base, the third out for Arizona. Still a tie score, 1–1.

The end of the game and the season was at hand, and Fox, the network broadcasting Game 7, needed to prepare for the postgame trophy presentation and interviews; a stage had to be prepared in case the Yankees won. A Fox crew entered the visitors' clubhouse, ready to do its work.

But Steinbrenner, nervously moving through the clubhouse, saw them and exploded; he wanted them out. As far as he was concerned, it would be inviting bad luck to set up for a postgame celebration when the Yankees hadn't won anything; the game was tied, with so much at stake.

Steinbrenner insisted that the Fox crew stay out, and he loudly chastised his own attendants, and then Phyllis Merhige, a Major League Baseball official. Get them out of here, he yelled, and the Fox people departed. For the moment, Steinbrenner had managed to keep the TV crew out of his bunker. To bring a victory stage in here—well, he believed that would jinx the Yankees.

CHAPTER 18

JOHN STERLING hunted down Joe Torre before every game, stepping briskly through the halls of Yankee Stadium, wielding a microphone and a digital recorder. Sterling, the Yankees' radio announcer, hosted Torre's daily pregame show, asking the manager about the issues of the hour, about injuries and streaks and slumps. Torre, who had worked as an announcer for the California Angels in the years between the Atlanta Braves firing him and his hiring by the St. Louis Cardinals, treated broadcasters and reporters respectfully, understanding from his own experience the rhythms and responsibilities of their jobs. He was especially fond of Sterling and teased him good-naturedly, noting to other reporters those afternoons when Sterling was particularly well dressed.

Before World Series home games, Sterling would tape his show in Torre's white cinder-block office, to avoid the crush of media waiting outside the clubhouse, and when he walked through the door just prior to the Subway Series in 2000, Mel Stottlemyre was sitting on the couch. He was not supposed to be there.

Stottlemyre was being treated for multiple myeloma—cancer of the bone marrow—and because his immune system was weakened, his doctors recommended that he avoid contact with other people. But Stottlemyre, who had ties to both teams, having pitched and coached for the Yankees and coached for the Mets when they won the World Series in 1986, could not stay away. His duties were being handled by Billy Connors, but he hated being away from the pitchers and the action; during each of the games, he stayed long enough to watch the first innings in the manager's office, surrounded by 55,000 people in the stands above him. Prior to games, he spent hours with Torre, whose friendship was so important to him now; Stottlemyre's voice would crack when he spoke of the way Torre had supported him that summer.

It was shortly after Torre had surgery for prostate cancer, in the spring of 1999, that Stottlemyre told him of his own condition, which would be monitored for a year before he required more extensive treatment. Darryl Strawberry's cancer was diagnosed five months before Torre's, and less than three years after Torre's brother Rocco had died; another brother, Frank, had required a heart transplant in the midst of the 1996 World Series. The fathers of four Yankees veterans passed away during the championship run: Maury Brosius, Chick O'Neill, Ambrosio Sojo, and Bernabe Williams. Real life constantly invaded the Yankees' baseball world, and after Mike Stanton left the team, he concluded that the reason this group of teammates had become so close was that they had needed one another so often.

It was Stottlemyre's nature to always look for the good in any situation, to look for the good in his pitchers. His optimism was robust, resolute; David Cone thought he was the most upbeat person he had ever met. But he was not a Pollyanna, oblivious of reality; if a pitcher threw badly, he would note his mistakes but refrain from reviewing them after the game, allowing the pitcher a night to exhale. Then he would come back the next day enthusiastically, ready to discuss problems and work on adjustments, sounding confident that a solution was inevitable. He was not a holder of grudges, and unlike many coaches, Stottlemyre did not resent struggling or unreliable players; he tended to view bad behavior as a clue to a personality puzzle that needed solving. What Mel Stottlemyre believed, his son Todd said, was that finding the negative in people was a waste of time.

During the 2000 season, when Stottlemyre was going through his treatment for cancer and had lost much of his hair, Orlando Hernandez came back from rehabilitation for arm trouble and complained obliquely that there were those in the organization trying to undermine him. It became apparent that his anger was directed partly at Stottlemyre, who was completely at a loss as to what Hernandez might be talking about. But instead of reacting sharply—and others in the clubhouse would not have blamed him if he had—Stottlemyre said he was sorry El Duque felt betrayed, and that it was obvious they needed to talk. He waded through Hernandez's shifting moods and seemingly indefinable ailments, maintaining a working relationship. Stottlemyre once allowed, through a small grin, that in coaching El Duque he had a lot of practice in mind reading, "although I don't know if I'm any better at it than I was before." He encouraged Andy Pettitte, who tended to berate himself, tolerated David Wells's aversion to authority, gave Roger Clemens the specific technical observations that he craved, and allowed Mussina to ostensibly coach himself. Hideki Irabu, like Hernandez, could be a total mystery, but Stottlemyre would go back to him daily, talking cheerfully with his hand on the pitcher's elbow or shoulder—he often made contact with the players in this way when he talked to them face-to-face—and wearing a broad, empathetic smile.

He liked players, and his relationship with his own sons helped him, Stottlemyre explained; Mel Jr. and Todd pitched in the majors, and through them he had a better understanding of the current generation. Stottlemyre had been a sinkerball pitcher during his own 11-year playing career with the Yankees, with enough self-confidence to start three World Series games in his rookie season of 1964, after being called up in August. But in his time with the Yankees, he would coach pitchers who were wide-ranging in style and personality, from Cone to Pettitte to El Duque and Clemens and Mussina, without ever forcing his own pitching methods and philosophy on them. "He understands there is change," Todd Stottlemyre said. "Some changes have been for the better, and maybe some changes are not, but there are changes and he's adapted."

Stottlemyre tended to spend more time with pitchers who were struggling, commiserating with them. If a pitcher was getting racked and Stottlemyre visited the mound, he would speak positively, mix in a little humor, and with Cone, Pettitte, or Clemens—pitchers he knew well— he might raise his eyebrows and let them know they were in jeopardy of being relieved. "He wouldn't really say anything," said Cone, "but you could tell by the look on his face."

Stottlemyre served Cone as pitching coach for the better part of a decade, and in all that time, Cone recalled only one instance in which he saw him truly angry. While still with the Mets, the two were watching the St. Louis Cardinals on television during a pennant race, and when the Cardinals won their game and damaged the Mets' playoff chances, Stottlemyre shouted angrily, his tone surprising Cone. He held his temper, Todd Stottlemyre thought, partly out of deference to others. It was his father's way to remain steady and strong. In their conversations after Stottlemyre was diagnosed with cancer, Todd would ask his father how he felt, and Mel would say he felt great and then ask his son how he was doing in his arm rehabilitation: *How's your arm? What are you doing in rehab? You've got to work hard, you've got to get your rest.*

"Immediately after his diagnosis, it was almost as if he was the support for our family dealing with his cancer," Todd Stottlemyre recalled. His father never feared responsibility and was not afraid to carry the burden of his diagnosis, Todd Stottlemyre said, "and then look at his family and say everything is going to be OK. There wasn't one day where I caught him down. Do I think there were times when he had down days? Yeah, but he wasn't going to let his kids see his down days, or anybody else. That just wasn't part of his character."

For a year, Torre kept Stottlemyre's secret, but when his condition worsened and it was determined Stottlemyre would require treatment that would prevent him from coaching for days at a time, Torre called a meeting and told the team of the diagnosis. He encouraged the players to talk to Stottlemyre if they had any questions. Clemens, the starting pitcher that day, was badly shaken, and he asked Stottlemyre to explain his condition before he warmed up. Stottlemyre responded to Clemens and other players as he did to his own son, offering a brief synopsis and adding that he felt fine before focusing on Clemens's situation. The treatment caused him to tire more easily and prevented him from throwing batting practice, something he loved to do. (Stottlemyre remained in excellent condition after his playing days ended, and hitters thought his batting practice pitches had more lateral movement than some American League pitchers'.) But he stayed upbeat, kept asking his pitchers how they felt; there was never any question that he would remain pitching coach through the summer, even when he was away from the team for treatment. "He's John Wayne," Torre once mused.

The Yankees would designate specific road trips on which families of players were allowed to travel with the team; otherwise, it was understood that wives and children should travel separately. But Torre suspended that rule in the summer of 2000 for Jean Stottlemyre; she was allowed to travel with her husband, to help him. When Sterling asked Mel Stottlemyre about his condition, Stottlemyre was absolutely direct, acknowledging the conventional wisdom that people with his illness did not live long, mentioning a specific time frame. The only time Sterling ever saw Stottlemyre break down after his diagnosis, he recalled, was at a charity event, while Stottlemyre watched a video presentation of young leukemia patients. Jason Stottlemyre, Mel and Jean's third son, had died in 1981 of leukemia when he was 11 years old.

TORRE HAD known Stottlemyre and Don Zimmer only as acquaintances when Steinbrenner hired him to manage the Yankees. In other circumstances, Torre might have been reluctant to work with two coaches unfamiliar to him, particularly a pitching coach and bench coach, two crucial positions on any staff. But Steinbrenner wanted Stottlemyre, and Torre knew that Zimmer had worked for Steinbrenner before, so he embraced both. The three men became friends quickly, sat next to one another during games, and chatted in low voices in the Yankee Stadium dugout. They spent time together away from the park, as well, going to the race track, sharing lunch and dinner.

Torre quickly trusted Stottlemyre—no small matter in the relationship between a manager and a pitching coach—and he came to rely on Zimmer, who had joined his staff with nearly a half-century in professional baseball and a reputation as an unconventional thinker willing to take chances. Bob Watson would see the Yankees put on a risky play—a squeeze bunt, a hit-and-run in a situation when most teams would never have the base-runners moving with the pitch—and assume that Zimmer had whispered a suggestion in Torre's ear.

Zimmer had played with Jackie Robinson and was a member of the 1962 Mets. He played in Cuba before Castro's revolution and with the Washington Senators after John F. Kennedy's election. When Carlton Fisk hit his home run to end Game 6 of the 1975 World Series—history's fall classic—Zimmer, then Boston's third-base coach, followed Fisk to home plate. He retired briefly before the 1996 season and received a single Social Security check of about $1,000, the only wage he got in his life outside baseball. He was a loyal person—he and his wife, Soot, maintained a Christmas card list of about 300—and sensitive, reacting sharply when he felt slighted. Before joining the Yankees, he had been the bench coach for Colorado manager Don Baylor, and when he came to believe that Baylor was no longer listening to him, he informed general manager Bob Gebhard that he intended to quit in the middle of a game. True to his word, he left the Rockies' bench in the fifth inning.

Zimmer was close with many of the Yankees, Paul O'Neill, Joe Girardi, and Derek Jeter in particular, sharing a daily game of bridge with a regular group that included Brosius, O'Neill, Girardi, and Kenny Rogers. But some members of the organization—players as well as staff—were leery of Zimmer, finding him hard to please, and were sure his untempered judgments of them affected Torre's thinking. "The source of trouble," one member of the organization said, when Zimmer's name came up in conversation. He was outspoken in staff meetings, whether making a strong case on behalf of catcher Joe Girardi or expressing doubts about Alfonso Soriano's ability to play the infield. (In the first year after Girardi left the Yankees, the team went into the 2000 season with marginal journeyman Chris Turner as a backup—partly, some executives figured, to make sure Posada understood he was absolutely the No. 1 catcher, and partly to ensure that Torre and Zimmer could not rely heavily on an alternative to Posada, as they had done with Girardi.) When Zimmer had disagreements with Steinbrenner, he sometimes rebutted him bluntly and publicly, through reporters. Having turned 70 years old in 2001, he no longer had to work, and he would not be pushed around.

But Zimmer was absolutely devoted to Torre; the two called each other almost daily when they were on vacation before spring training in 1999, and Zimmer was numb when Torre told him of his cancer. Torre summoned some players—Cone and Clemens and O'Neill and Girardi—into his office at the Yankees' spring training complex and asked them to pass the word to the others before the Yankees' two split-squad exhibition games that day. Girardi, feeling shaken, rode the bus from Tampa to Fort Myers thinking about what he would say to the players: "Our team really counted on Joe, because Joe always made sure that everything was OK. He had that quiet calmness to him, and all of a sudden, with him being sick, it scared a lot of us."

Zimmer had just had knee surgery, but Steinbrenner went to his hotel room and banged on the door. "Get your ass out of bed," Steinbrenner said. "You've got to run this team now." Hobbling on his bad knee and in terrible pain, Zimmer managed the Yankees until May 18. After a 16-7 start, the team began to struggle, and Zimmer clearly missed his friend, reaching the verge of tears several times as he spoke about Torre. His instinct was that it was wrong to use the manager's office during Torre's absence or sit in the front seat reserved for the manager on the team planes and buses. He became increasingly tense without Torre around, once surprising his players by calling a meeting after a terrible loss in Texas to tell them he was retiring the next day; he had assumed, wrongly, that Torre was coming back. Torre once visited the team while still recovering, and Zimmer sat next to him and smiled broadly, ecstatic to have his friend close by.

His knee would swell excruciatingly during plane flights, and he told reporters he was going home to Florida as soon as Torre came back. But once Torre returned, the talk of retirement evaporated, and he stayed on as Torre's bench coach.

On the day Torre was diagnosed with prostate cancer, Westchester County's *Journal News* columnist Ian O'Connor phoned Maury Brosius, who was battling colon cancer. O'Connor had developed a rapport with the father of the Yankees' third baseman and wanted to ask what Torre might expect. The last time O'Connor and Maury Brosius had spoken, Brosius's cancer was in remission, and he was optimistic about his chances. "How long," O'Connor asked, "does your doctor say you have to go through treatment before you beat this thing?"

"I'm not going to beat this thing," Maury Brosius said. His cancer had spread, and doctors had recently told him they didn't know how much longer he would live. Maury asked O'Connor not to write that because he had not yet told his son or the rest of his family about his latest prognosis. "Before I'm gone, write something nice about me," the ailing man asked O'Connor.

The next time the reporter saw Scott Brosius, standing at the player's locker with a small group of reporters, he felt awkward, wondering how much he knew. But that summer of 1999, Brosius left the team several times to be with his father in his Oregon home. There was no protocol in baseball for someone with a sick family member, and while the baseball culture was softening—leaving the team to witness the birth of a child had become an accepted practice—the sport's old guard tended to look dimly on players who missed games. An accountant who left work for personal reasons could make up for lost time when he came back, but a ballplayer had no way to compensate for games missed. Each time he asked, however, Torre quickly told Brosius, who had already lost his mother to cancer, that he should take the days he needed. It made no sense to keep him with the team if his mind was in Oregon, Torre thought, and if the Yankees denied him permission to leave and prevented him from seeking emotional peace, he would resent the team and the game. "I don't think I could have been treated any better or with any more understanding when I was going through that with my dad," Brosius would say years later. "Joe would see you as a player, but he'd look through that and see you as a person as well."

When the third baseman was with the team, father and son talked every night by phone. Maury Brosius's condition worsened. When Scott happened to wear his uniform with his socks drawn high one day, Maury reminded Scott that this was how he had taught his son to wear the uniform; Brosius wore his socks high thereafter. Late in August of 1999, O'Connor wrote about Maury Brosius and his son. "Scott was forever there, Maury said," O'Connor wrote. "Even with cancer snaking its way across the Yankees' clubhouse, visiting Torre and Darryl Strawberry, Scott stood strong against the fates, offering reassurance from thousands of miles away. 'He has so much courage,'" Maury said.

Maury was in extraordinary pain, and Scott asked Torre for permission to go home again. For five days father and son talked, having the conversations they wanted to have, Scott Brosius recalled, and said goodbye. When he returned to the Yankees, with Maury waning, the son felt blessed to have seen his father once more. "God has done some pretty great things for us," Scott Brosius said. "I'm pretty sure that going home when I did was the right time to go, and today was the right time to come back." Maury Brosius passed away a week later, and when Brosius asked for time to tend to his family, Torre agreed.

AMBROSIO SOJO died unexpectedly just before the start of the 1999 World Series, and Luis Sojo flew to Venezuela for the funeral, missing Games 1 and 2. Then, just a few hours after the completion of Game 3, Paul O'Neill's phone rang at 2:30 a.m.: his father had died, after months of declining health. O'Neill decided to play in Game 4, determining he would not tell anyone with the Yankees about his father until afterward. But shortly thereafter, Torre left a message on O'Neill's machine, offering to help in any way he could; the Yankees' organization had been monitoring Chick O'Neill's condition. Torre had been through so much adversity in his life, O'Neill would write in a book published after he retired, "that I later came to think that, without saying it in so many words, he was here to serve as a guide to show me how to handle this most challenging time in my life."

When the last out of Game 4 was made, Torre embraced O'Neill in the infield and spoke of his father, and O'Neill broke down and ran off the field, overcome. He found an empty room and sat and thought of Chick O'Neill. His instinct, after a World Series game, was to phone his father, and, for the first time, it hit O'Neill that he would never be able to call him again. At that moment, Clemens opened the door. Clemens's own father had passed away from a heart attack when he was a boy, and when teammates brought their fathers around the clubhouse, Clemens would wish his own father had gotten a chance to see him pitch. Clemens reached out to hug O'Neill, offering condolences. Brosius entered, and then Sojo, teammates who needed one another.

O'NEILL, BROSIUS, and Sojo were in the dugout as the eighth inning began in Game 7 of the 2001 World Series, their last innings as teammates. Torre leaned against the front railing, flanked by Stottlemyre on his left and Zimmer to his right.

Alfonso Soriano led off for the Yankees. He had three strikeouts and no hits in his seven at-bats against Curt Schilling, and now, in his eighth at-bat, he quickly fell behind in the count no balls and two strikes, taking a 93 mph fastball for strike 1 and flailing at a splitter for strike 2. Don't get beat in the strike zone, Schilling told himself.

Most of the season, pitchers had played on Soriano's habit of chasing pitches out of the strike zone, and he figured Schilling would do the same, probably down low. Schilling threw a splitter outside, a couple of inches off the ground, and Soriano chased it, barely fouling it off. Schilling tried climbing the ladder, changing the plane of his pitches, and fired a chest-high fastball, 94 mph; Soriano swung, another foul.

Torre, Zimmer, and Stottlemyre talked at the dugout railing about when they should call on Rivera if the score remained tied, a difficult decision. Maybe Soriano will make the decision for us here, Torre said, suggesting that the second baseman would hit a home run.

Schilling had thrown 94 pitches, but he felt good, adrenaline flooding his body. Damian Miller squatted and signaled for a fastball. Schilling shook off that sign. Miller called for a splitter, and Schilling nodded and threw, another splitter diving shin-high, a good two-strike pitch so low that Miller jerked his glove toward the ground, the laces scraping the dirt. But Soriano swung, an uppercut, lifting his bat high in a follow-through; he knew he had just hit the home run that would beat the Diamondbacks. Zimmer began screaming, telling the ball to get out, and

Torre instinctively hit Stottlemyre in the bicep—*Look at that, will you look at that, can you believe that.*

Schilling's head jerked upward, following the flight of Soriano's drive, which carried 15 rows into the stands in left-center field, a monstrous home run. Zimmer raised both index fingers high over his head. Torre, the stoic manager, pumped his fist, his lips pursed tight; it was apparent that he was barely containing tears. Schilling glanced repeatedly at where the ball landed. He could not believe Soriano had hit that pitch—a pitch so low—that far. The Yankees had the lead, and a halogen thought filled Schilling's head: Rivera's coming into the game.

Most of the Yankees were tumbling out of the dugout to congratulate Soriano, but Stottlemyre quickly turned to Torre, patting him twice on the back, to confirm what he already knew, that Rivera would pitch the last two innings. Soriano crossed home plate, right hand raised, high-fived Brosius and Justice, and then was swallowed by teammates in front of the dugout. "Attaboy, Sori," O'Neill shouted. Soriano paced in the dugout, slapping teammates, overcome by the moment. He turned and looked out toward the mound, toward Schilling, and shouted, "Don't throw that shit in here!"

Schilling struck out Brosius and allowed a pinch-hit single to Justice. Then Brenly came to the mound and said it was time to bring in a fresh arm. "Hell of an effort, Big Man," the manager said, slapping Schilling on the shoulder. "That ain't going to beat us, Big Man."

Luis Gonzalez, Steve Finley, and Danny Bautista, the Arizona outfielders, gathered in center field. "Listen, we're going to win this game," Finley said. "We've got to find a way. We're going to find a way."

In the dugout, Schilling was devastated. He pulled on a jacket and slumped against the bench. On any other day, Schilling would have retreated to the clubhouse for his usual postgame treatment. But now his season was over, and there was nothing more he could do. He stayed in the dugout, bug-eyed and still stunned by Soriano's home run, and watched relievers Miguel Batista and Randy Johnson close out the Yankees in the eighth. Schilling had the same thought over and over: I cost us the World Series.

Chapter 19

The Yankees' closer preferred to watch the first few innings of each game on a television in the clubhouse, so he could see how the home plate umpire was calling the inside and outside corners of the strike zone. Around the fifth inning, Mariano Rivera would jog to the bullpen, striding easily. (The pitchers did wind sprints together in spring training, Roger Clemens and Andy Pettitte pounding steadily like oxen, David Cone stepping stiffly, never quite lifting his knees. By comparison, Rivera moved like a race horse, bouncing on the balls of his feet, balanced, with a high center of gravity. The others sometimes cussed at him good-naturedly because of how easy he made it look and how slow he made the rest of them appear.)

In the seventh inning, Rivera would stretch his legs and shoulders, pulling at his elbows, bending back his wrists. When it seemed likely he would pitch, he would cup a three-pound iron ball in his right hand and whirl his arm from side to side, back and forth, then in circles. His arm properly prepared, Rivera would reach for his glove to warm up.

He always threw to the same catchers in the bullpen—catching instructor Gary Tuck for several years, and then Mike Borzello—and almost always warmed up the same way, throwing high fastballs with his first two tosses, his fingers surrounding the seams of the ball, his motion comfortable and loose, the catcher standing. The catcher would then squat, and Rivera would throw five or six more fastballs down the middle before he began to focus on the corners, aiming cut fastballs as if he were trying to throw inside to a left-handed hitter. After a couple of those, Rivera would aim at the other corner.

Other relievers noticed that Rivera almost never glanced at the field to follow the action. Tony Cloninger, the bullpen coach, would keep him apprised, speaking evenly like a jockey talking into the ear of his mount. This way, Rivera could focus on his mechanics and the catcher's glove, and think about the hitters he would probably face. Rivera followed the series of fastballs with a couple of sliders, if time permitted, and finished his warm-up with fastballs down the middle. He never seemed hurried, and his stature as a reliever and competitor had grown to the point that umpires never nudged him along, even when he stalled by taking extra warm-up pitches after he'd been called into the game, a habit that bothered opposing managers. "This looks like this guy makes his own rules," Lou Piniella once complained.

Barely 60 seconds after Alfonso Soriano's homer off Schilling disappeared into the crowd, Rivera began throwing in the visitors' bullpen, preparing to pitch the last two innings and finish off the Diamondbacks. Through four years of playoffs and World Series, Joe Torre had managed his starters and middle relievers and hitters to get the Yankees into exactly this situation: six outs or fewer remaining, Rivera on the mound. Just put the game in his hands, and the Yankees would win.

Rivera had pitched in 38 postseason games since allowing Sandy Alomar's game-tying home run in the 1997 playoffs, and the Yankees had won 36; other pitchers lost the other two games. He had inherited one-run leads in seven games, two-run leads in 11 games, three-run leads in five games, and converted each of these save chances. In four other games, he had been the winning pitcher. More than any other player, some opponents believed, he had been directly responsible for the Yankees' championships. Derek Jeter was a terrific player, yes, and Bernie Williams was an elite center fielder, and the Yankees had more than their share of All-Stars. But other contending teams had deep lineups, too, and some had good starting pitchers, like the Yankees. Only the Yankees had Rivera, the dignified closer with the savage cut fastball that turned bats into scrap wood. "It's obvious they've won the world championships they have because of him," Jim Thome, the Cleveland first baseman, once said.

Over the course of Roger Clemens's career, opposing hitters would mention to him what a relief it was to see him leave a game in the late innings. But once Clemens went to the Yankees, it was a different story. "They would rather see me stay in the game being tired," he said, "than to see Mo come in.

"If you put a microphone in our dugout when he came into games during that stretch—I mean, you talk about carefree . . . [Torre] would hand him the ball, and it was over. I mean—*over*. And you know what, *they* knew it was over. They can go up to the plate and say to themselves, 'I'm not going to give this at-bat away, and I'm going to battle as hard as I can.' But then, after one pitch, it was *over*. He was that nasty, with one pitch."

The one pitch was Rivera's cut fastball, a model of high velocity and freakish movement, veering sharply into the hands of left-handed batters and away from right-handed batters at about 95 miles per hour. Some pitchers could throw as hard or harder than Rivera, but their fastballs did not possess the radical movement that his cutter had.

In this era of offense, Mike Mussina thought, Rivera was the only pitcher who dominated hitters day after day, season after season, with one weapon. Even the best pitchers worked like fugitives, always on the move: if they didn't constantly adjust the location and speed of their pitches and the sequence of their pitch selection, the hitters would eventually catch up to them. But with Rivera, the best batters in the world knew exactly what he was going to throw and where he would throw it, and it didn't matter.

Pedro Martinez and Greg Maddux threw the best changeups in this generation of pitchers, Randy Johnson the best slider; Robb Nen probably had the best fastball. But all those pitchers complemented those weapons with other weapons. Rivera overwhelmed hitters throwing only the cutter. "You know he's going to throw you a fastball," Seattle outfielder Stan Javier said, "and you still can't hit it. He's the only pitcher in baseball you can say that about." Jorge Posada sometimes didn't even bother giving a sign, merely beckoning with a wave of his glove and bare hand: *Bring it on.*

Rivera never smiled on the mound, never looked concerned, never grimaced, never glared. It was as if the hitters were irrelevant, invisible; it was as if he was just playing catch with Posada. You might score against Rivera, and every month or so during the regular season, you might beat him. But you would never get to him and have the satisfaction of seeing him wince. Goose Gossage, the retired All-Star reliever, loved watching Rivera, loved the way he went about his work, and he tried to imagine what opponents must have thought when Rivera came into a game. "They're sitting in the dugout thinking, 'We've got no fucking chance,'" Gossage said one spring, his voice rising, his eyes widening above his thick mustache. "It's fucking *over*. This guy walks in and they are *fucking done.*"

Rivera did not have a particularly strong arm as a youngster, but he always had great accuracy. As a boy, he had spent many hours throwing on the beaches of Panama, hurling rocks at cardboard or a tightly wound ball of string at tiny inner tubes. When Mariano was a teenager, he began working on his father's fishing boat and could not believe how difficult it was; this was not a life he wanted. He signed with the Yankees when he was 20 years old, a conventional starting pitcher who had excellent control and, as Gene Michael recalled, a serviceable fastball. Rivera allowed only 17 hits and three walks in 52 innings for Class A Tampa in 1990, but would require major elbow surgery two years later. He made his major league debut in 1995, but initially struggled and was sent down to Class AAA Columbus. It was during his time with the Clippers that he experienced a sudden and inexplicable increase in his velocity; years later, Michael and Rivera guessed that it was probably because his body had filled out or because he had fully recovered from his operation. The Yankees promoted him to start against the Chicago White Sox on July 4 of that year. The Chicago scouting report had described him as a pitcher with an average fastball "and a great changeup," remembered Robin Ventura, the White Sox third baseman. But against the White Sox,

Rivera threw fastballs that exploded through the top of the strike zone or broke into the hands of left-handed hitters—a natural cutter. He struck out 11. "Not a very good scouting report," Ventura drolly recalled.

Rivera had strong legs but a relatively thin and wiry torso—a body, Clemens thought, that helped him deceive hitters because he never looked the part of a power pitcher (and hitters faced closers only a few times each season, not enough chances to get comfortable against Rivera). He had a smooth and easy motion, throwing the ball without drawing his arm far from his body; he looked more like an infielder flipping the ball to first base than a power pitcher. But he would release his fastball, so relaxed and easy, reaching out, finishing with his arm extended. "It's like his arm has an extra extension that pops out of his shoulder," Cone said. "And there is that great wrist action; his wrist is like a blur at the end of the pitch." And suddenly, his fastball would be on top of hitters, overwhelming them.

Rivera relieved in nine of his 19 appearances for the Yankees in 1995, and the next season Torre would use him in middle relief, as a setup man for veteran closer John Wetteland. Rivera was dominant, striking out 130 in 107⅔ innings, and he became known for his ability to throw high fastballs—a four-seamer, the players called it, because the pitcher held the ball across the seams—through the upper half of the strike zone. Rivera would get ahead in the ball-strike count, put the hitter on the defensive, and elevate his subsequent pitches, going a little higher each time. But in 1997, Rivera began refining his cut fastball while playing catch with Ramiro Mendoza.

A cutter is something of a hybrid, bred from a fastball and a slider. When pitchers throw fastballs correctly, they propel the pitch with the full force of their fingers, wrists and arms directly behind the ball. When they throw sliders, they essentially use the force of their fingers and wrists on one side of the ball to spin it, in the same way a billiard ball spins when hit indirectly by a cue stick. A well-thrown slider moves laterally or downward with diminished velocity. To throw a cut fastball, pitchers use their fingers to drive down on the ball as it rolls out of their fingers, creating some additional backspin and lateral movement with a loss in velocity. But Rivera's cutter had full velocity.

Most pitchers release fastballs with their fingers essentially aimed straight at the catcher, draped over the top of the ball, but Rivera threw his fastball with his fingers cocked inward—aimed at 11:00 on the face of the clock, rather than at 12 o'clock. That meant that while the ball was flying toward the hitter, it was actually rotating slightly to the side, something that Mussina noticed while playing catch with Rivera. Mussina thought the axis of Rivera's cutter was tilted off-center, which caused the unusual movement. It was like a car skidding across ice, the front veering to the side, the whole thing fishtailing. And Rivera, who had spent all those hours as a child throwing rocks on the beach, could control it superbly.

Because of the cutter, Rivera went from being a solid closer in 1997 to being all but unhittable in the summer of 1998. Rivera usually aimed the pitch at the inner half of the plate against lefties, and once the hitter decided to swing—and this choice had to be made when the ball had covered less than a third of the distance to home plate—he thought he was swinging at a pitch in the strike zone. But the cutter would veer very sharply and very late in its journey, just as it reached the dirt area in front of home plate, and the hitter had absolutely no chance to adjust, the way he might adjust against a slower slider or curveball. "When he throws it, you think it's straight," said Arizona shortstop Tony Womack, "and the next thing you know, it's on your thumbs."

The pitch destroyed bats, swerving into the handles of left-handed hitters or against the far end of the barrels of right-handed hitters. He often shattered two and three in an inning; Chuck Knoblauch once joked that Louisville Slugger should sign Rivera to a personal services deal because of the volume business he created for the bat company; in the summer of 2001, he broke 44 bats, including five in one game against Toronto. Boston outfielder Troy O'Leary, one of the few left-handed hitters who had some hits against Rivera, would not use his favorite bats—Model P72, all black—when he faced Rivera, sacrificing lesser wood instead. In the last inning of the 1999 World Series sweep over the Braves, Rivera broke the bat of Atlanta slugger Ryan Klesko, who fouled off the pitch and had to get another. Rivera broke that one, too, and another, as Klesko finally popped up to second base. The Braves were getting steamrolled in the World Series, and yet several of them could be seen in their dugout, smirking at Klesko's futility against the cutter. "What do you expect?" Klesko huffed the following spring. "The guy throws 97 mph cutters."

Some left-handed hitters tried moving toward the front of the batter's box, closer to the mound, to get at Rivera's cutter a little sooner. But adjustments didn't seem to help. "It just keeps coming at you," said Toronto catcher Darrin Fletcher, a left-handed hitter. "You think it's over the inner half of the plate, and it comes after you. We have this saying that a pitcher 'gets in your kitchen.' Rivera's cutter continually gets in your kitchen, and you cannot get it out."

In 1998, his first season fully relying on the cutter, Rivera struck out only 36 and allowed only 48 hits in 61⅓ innings; hitters were making contact against the cutter, but usually imperfect contact. In 1999, when Rivera refined his cutter, left-handed batters hit only .143 against him, with 18 singles, one double, and one home run in 140 at-bats. They had to swing because Rivera's control was stunning: he went more than a calendar year—from July 9, 1998, against the Blue Jays, to September 11, 1999, in Fenway Park—without walking the first batter he faced.

Hitters tended to dribble grounders and fist pop-ups against Rivera, and that forced the Yankees' fielders to alter their standard position. When most other pitchers were on the mound, Tino Martinez, the first baseman, would usually play deep when a strong left-handed hitter was at the plate. But when Rivera pitched, Martinez would take several steps forward, to prepare for a slow roller. All the infielders had to move in a little, and with left-handed batters at the plate, the Yankees' left fielders would come way in, almost as if a pitcher was hitting. Batters rarely hit the ball hard.

Rivera had been on the mound at the end of the World Series in 1998 and in 1999, always in the center of the Yankees' celebrations. He was there in the last inning of the 2000 World Series, as well, and needed one more out when Piazza came to bat as the possible tying run. It was easier for right-handed batters, like Piazza, to hit the cutter. You've got to get him to throw the ball in the lower half of the strike zone, Piazza believed, and take a quick swing. "Take a long swing and the cutter will chew you apart," Piazza said later. "His velocity will do the work for you. Just put good wood on the ball."

Piazza swung viciously, his front leg straightening and bracing his body, and as the ball rocketed toward center field, Rivera flinched. For an instant, Torre thought the ball would climb over the fence to tie the game, but Bernie Williams retreated in center field, stopped and made the catch, and for the third time in three years, the Yankees had won the World Series. Rivera was overrun in the middle of the infield by celebrating teammates.

Torre had used Rivera for multiple innings in middle relief throughout the 1996 season, and after he became the closer, Torre occasionally would call on him in the eighth, and Rivera never complained, never balked, as other closers would have. His job, he thought, was to do what the manager asked him to do. He came in to pitch in the eighth inning in 15 of his 28 postseason appearances from 1998 to 2000. It was during this time that the idea of being a closer who threw the ninth inning, and only the ninth inning, stopped being so fashionable.

Rivera had more responsibility during the 2001 season, with Nelson gone and Torre mostly relying on Mike Stanton and Ramiro Mendoza in middle relief, but the quality of his cutter was intact. Steve Rippley, the home plate umpire for Game 7, had worked most of his career in the National League, but after interleague play began and the league umpires were integrated, he had worked some Yankees games for the first time and was taken aback by the movement on Rivera's cutter; there was nothing else like it, he thought. And now, with the Yankees batting in the top of the eighth inning of Game 7, Rivera was warming up to get the last six outs.

Because Soriano had slammed his home run with nobody out in the eighth and Bob Brenly had subsequently made two pitching changes to get through that inning, Rivera had ample time to warm up and complete his routine. He stood and waited on the bullpen mound, arms folded, and after Knoblauch flied out to end the top of the eighth, Rivera stepped through the gate and onto the field, head down, and began his jog to the mound.

A couple of years after Rivera became the Yankees' closer, the scoreboard production staff at Yankee Stadium debated what music should accompany him as he entered to pitch in home games. Players usually selected their own music, but Rivera didn't care. Mike Luzzi, a scoreboard technician, suggested "Enter Sandman," a song by Metallica. Mike Bonner, the assistant director of scoreboard operations, asked Rivera if that was OK, and the pitcher shrugged. He didn't really like music that much, anyway; go ahead and play what you want, he said. Even three years later, Rivera still had no idea what his entrance song was called, nor had he bothered to listen to it. A reporter told him that the reason they picked "Enter Sandman" was because he put the opposing hitters into a frightful dreamland: "Sleep with one eye open, Gripping your pillow tight," the lyrics went. Rivera thought about this and nodded; he liked the notion. And whenever Rivera stepped onto the field at Yankee Stadium, head down and glove in hand, ominous guitar strains filled the air. Enter Sandman. Enter Rivera.

There was no accompanying music for Rivera in Bank One Ballpark, but the air was thick with gloom when he came out of the Yankees' bullpen, the unbeatable pitcher, the pitcher who never gives up runs. "If you gave every team in baseball the opportunity to go into the last two innings with a lead and Mo pitching for them," Jeter would say later, "then every team in baseball would take that. I don't care who the team is, who their closer is. They would take that scenario." Some Diamondbacks said months later that they still felt hopeful because Arizona had come back to win so often. Others, like Curt Schilling and Damian Miller, felt crushed watching Rivera come into the game. "We were like, 'Oh, shit,'" said Miller.

Torre had changed his outfield, Shane Spencer moving to right field and Chuck Knoblauch taking over in left, after Knoblauch had pinch-hit for Paul O'Neill in the top of the eighth against Johnson. O'Neill had been in the on-deck circle, ready to hit, when he was called back, and now O'Neill's playing career was over. He had gone back to the dugout and set down his helmet. He held on to the bat just a little while longer, taking a couple of short practice swings.

Luis Gonzalez led off the bottom of the eighth, and with the count 2 balls and 2 strikes, he swung at a pitch he thought would cross the inner half of the plate. But Rivera's cutter veered and bore inside, smashing Gonzalez's bat on the handle, ricocheting foul. Gonzalez headed back toward the dugout to trade in his shattered bat. Rivera fired another cutter, 95 mph, the pitch darting inside, and Gonzalez swung over the top of it, missing it badly. One out. Brian Cashman was counting down; the Yankees needed only five outs for a fourth consecutive championship.

Matt Williams, the next hitter, took a strike, then fouled off a fastball, swinging late. Rivera looked in for a sign from Posada, and with Williams's eyes focused on the pitcher, Posada raised his glove high. He tapped his glove, raised it again, chest high, his message to Rivera obvious: throw your fastball high. Rivera launched a four-seam fastball, chest high, and Williams, completely overmatched, swung under it for strike three.

Steve Finley lined a single to right, breaking his bat in the process, but Rivera threw a strike to Danny Bautista, then another. No balls and two strikes. Posada raised his glove again, shifted his body to set a target inside, and Rivera threw a high fastball. Bautista swung late, missing, another three-pitch strikeout. Rivera had struck out the side, blowing away the Diamondbacks. He ambled off the mound, head down.

In the Yankees' clubhouse, Major League officials ended the standoff with Steinbrenner and ordered the network workers to set up the trophy presentation stage. Fox had to get ready for the postgame show. The Yankees had taken the lead, and with Rivera needing only three more outs, they were minutes away from another celebration.

Steinbrenner loudly protested the intrusion; others in the room watched him snap at Rick Cerrone, his media relations director, and Rob Cucuzza, the team's equipment manager. There's nothing to be done, they explained to Steinbrenner; the TV people have a job to do.

Steinbrenner was furious, superstitious. "I'm telling you," he said, "this is bad. They shouldn't be in here."

CHAPTER 20

CHUCK KNOBLAUCH and Scott Brosius ran off the field together after the eighth inning of Game 7, each with one inning remaining in his career with the Yankees. The two players had joined the Yankees at the same time, for the 1998 season, and prior to Game 5 of the 2001 World Series, they had reminisced in the clubhouse about their years with the team—four incredible seasons, they agreed. The record-setting year of 1998, two perfect games, three championships in the first three years, this World Series. A few hours after that conversation, both were instrumental in the Yankees' comeback victory against Arizona.

Brosius would leave on his own terms. He was now 35 and had come to hate the months away from his children in Oregon; within a couple of weeks he would make the choice to retire and go home for good. There had been modest expectations in New York for Brosius, a strong defensive third baseman who hit .203 for Oakland in 1997, and yet in his first year with the Yankees, he had batted .300 with 98 RBIs and been named the MVP of the World Series against San Diego; he would make the All-Star team and win a Gold Glove. Nothing else in baseball, he figured, could match his years with the Yankees.

Knoblauch was two years younger than Brosius and not ready to retire, but soon he would not have a choice because of the throwing neurosis devouring his career. His unusual problem dominated his days with the Yankees and obscured what he had accomplished earlier in his career. In his first seven seasons, with the Minnesota Twins, Knoblauch had 1,197 hits and 713 runs scored, and he was a prototypical leadoff hitter and just 29 years old when the Yankees swapped prospects and $3 million for him. His career path, to that point, was of a borderline Hall of Fame candidate. Everything in his background, makeup, and physical conditioning suggested Knoblauch was the type who might play 20 seasons.

He was the son of a Texas baseball coach. When Chuck was a boy, Ray Knoblauch had built a mound for his son, a strip of rubber across the top, and home plate set at regulation distance for Little League. A hardened taskmaster, Ray taught his son about hitting and running and playing the infield, schooled him in the intricacies of the game that other coaches did not even notice. Ray Knoblauch coached Chuck at Bellaire High School in Houston, and even after his son turned professional, he continued to be a presence in Chuck's baseball life, traveling to see him play.

Chuck Knoblauch's agents negotiated his first contract with the Twins in 1989 and asked that he be invited to spring training the following year. Andy MacPhail, the general manager, thought about this and offered an incentive: if Knoblauch could hit .275 in Class A in his first professional season, he could go to spring training with the major league team. No, Knoblauch said, make that .300—creating his own higher standard—and he batted .308 for Kenosha and Visalia and went to spring training.

Knoblauch had played shortstop at Texas A&M, but the Twins already had a shortstop in Greg Gagne and needed a second baseman. They asked Knoblauch to make the switch during an instructional league camp, and Tom Kelly, the Twins' manager, watched him in the first days of the transition and was impressed by his athleticism and the questions he asked about playing second base. Kelly could see that Knoblauch knew and loved the game, and Kelly could see that he was as tough as the scouts had reported. He teemed with confidence; he was absolutely sure of his ability. He played in Double-A in 1990 but jumped to the majors the next season, batting .281 with 25 stolen bases. The Twins won the American League pennant, and in the World Series, Knoblauch—23 years old—was widely heralded for faking a play and confusing Atlanta base-runner Lonnie Smith, who slowed and failed to score the run that might have won the World Series for the Braves.

Knoblauch had a gift for disrupting opponents, wearing down pitchers with prolonged at-bats. He was five feet nine and 175 pounds, and because of his size and his serious demeanor, opposing players viewed him with grudging admiration as an indomitable pest. A starting pitcher might breeze into the fifth inning, his pitch count relatively low, and then Knoblauch would come to bat and foul off three or four pitches with a full count, shaking the pitcher's rhythm and tiring his arm. He would take huge leads, daring the pitcher to pick him off, diving back into first base and then edging off even farther, without so much as bothering to brush the dirt off his uniform. Knoblauch was called a little fucker many times, and mostly it was meant as a compliment.

Ballplayers use all sort of rituals and methods to give themselves a psychological advantage. Some Yankees, like David Wells, used music, turning the stereo volume knob clockwise and allowing the sound and the words to drive their adrenaline to a peak. Friends of Baltimore third baseman Cal Ripken thought his consecutive-game streak gave him an extraordinary mental edge, and as suggestions were floated in 1997 and 1998 that Ripken needed to rest a day or two every week, those same friends disagreed strongly. They believed Ripken drew energy from his own streak, pushed and drove himself to live up to the immense standard he had established. If he rests, one friend said, then he's not Superman anymore, and he'll wilt.

The mental trigger in Knoblauch seemed to be a perceived affront. He defiantly entrenched himself at the front of the batter's box, hovering over the plate, and when pitchers threw inside, Knoblauch wouldn't budge. He might spin his torso, he might bend back, he might take a ball in the ribs, but his feet would remain rooted: You will not move me. Between pitches he stepped out of the batter's box, adjusted his batting gloves, tapped his spikes with his bat, reset his stance, touched the barrel of his bat with his right hand, tapped the top of his helmet with his left hand. The pitcher would wait on the mound for him to complete his ritual, unable to establish his own tempo; Knoblauch refused to be hurried. "I really don't know exactly what I do, because I'm really thinking about the pitch," Knoblauch once explained. "Maybe the pitch or the count, or maybe it's to slow that pitcher down and get him out of his rhythm. It's all about getting comfortable. It's kind of a fidgeting routine while your mind is at work."

Knoblauch signed a five-year, $30 million contract with Minnesota before the 1997 season, but in the first year of the contract, he asked for a trade. He was tired of losing, and by the end of that season, his teammates were tired of him, frustrated by his contentiousness, his helmet throwing. "I want to win, and I'm sure when we weren't, I wasn't very much fun to be around," Knoblauch said. Twins general manager Terry Ryan talked to the Yankees, the Indians, and other teams about Knoblauch that winter, without completing a trade. But there was a push within the Minnesota organization: get him out of here before spring training begins because he's going to be a distraction. The deal was finished about a week before camp opened.

Knoblauch shaved his beard in adherence to the Yankees' policy on facial hair and arrived at training camp deferential and polite. Right away, it was apparent how he would jump-start the offense; in a lineup filled with dangerous hitters, Knoblauch would lead off, take pitches, work the count, tire the pitcher a bit, and perhaps reach base. He averaged four or more pitches per plate appearance, giving other batters an extended opportunity to see the opposing starter. He worked with Jeter on turning double plays and sharing responsibility around the second-base bag, a seemingly easy transition. His throwing arm was considered one of the best among players at his position.

Late in that first spring training, Knoblauch's throwing motion shortened on plays when he had extra time: rather than extending his right arm and whipping the ball, he was flipping it to first base as if he were throwing a dart, his elbow bent. It happened occasionally, maybe a half-dozen throws in all, and affected his accuracy only once or twice. Once he threw the ball into the dirt, and years afterward Chad Curtis recalled clearly how Knoblauch returned to the dugout making fun of his own terrible throw, mimicking his delivery. He and the other players had laughed easily, and why not: Knoblauch had won the Gold Glove the year before, and teammates figured that the funky throws were caused by some sort of mechanical flaw that he would correct.

In the Yankees' third game of the regular season, Knoblauch launched a routine 30-foot throw to first, high over the head of first baseman Tino Martinez. "I could've done some different things," Knoblauch said after that game, referring to his throwing mechanics. "That's why they're called errors. They're bad plays. I got the first one out of the way." There would be many more to come.

In that same game, Knoblauch had been picked off twice by Jimmy Haynes, a gangly right-hander with a slow delivery to home plate. He would have only six stolen-base attempts the rest of the month, establishing a pattern that lasted throughout his four seasons in New York. Knoblauch, the brazen and arrogant base-runner for the Twins, seemed reluctant to take risks on the bases for the Yankees.

Some great base-runners steal bases instinctively; others are adept at calculating the most advantageous moment to run. Knoblauch was both quick and smart, and he averaged almost 40 steals a year in his first seven seasons in the majors. In his last season with the Twins, he attempted 72 steals, 62 of them successful for a remarkable 86 percent. But he attempted only 43 in his first season with the Yankees and 37 in his second season. He reduced his leads drastically, and as he crept away from first, he'd lock his hands on his knees, making it all but impossible for him to get a good break from first base.

Torre wanted him to be aggressive on the bases, but sometimes Knoblauch would get the sign to run and would not, explaining afterward in the dugout that he hadn't been able to get a good jump. His Yankee teammates who had watched him wreck the concentration of pitchers when he was in Minnesota were perplexed: why won't he run? In a game against the Mets, Knoblauch rounded first base and brushed against first baseman Todd Zeile. Thrown out at second, he sprinted toward the Yankees' dugout without arguing about what Zeile had done, without noticing that first-base coach Lee Mazzilli had badgered the first-base umpire into citing Zeile for interference.

He wanted to get off the field before anybody noticed his mistake, a teammate guessed. It seemed as if Knoblauch, with the Yankees, was afraid of making mistakes, his dread betrayed by his stiff throws and timid base-running.

His teammates weren't sure how to react, because Knoblauch's intensity and shifting moods created an emotional moat—a canyon, really—around him. On days when he seemed at ease, he could chat for hours, sharing stories in his soft voice. "At heart, you could see that he was a good guy, deep down," said one teammate. But the next day he was apt to walk by the same teammate without even making eye contact.

Tim Raines joked with many of his teammates good-naturedly about awkward plays or futile swings or bad haircuts—anything to get a laugh and lighten the mood. He was the only Yankee known to have teased Paul O'Neill during one of the right fielder's rants on the bench. But Raines had a strong sense of when he might be in jeopardy of crossing a line, and because of this, he never joked with Knoblauch about his throwing. Knoblauch was so serious, Raines explained, that you weren't sure from day to day whether he could laugh about his throwing problem. So Knoblauch would return to the dugout after making a horrendous throw and there was rarely any acknowledgment; it was as if he had a huge pimple on his forehead and everybody saw it, but nobody would say anything.

You just felt bad for him, O'Neill said. First baseman Tino Martinez recalled years later, "It was hard to watch, because he was such a great defensive player and a great hitter, and to see him go through that every day, that really bothered me." Teammates realized how proud Knoblauch was and understood that encouragement might embarrass him deeply. Mostly, they left him alone.

In past years, he had been able to talk to his father, his baseball mentor, but while Knoblauch was with the Yankees, that became impossible. In 1996, Ray Knoblauch began having trouble communicating certain words and phrases, and his son arranged an appointment for him at the

Mayo Clinic in Minnesota. Doctors showed Chuck the pictures taken from the brain scan and explained what the dark spots probably meant. When they talked with Ray, though, they would not use the word *Alzheimer's.*

Ray Knoblauch was faring badly when he visited Chuck in his first spring training with the Yankees, but he could still recognize his son and, Chuck thought, could still watch a baseball game and grasp what was happening on the field. The two met again in August, in Arlington, Texas. "It was the first time I saw my dad as an old man," Chuck Knoblauch said that year. "In the 30 years I'd been alive, my dad always looked exactly the same. In Arlington, he was walking around really gingerly, like he might fall down, really tired, laying around."

Knoblauch made 10 errors before the All-Star break that first year, including six while throwing the ball, and was batting .263; the year before, he hit .291 for the Twins, and he had a career average of .304. A couple of days after the break, Knoblauch ducked his head into Torre's office and asked to meet with him the next afternoon.

Torre, sensing he needed to talk, replied, "How about now?" Torre had not thrust himself on Knoblauch through his early-season struggles, waiting instead for Knoblauch to come to him, and now that he had, the two spoke for a half-hour. Torre related the pressure he felt after being traded to St. Louis before the 1969 season, and he reminded Knoblauch of all the good things he was doing for the team, his high on-base percentage and extended at-bats. And Torre mentioned to Knoblauch that despite his throwing problems, the Yankees were thriving; he was the second baseman and leadoff hitter for a team on pace to set a single-season record for victories.

"It takes a little time when you get to a new ballclub," Torre said afterward. "You put a lot of pressure on yourself. It's stupid to do, but you don't know that when you're in that body and you're trying to impress somebody." Torre encouraged him to just go have fun. Knoblauch sometimes threw tentatively, but he would make only three errors the rest of the season, and in the World Series, he slammed a game-tying three-run homer in Game 1.

Knoblauch went through a divorce after the 1998 season, and his throwing problem erupted again the following spring, while Torre was away from the team. By the time Torre rejoined the Yankees in Boston on May 18, Knoblauch had already committed six of the 26 errors he would make in 1999. To some teammates, he seemed more isolated than ever.

The throwing jitters of the former Gold Glove winner became notorious. Murmurs of anticipation from the crowd began rising every time the ball was hit to Knoblauch, whether at Yankee Stadium or on the road, and when he successfully completed the easiest throws—throws most Little Leaguers could make—fans roared facetiously. Knoblauch and the team began receiving dozens of suggestions for solving his problem, from coaches, from teenage fans, from psychologists. Derek Jeter thought it was possible that if Knoblauch had started having the throwing jitters in some other place, the problem might have been contained. "You don't expect it to happen to superstar-type players," Tim Raines said. "If he was just a regular player, nobody would've said anything about it. If he wasn't on the Yankees, an All-Star, a Gold Glove winner, no one would've said anything."

Because of his wealth and his contentiousness, and the fact that he played a sport for a living, Knoblauch was an unsympathetic figure; he had signed on the dotted line of baseball's Faustian pact, receiving enormous sums of money in return for accepting the verbal abuse from hostile fans and submitting to daily questions from prying reporters. Few people, if any, could relate to what he was experiencing. Every day, tens of thousands of people watched Knoblauch go about his daily work, expecting him to fail in the simplest task, cheering or booing when he proved them right.

During David Cone's perfect game against Montreal in July, the Expos' players, desperate for a base-runner, joked on their bench that somebody should hit the ball to Knoblauch. But Knoblauch had backhanded a grounder in the eighth inning and thrown to first for the out. He had always played well in important games, reacting to the moment; this would be the last of his strengths consumed by his neurosis.

By the summer of 1999, there was no pretending; Knoblauch acknowledged the problem and would spend hours trying to correct it, working with Willie Randolph, the team's infield coach. Besides trainer Gene Monahan and hitting coach Chris Chambliss, Randolph was this team's only lasting tie to the championship seasons of the 1970s, when he was the Yankees' second baseman. He was serious and diligent, still in excellent physical condition a decade after retiring as a player, exuding an air of professionalism. Randolph had repeatedly interviewed for managerial jobs unsuccessfully; executives with two interested teams felt that he had such a strong belief in the Yankee approach of right and wrong that he would never be happy with another organization. Budgetary constraints were a reality elsewhere, the executives noted, and they worried that Randolph—accustomed to competing for championships annually—did not have the patience to watch young or mediocre players slog through lost seasons. The Cincinnati Reds intended to offer Randolph a job as their manager, with thick strings attached: his coaching staff would be chosen for him. Randolph badly wanted to manage, something he had never done before, and many candidates in his situation would have jumped at their first shot at managing. But he turned down the job, feeling that he would not have a legitimate chance to succeed when surrounded by a staff he did not know.

Randolph would talk to Knoblauch about his mechanics and hit him thousands of ground balls, in hopes of making the act of throwing a baseball natural again—action without thought. Knoblauch tried dropping his elbow and flinging the ball almost sidearm; this at least got him away from the dart-throwing mechanics that led to the errors. Randolph worked to rebuild his confidence, pumping him up, encouraging him while trying not to embarrass him. The whole process was similar to the treatment of an alcoholic; you had to take it one day at a time, Randolph felt, and even if Knoblauch had a good day or a good week or a good month, it was always possible his next three-error game would still come the next day.

But no matter how much he talked to Knoblauch or worked with him, Randolph couldn't imagine having trouble making simple 70-foot throws. He had never experienced anything like it. Randolph fully invested his time in Knoblauch, who was mostly receptive, probably more than anyone on the team expected, considering his defiant nature, but he never felt they had gotten a firm hold of the problem, because it had nothing to do with throwing mechanics or fielding drills. Randolph was essentially powerless, like a noted professor trying to teach a troubled savant the ABCs all over again.

Tino Martinez was one of the few players who seemed to reach Knoblauch. Just throw the ball as hard as you can, Martinez told him. Don't worry, I'll catch it. But the problem festered.

At first, Knoblauch had struggled making routine throws, easy grounders that afforded him time to think about the mistake he might make; if he had to pursue a grounder and rush a throw or turn a double play, he would be OK. But then he began having problems with difficult throws as well. In Boston for Game 4 of the AL Championship Series, Martinez rolled the ball to the other infielders to keep them warmed up between innings, and Knoblauch bounced a throw back to Martinez. The Fenway crowd jeered and then roared when his next practice throw sailed 20 feet wide, bouncing against the photographers' well. Knoblauch struggled with throws in the game, and Torre spoke with him before Game 5 about using Luis Sojo as a late-inning defensive replacement. "You're the manager," Knoblauch told Torre. "Do what you want." Knoblauch led off that night, greeted by a derisive roar from the Boston crowd, and slammed a single through the middle, defiant as ever.

Knoblauch received some counseling before the 2000 season, and the throwing problem was dormant in the first month as he found a comfortable rhythm, catching the ball, stepping, and firing to Martinez. He was off target a few times and made some errors, but he seemed to be free of the torment. But on May 21, in Cleveland, he threw a relay to home plate far over Posada's head, and three days later, returning an easy grounder in the eighth inning of a game in Chicago, his problem paralyzed him: his throw covered about half the distance to first and rolled into foul territory, far to Martinez's right. Knoblauch nearly fired his glove in disgust, and after the game he spoke with Torre about the possibility of retirement, his repressed anger finally tumbling out. "I certainly don't need the frustration," he said. "I don't need it. I know baseball is a small part of life, but when you're playing it, it's a big part of life. It's what we do." Knoblauch felt he had two choices: "You keep going out there or you take it to the house."

On June 15 he made three errors in the first six innings, returned to the dugout before the Yankees were to bat in the bottom of the sixth, and beckoned to Torre to follow him into the runway. Knoblauch said he thought he was hurting the team; Torre suggested that he go home to avoid the crowd of reporters who would be at his locker after the game. Knoblauch returned to the clubhouse, smashing equipment, dressed, and walked out of Yankee Stadium. He phoned his mother, Linda Knoblauch, who told him her instinct was to fly to New York to hug him, but she had to remain in Texas to tend to Ray. "I've asked her to come, but she can't," he said two days later.

Knoblauch went on the disabled list with elbow trouble in August, and as his rehabilitation stretched longer than expected and the playoffs approached, Steinbrenner began griping to friends that the second baseman was simply afraid to play. The complaints made their way into print, and Knoblauch returned angry. He changed the music that accompanied his at-bats to Eminem's "The Way I Am." The song, Knoblauch confirmed to Jack Curry of the *Times*, was a retort to those who judged him: Steinbrenner, the media, the fans.

'Cause I am, whatever you say I am
If I wasn't, then why would I say I am?
In the paper, the news everyday I am
I don't know it's just the way I am

"You get fed up with everything," Knoblauch told Curry. "It's not one particular thing. It's everything. The song speaks the truth. You are who you are. If somebody likes it, great. If not, that's great, too. Life goes on. Everybody is who they are, they believe in what they believe in and they do what they need to do."

By the end of the 2000 season, Knoblauch was a virtual statue at his position, seemingly frozen by fear. Teammates wondered if he was afraid to reach grounders because he knew that after gloving the ball, he would have to make a throw. The Yankees played 11 playoff games in 2000, five more in the World Series, and Knoblauch never played an inning at second base. Torre spoke openly late in the 2000 season about using him in left field.

But Brian Cashman didn't want to shift Knoblauch; when he batted about .270, drew walks, and stole a few bases, he was still a quite effective offensive second baseman. Left field typically was a position for power hitters, and if Knoblauch made the switch, the Yankees would immediately lock themselves into having one of the worst offensive left fielders in the league. Cashman met with Knoblauch after the 2000 season, and at the end of a tense conversation, Knoblauch agreed to try second base again for 2001.

He received more counseling, and about a month before spring training began, he went to Tampa to work with infield instructor Mick Kelleher on his fielding, diligently taking ground balls, making thousands of throws. Knoblauch spoke hopefully about the forthcoming season in the early days of spring training. He was going to get back to stealing bases, he said, get back to being aggressive on the bases. He looked OK in the infield workouts, throwing with a low arm angle but with relative accuracy. But in the first exhibition game of spring, he threw the ball away; regression quickly followed.

Midway through spring training, the Yankees were in Fort Myers to play an exhibition against Minnesota. Twins fans had targeted Knoblauch with irate jeers and boos since he forced his departure from Minnesota, and when he bounced a throw to first base in the second inning, they cheered. Two innings later, Knoblauch threw high for an error, then bounced another throw to first in the fifth, shouting when Twins catcher A. J. Pierzynski was called out. He fired wide of first in the sixth, for his fourth bad throw in six innings. He was broken, and the Yankees decided he could not be fixed. The coaching staff met and determined Knoblauch needed to move to left field.

When Torre told him of the decision, Knoblauch—who had made himself into a star through defiance—seemed relieved. He had tried everything to battle the problem, taking extra ground balls and seeking counseling and enduring humiliation. He had battled his problem, Martinez would recall, and was an important part of what the team accomplished in the championship years. Baseball had been the focus of Knoblauch's life for his first 32 years, had served as a link to his father, and had made him wealthy, and ultimately, baseball crushed part of him. The throwing jitters had wrecked his career, but he felt that he tried as hard as he could. "The word *quit* isn't in my vocabulary; it's not that I'm quitting on second," he said the day Torre told him of the switch to left field. "I've done everything I possibly could to this point, and it's just not happening right now."

Shortly after acquiring Knoblauch in the trade with the Twins, the Yankees had agreed to give him a two-year, $18 million extension to buy out his right to demand a trade. But the deal, which would have extended his contract through the 2003 season, was never formally announced, as Knoblauch was overcome by his throwing problems. Randy Levine, who became the Yankees' president after the oral agreement between the team and Knoblauch's agents was reached, would insist there had been no such arrangement. But friends of Knoblauch believe he did, in fact, receive a large settlement from the Yankees under the table, a little more than 50 cents on the dollar—money paid off to end his time with the team.

Knoblauch batted .250 in his last season with the Yankees and was nearly traded to Seattle in midseason before Steinbrenner killed the deal, worried about what Knoblauch might do against the Yankees in the postseason. The promise of greatness remained in him; executives remembered what he had been, though nobody fully understood what had happened to him. Knoblauch did not like speculating about the source of his throwing problems. "What good would it do?" he asked. "It won't change anything."

But many of his teammates thought privately that his move from a small-market team to the spotlight of New York was at the root of his problem. Suddenly in a situation of enormous pressure—which he had created by demanding a trade—in the world's largest market, playing for the game's most powerful franchise, the insular infielder had been hit by performance anxiety, they thought. And this was at a point in his life when Knoblauch was, for the first time, without his father to lean on.

Torre mostly kept Knoblauch in the Yankees' lineup through the post-season in 2001. He didn't start Game 5, on the night that he and Brosius had talked in Yankee Stadium after batting practice, but would enter as a pinch-runner for David Justice in the seventh inning. The Yankees were trailing, 2–0, when Knoblauch batted in the ninth against Byung-Hyun Kim, striking out for the second out in the inning. But Brosius followed, attacking a hanging breaking ball for the game-tying home run. Knoblauch singled off Albie Lopez in the 12th inning, advanced to second on Brosius's sacrifice bunt, and scored the winning run when Soriano singled, bounding into the air after touching home plate. "We have this great desire to win, but it's almost like we want to win this one even more," Knoblauch said after that game. "If this is our last go-round with the Yankees, we can walk away and say that we won four World Series in a row."

Four championships in four seasons would be Knoblauch's ultimate vindication for his troubled years with the Yankees, and now, in the ninth inning of Game 7, he and Brosius and the other Yankees needed just three more outs to make that happen. As Randy Johnson pitched in the top of the ninth, Brosius leaned against the front railing to the dugout, next to Derek Jeter. Brosius had his hat off, a small smile on his face.

Johnson had thrown 104 pitches the night before, in Game 6, but there was no reason to save his arm. Throwing fastballs in the low 90s, mixing in an occasional slider, Johnson retired Bernie Williams on a short fly to center and Martinez on a grounder to shortstop. Rivera rested on the bench in the Yankees' dugout, cap and glove at his side, head down, staring at the ground. His teammates gave him plenty of space; no one came near him. Johnson pitched to Posada, reached two strikes. Rivera lifted his head, looked directly into one of the Fox network cameras set up in the far corner of the dugout, and quickly averted his eyes. Posada struck out, and Rivera gathered his equipment and walked back to the mound, tossing his warm-ups easily, lightly, needing three more outs to hold the Yankees' 2–1 lead.

Mark Grace would lead off the bottom of the ninth—perhaps the best player to start the inning for the Diamondbacks, Arizona manager Bob Brenly thought; he was a good contact hitter and would not be intimidated by the moment. Grace, a left-handed hitter, had not started Game 6 against Pettitte, and Brenly could have used powerful young slugger Erubiel Durazo at first in Game 7. But Brenly had a good feeling about Grace, his defense, and his experience. "The guy deserved to be on the field for a Game 7 of the World Series," Brenly said months later.

Grace had never faced Rivera before Game 5 and found that watching him on television hardly compared to actually seeing his cutter head-on. "You know what he's going to do," Grace said. "He's going to try to bully you inside with those Frisbee cutters, and you've just got to be ready for it."

Grace had grounded out in that at-bat and decided that it was a mistake for a left-handed batter to try to pull the cutter into right field. If you did that, he thought, you had to start your swing very early to get the barrel of the bat out in front and your swing would get too long, and the cutter would jam you. If you tried to pull the cutter, it would be like trying to fend off a mosquito with a long boat oar; a fly swatter was much more effective. It was smarter, Grace thought, to be short and quick with his swing and try to punch the ball into center or left field.

Grace took a cutter inside, 92 mph; ball one. Rivera fired another, and Grace threw his hands quickly, close to his body, and smacked a liner into center field, the ball falling for a single.

Grace rounded first base, and in the visitors' clubhouse, where the victory stage was set up, Steinbrenner jabbed a finger at the attendant standing next to him. "If we lose this," he said, "it's all your fault."

CHAPTER 21

CURT SCHILLING was sitting on the Arizona bench when Grace's single fell into center field, and so he remained there, figuring it was a lucky spot. With his teammates crammed against the railing at the front of the dugout, he would have to peer around them and through their legs to watch the last half-inning play out. But he would not sit anywhere else.

Before Grace batted, David Dellucci was told that he would go into the game no matter what Grace did. If Grace made an out, bench coach Bob Melvin told Dellucci, he was going to pinch-hit for Damian Miller, who was scheduled to bat second in the bottom of the ninth. If Grace reached base, Dellucci would run for the slow-footed Grace. So now Dellucci ran to first base, 28 years old, a career role player, his mouth dry, his stomach tumbling. As he ran to first, he slapped hands with Grace and reminded himself to absorb the moment, to give himself a memory he could recall years later. And then he began internally reviewing as many possible scenarios as he could—what he should do if the ball was popped up, how he should get his lead. Can't get picked off, Dellucci reminded himself.

Miller remained in the game to attempt a sacrifice bunt, a play he rarely tried as the No. 8 hitter in the Arizona lineup, because pitchers usually batted behind him. Miller had four sacrifice bunts during the regular season, seven in his career, and his responsibility was to bunt against a hard-throwing pitcher who was also one of the best fielders of his generation. A bunt back toward Rivera would almost certainly result in an out, and possibly in a double play. In 455 major league games, Rivera had made just one error, despite the many slow grounders caused by his cutter. He shagged fly balls during batting practice, and rather than stand in one place and wait for the long drives to come to him, Rivera sprinted deep into the alleys to chase down balls, with remarkable range. Teammates were convinced that in addition to being the best closer in baseball, Rivera might also have been one of the sport's best outfielders.

Miller's best bet was to push his bunt toward first base, along the line, making it difficult for Tino Martinez or Rivera to throw to second base for a force. Failing that, he could bunt along the line toward third; Brosius would be charging from third base, but Miller probably would succeed in advancing the runner. What he could not do was bunt the ball back to Rivera; that would be trouble, he knew.

Rivera's first pitch cut away from Miller, who beat it into the dirt, foul. The next pitch, another cutter, flew right at Miller, then broke over the inner half of the plate. Miller bunted the ball with the meat of the bat, too hard—right back to Rivera. "It might have been a single up the middle if Rivera hadn't fielded it," Miller joked a couple of years later.

Rivera pounced off the mound, attacking Miller's bunt, turning his body counterclockwise, setting his feet so he could quickly throw toward second base. He reached the ball with plenty of time to force out Dellucci at second; there was a chance, as well, that Jeter might be able to throw to first for a double play.

But as the baseball bounded toward the mound, it attacked Rivera. When a ball is bunted onto grass, it quickly loses speed, but Miller's bunt careened along the swath of dirt that extends from home plate to the pitcher's mound in Bank One Ballpark—one of the features designed by a former Yankee manager to make the place unique.

Buck Showalter's strip of dirt.

The ball bounced low, like a rock skipping across a pond, and maintained its speed, rolling up the pocket of Rivera's glove, to the heel, nearly escaping. Rivera seized the ball with the heel of his hand, rather than at the base of his index and middle fingers. His fingers circled the ball along its lower half, his hold imperfect, and he whipped the ball toward second base, trying for a force play.

Dellucci had gotten a good lead, moving away from first base as Rivera began his delivery, and when he saw Miller's bunt go down, his thought was clear: I have to get to second. Even if he couldn't get there in time to be safe, Dellucci wanted to disrupt Jeter, who was covering the bag, maybe prevent him from turning a double play. But as Dellucci raced toward second, he saw Jeter leaning toward him, his right foot anchored on the base, reaching with his glove.

Rivera's throw sailed, veering up and away from Jeter. The Yankees' shortstop extended his body toward first base, and Dellucci, bearing down on second and beginning his slide, saw Jeter's left shin "sticking out there," Dellucci recalled months later. It was a perfect target for a runner desperate to break up a play, and Dellucci spiked Jeter on the left ankle, cutting down the shortstop through his baseball shoe as the ball nicked his glove and caromed into short center field. The fans in Bank One Ballpark roared as Jeter rolled around on the dirt, writhing in pain. Both runners were safe. Months later Grace would rave about Dellucci's determination and presence of mind; the inning might have played out differently if not for Dellucci's play, Grace thought.

Jeter pushed off the ground, limping. He thought his foot might be broken—he would have X-rays days later—but there was no chance he would leave this game, no chance anybody would think about taking him out. He walked slowly to the mound to listen to Torre, who had come out to try to settle his players, his right hand on Martinez's shoulder. The Diamondbacks were going to try another bunt, that was obvious, and Torre told the players on the mound to make sure to get one out. "Let's not take any chances," he said.

With runners at first and second, nobody out, Brenly needed a sacrifice bunt and he installed Jay Bell as the pinch-hitter. The 35-year-old infielder had lost his job as an everyday player, but he was an excellent bunter, leading the National League in sacrifice bunts in 1990 and 1991, when he was with Pittsburgh. He had more successful sacrifice bunts than any other active player.

Bell faced the same pitfalls as Miller before him—the pitcher was athletic, the pitcher threw hard. The movement of Rivera's cutter didn't bother Bell, but trying to control a bunt against a 95 mph fastball was like grabbing a rattlesnake by its trunk. And everyone in the park knew Bell would be bunting; Rivera was sure to be bounding off the mound as soon as he released the ball.

Bell turned and squared, holding the bat in front of him, trying to aim the ball away from Rivera. Instead, he pushed it directly back toward the mound, and Rivera, who had made up his mind to rush the third base line, swooped on it. Bell broke out of the batter's box, one thought filling his head: I screwed up the World Series. He knew immediately he had failed to advance the runners, with baseball's best closer on the mound.

Rivera picked up the ball after its second bounce, whirled, and fired toward third base, the ball arriving well ahead of Dellucci, for the first out. The throw sailed a bit, and Brosius, with one foot jammed against the bag, had to reach slightly to his left to make the catch. Brosius immediately glanced at second, to locate Miller, now the lead runner. And then he looked at first, where Bell was arriving.

The following spring, Rivera would tell Jack Curry of the *New York Times* that he had expected Brosius to throw to first, to try for a double play. "The ball hit Brosius in the chest and he just took his foot off the bag," Rivera said. "I was waiting for the ball to cross to me. When you're a pitcher, you always wait for the ball to cross you. I was like, 'Where's the ball?' I saw Brosius with the ball, I said, 'Uh, oh.' I tell you what, that was a double play."

Rivera later asked Torre whether a double play could have been made, and Torre's response was, "Absolutely."

Torre thought his advice to the players gathered on the mound—make sure of one out—might have been strictly interpreted by Brosius, when in actuality the words were meant mostly for Rivera. "I'm not sure if that was in his head," said Torre. "I was really referring to Mo [Rivera]."

In days to come, Bell would watch the replays and read Rivera's comments, and he believed Rivera was wrong, that the ball hadn't hit Brosius in the chest. He had had to reach to his left to catch the throw, which changed the circumstances, Bell thought. "There's no question with Brosh, that if he gets the ball thrown directly at him, he comes off and throws to first base," said Bell, who had come to know Brosius through the years. "But where the ball was thrown, on the second-base side—if he comes up and throws wildly to first base, a run scores and there's a man on third. It's not slow motion; you're having to think very quickly.

"I read what Mariano said, and he was looking for different things. Well, if Mariano had made a good throw to second base, he wouldn't have been in that situation. If he had a good throw to third base, there would have been a double play. But that's just the way baseball goes."

Brosius said his thought was, "'We've got the best closer in the game, we've got to make sure we get an out.' I'm not worried about the double play. We've got the best guy in the game on the mound.

"When you watched it on TV replay—and I watched it a couple of times—it didn't seem that glaring to me, watching Jay run to first base after he bunted. It didn't seem like I got the ball so fast that I had all the time in the world. If I had to do it all over again, I would do it the same way, just get an out."

Brosius saw the *Times* article and thought the headline—"Rivera Places the Blame in Brosius's Hand"—was unfair. "I thought that was out of character for Mo, a guy who never placed blame, and when I looked through the piece, he never said that [I lost the game]," said Brosius. "What he did say is that we maybe could have turned two. That's his opinion." And for Brosius, that sufficed. He saw Rivera the next summer, but the two men never discussed the play.

Schilling wondered, months later, if there was another factor affecting the Yankees. They had struggled defensively throughout the postseason and in the World Series, committing eight errors against Arizona, far more than in any series during their run of championships. The Diamondbacks made only three errors, all in Game 3. For the first time in years, Schilling thought, the Yankees might have been playing to avoid mistakes.

One out, runners at first and second. The slow-footed Miller, who had advanced to second on Bell's bunt, was replaced by pinch-runner Midre Cummings. Arizona shortstop Tony Womack walked to the plate.

Rivera had thrown 14 pitches in the eighth inning, and after three batters in the ninth inning, he had accumulated a total of 19—a sprinter now asked to run a little farther.

Womack was a pesky left-handed hitter with little power but great speed, and Bell thought he had been the Diamondbacks' best player in the playoffs. He'd had the series-clinching hit against St. Louis in the Division Series, contributed to the wipeout of Atlanta in the Championship Series, and had seven hits in the World Series. Womack was a good hitter for Arizona in this situation, because he typically made contact, would probably put the ball in play, and was unlikely to hit into a double play.

Five feet nine and 170 pounds, Womack figured out early in his career that pitchers would forever try to jam him with fastballs. If they pitched away from him, aiming at the outside corner, then they'd play into his hands: he'd just slap at it or bunt and run. If they pitched carefully and walked him, he'd probably steal second. So they would usually try to hammer him inside with fastballs, knock the bat out of his hands. Rivera pitched inside to left-handers with his cutter, anyway, and Womack was sure he would probably not change that in this situation.

Rivera threw a cutter and Womack took it, the ball drifting inside for ball 1, the 93 mph pitch lacking the sharp break of his best cutter. Rivera's next pitch was 91 mph, another cutter that moved lazily for ball 2. His pitch count had climbed to 21.

Womack took a strike, and then Rivera tried a four-seam fastball, rather than the cutter, a fastball that stayed straight. Finally, a pitch to hit. Womack swung and fouled it back, and tried to reassure himself. That's not the only hittable pitch you'll see, he told himself. You'll get another.

The count was 2 balls and 2 strikes. Mary Cashman turned to her husband and held up four fingers: Four more strikes, she said, counting down as he did. "The four toughest strikes in the history of baseball," Brian Cashman replied.

There were no adjustments to be made against Rivera, Womack

thought. You would look for the ball coming out of his hand, you would read its trajectory—inside fastball, almost every pitch—and what happened after that was a bit out of your control. If the ball cut hard, it might hit your thumbs, and if it didn't, well, then you might swing out in front and pull it.

Rivera paused, looked to Posada for the sign, and threw, another cutter, a high one. Womack pulled his hands in and mashed the ball into right field, dumping it down the line. Cummings scored the tying run from second base, Bell raced to third, Womack sprinted into second. The fans who had been standing and waiting for something good to happen erupted, and the sound of thunderous celebration reached the visitors' clubhouse, where Steinbrenner raged about the TV stagehands. "God damn it!" he screamed. "I knew it! I knew they would jinx us!"

"You just hope you get the 94 mph cut fastball instead of the 97 mph cut fastball," Womack would say months later. "And I think that's the one I hit, 94."

The pitch was clocked at 92 mph. This was the 97th inning Rivera had thrown in 2001, exceeding his record as the Yankees' closer; in 1998, he'd thrown just 74⅔ innings. He would not say so afterward, but teammates thought he was worn out; this was the sixth time in this postseason he was needed for five outs or more. As Rivera blew away the Diamondbacks in the eighth inning, seven of his 14 pitches had reached 94 or 95 mph. In the ninth inning, he would hit 94 mph only once.

One out, runners at second and third, Yankees 2, Arizona 2. Rivera was impassive as he walked back to the mound after Womack's hit, but the double had been devastating. Even if Rivera could get the last two outs in the inning without allowing the winning run, the Yankees still would have to rally their flagging offense for another run.

Womack took his lead at second. He looked at the next hitter, Craig Counsell, and thought, Finish them now. Don't let them get to a 10th inning, not after what they did in New York. Counsell fouled off a fastball, but when Rivera threw inside with his next pitch, he hit Counsell in the right hand. The bases were loaded, with Luis Gonzalez coming to bat.

Several of the Yankees' minority owners stood in the entrance to the visitors' clubhouse, and they were warned by attendants: if Arizona wins, we're going to carry this stage out of here as quickly as possible, so get out of the way.

One out, bases full, possible winning run at third. Posada went to the mound, the infielders joining him for a meeting about positioning. To Torre, there was really no choice in the matter. He might have had Soriano and Jeter positioned at double-play depth, but because Rivera's cut fastball caused so many badly hit grounders, there was a possibility Gonzalez might hit a slow roller to second or short and there would be no chance to get Bell at home plate. Rivera had produced five double-play grounders in the last month of the regular season, including four in the last six weeks of play, but most of his pitches put in play were dribblers. Torre wanted the infielders to play in.

Gonzalez watched the conference from the batter's box, reaching down to swipe the dirt with his left hand. He saw Jeter and Soriano position themselves a foot or so off the infield grass, and Gonzalez decided to choke up on the bat an inch or so; he had to make sure he hit the ball. What he could not do was strike out. Anything but a strikeout.

Gonzalez had slugged 57 homers during the regular season, batting .325, but Pettitte hit him in the right wrist in Game 2, an injury that prevented him from taking batting practice the next two days; there had been some doubt about whether he would play in Game 3. The Yankees quickly exploited the problem, attacking Gonzalez with fastballs at his hands, and as he faced Rivera, he had only six hits in 26 at-bats in the World Series, and 11 strikeouts.

Rivera whizzed a cutter inside. Gonzalez swung, got jammed, and fouled off a pitch to the left side. He looked down and checked the handle of his bat; it was still intact.

Bell, at third base, turned and made eye contact with third-base umpire Ed Rapuano in a wordless exchange; what a game, what an incredible World Series. Bell had grown up hating the Yankees for beating the Dodgers, his favorite team, in the 1977 and 1978 World Series, and now, almost 25 years later, he had the power to beat them, if he could reach home plate.

Rivera looked for the sign, just in time to see Gonzalez call for time.

Gonzalez readjusted his batting gloves. Torre leaned across the front railing of the visitors' dugout, Zimmer on his right, Stottlemyre on his left. Paul O'Neill was at the railing as well, arms folded over the front. In the home dugout, Schilling had finally given in to temptation, vacating the back-row seat on the bench to go to the railing.

Rivera spat, waiting. He took Posada's sign, lifted his left knee and threw, that nice easy motion, and his cutter began veering inside as it neared home plate.

Gonzalez swung, gritting his teeth as he threw his hands and bat forward. The pitch struck his 34-inch bat and snapped it diagonally across almost half of its 10 grains, only 22 inches from the handle. The bat went limp in his hands as he finished the follow-through, as if he were swinging a wet rag.

The ball was in the air, rising, a little pop fly toward shortstop. If Jeter had been in his normal position, he could have ambled a step or two back and caught the ball. But all he could do now was raise his glove over his head helplessly and watch the Yankees' dynasty fall onto the outfield grass in Bank One Ballpark.

Gonzalez leaped into the air, screaming, "Yeah! Yeah!" The ball touched down a couple of feet beyond the infield, barely reaching the outfield grass, and Bell ran home, his arms raised. To Diamondbacks owner Jerry Colangelo, it seemed that Bell was moving in slow motion and took hours to finally reach home. Bell hit the plate with his left foot and fell into the embrace of Matt Williams, and soon the two men were swallowed by the first wave of Diamondbacks; a second wave rolled toward Gonzalez, who had rounded first base. Schilling rushed forward off the bench and raced across the infield, running just in front of Rivera, to be the first Arizona player to smother Gonzalez.

Knoblauch had picked up the ball with his right hand but knew it was too late and never threw it, running across the infield. Jeter limped to the dugout. Rivera lowered his head and walked off the field steadily, appearing the same as he always did at the end of an inning, except that he was stepping past players who had beaten him. Martinez jogged in from first base and met Rivera at the foul line, reaching his right arm around him, trying to console him. But Rivera continued, without hurrying, without slowing, into the dugout and down the runway. The half-inning had lasted just 14 pitches—nine minutes and 39 seconds.

The network and clubhouse attendants quickly lifted the foot-high temporary stage and bull-rushed it through the double doors. "Get out of the way!" one of them snapped as they bumped past some of the Yankees' traveling party. Knocking aside a couple of the men, they dumped the stage in the hallway.

Jeter sat on the bench, staring out onto the field—believing he should watch the other team celebrate and remember how he felt about losing. Torre stood at the railing, watching the Diamondbacks. There was no anger on his face, only a small smile. After a minute or two, he turned and walked to the clubhouse. O'Neill lingered in the dugout, staring at the field, pain filling his face. He had grown accustomed to success, playing a major role on winning teams, and now, as his career ended, he was on the bench, helpless. He stepped away from the railing, and Don Zimmer embraced him, the two men hugging as teammates for the last time. Rudy Giuliani stood in his box seat and clapped. The World Series had been so spectacular and resonated so deeply, he thought, that it almost didn't matter that the Yankees lost.

Greg Colbrunn, the Arizona first baseman, grabbed Jay Bell, who had botched his bunt. "Might be the most selfish play I've ever seen," Colbrunn joked; because of his mistake, Bell reached base and scored the run that won the World Series. Curt Schilling and Randy Johnson embraced, and Matt Williams tightly hugged Luis Gonzalez.

The last of the Yankees straggled in from the dugout. There was no screaming, no slamming of bats or spikes. Torre spoke to the players, talking about O'Neill, congratulating the players for their achievements, reminding them they had great reason to be proud. As he talked, Torre glanced at his shortstop; Jeter was enraged in defeat.

Steinbrenner stood nearby, anger littered across his face. Another member of the organization watched him and prayed: Please don't say anything. "He looked like he was going to jump into the middle of it and say something awful," said the observer. But Steinbrenner held his tongue, briefly, until after the meeting broke up. Then he said aloud, "There will be changes, that's all I can say. There will be changes."

Paul O'Neill went from locker to locker, hugging teammates. Derek Jeter answered some questions from reporters, then retreated into the trainers' room, his ankle throbbing, his anger barely contained. He couldn't believe they had lost, and his anger would stay with him for months. "I don't want to hear people say, 'We had a successful season, we made it to the World Series,'" Jeter would say later. "It doesn't mean a thing unless you win. You don't play to get to the World Series. You play to win a World Series." Jorge Posada and Tino Martinez seemed on the verge of tears. Mike Stanton was stunned. "You saw the light at the end of the tunnel," he said, "and it was taken away."

Steinbrenner began chastising a major league official, who had been yelled at by Steinbrenner before but never in front of so many people, the reporters, and players. "I'm done with you," Steinbrenner snapped, and later, he would confront Paul Beeston, the second-highest-ranked executive in baseball, barking about the network hands in the Yankees' clubhouse.

Reporters surrounded Mariano Rivera, leaning forward to hear the answers he delivered softly, evenly. The room was packed with journalists and cameras and hot television lights, and a thin layer of sweat formed on Rivera's forehead. Standing near the spot where he had made his pregame speech, Rivera stood for each wave of reporters, wearing a white dress shirt and tie, politely repeating the same explanations to the same questions. "We went through a good season," Rivera said. "I don't know, I'm not going to go back and say, 'Oh, we should have won.' This is what happened."

Roger Clemens came out of the Yankees' clubhouse, wearing a black suit, and was met by his mother, who looked at him with concern, knowing that he had pitched in pain. Then Clemens gathered his sons and went to the damp and raucous Arizona clubhouse to find Schilling. "I'm very proud of you," Clemens said, and Schilling was deeply touched. It mattered a great deal to Schilling what Clemens thought of him, and he thought those words—coming from one of the greatest pitchers of all time on that night—would resonate the rest of his life.

George Steinbrenner also made his way to the Arizona clubhouse, to find Jerry Colangelo and congratulate him and tell him he had always thought of him as a winner. Near dawn, Luis Gonzalez checked his cell phone and the first message was from Tino Martinez, calling with congratulations as the Yankees were on the way to the airport. Enjoy it, because you deserve it, Martinez said, and because you never know how many moments like this you will have in your lifetime.

Scott Brosius smiled slightly as he spoke with perspective immediately after the game, about what a great World Series it had been. The stark reality was that in those nine days of the 2001 World Series, Arizona had been a much better team than the Yankees, whose eroded offense and erratic defense had finally become too much for their pitching and their will to overcome. The Yankees batted .183 in the World Series and scored a total of 14 runs in seven games—one fewer than Arizona generated in their 15–2 victory in Game 6; the Diamondbacks scored 37 in the Series. Jeter hit .148, Knoblauch .056, Brosius .167, Martinez .190. The Yankees had typically worn down opponents by drawing walks and limiting their own strikeouts, keeping the ball in play and maintaining pressure on their opponents. In this World Series, they had accumulated just 16 walks and had 63 strikeouts. Their runs came freakishly—bloop hits, late-inning homers. If the Diamondbacks had lost the Series, Grace would acknowledge afterward, he would have been crushed, knowing how one-sided the play had been for most of the games.

But while the Yankees had been fortunate to be in position to win in the ninth inning of Game 7, some of the Arizona players felt they had been fortunate to conquer the closer who did not lose in that last inning. "I got lucky," Grace would say months later. "I think all of us got lucky."

The Yankees had four championships and would be regarded as one of the greatest dynasties in history, and had no reason for regret. But late that night, when Brosius finally got to bed, he could not sleep. It was the first time any loss had affected him in this way.

Colangelo couldn't sleep either. Before the Series began, he had told reporters that if the World Series played out the way he wanted, the Diamondbacks would win in the bottom of the ninth inning, scoring the decisive runs on a two-out hit by Gonzalez. As he stood at his seat and saw the inning play out, he said, it was almost as if a vision appeared before his eyes. After getting home shortly before daybreak, Colangelo watched the television replays of Game 7, over and over, until the phone rang at 7 a.m. It was the president of the United States. "What an unbelievable win," Bush told Colangelo. "You're supposed to call after the game in the clubhouse," Colangelo teased Bush. "No, no, that's your time, I wanted you to enjoy your time in the clubhouse," the president replied, before formally inviting the Diamondbacks to the White House.

Torre would call Gene Monahan during the off-season. *Too bad*, he joked to the Yankees trainer. *If we had won the World Series, we could have made you millions as a motivational speaker.*

ABOUT 36 hours after Luis Gonzalez's hit fell onto the outfield grass in Arizona, Paul O'Neill walked into the Yankees clubhouse to clean out his locker. A crowd of reporters had gathered for postmortems, the sort of pack that usually bothered O'Neill. But his mood was different now; he was a former player. His eight-year-old son, Aaron, was with him, skipping a class field trip to the Bronx Zoo. The father cleared his locker slowly, filling boxes, chatting amiably, cracking jokes that were mostly at his own expense. There were no more at-bats to torture him.

Aaron badgered his father to hurry, loading the boxes quickly, stepping inside the locker across dozens of pairs of old spikes, coat hangers rattling against his head. The boy found a pair of sunglasses and put them on, and when he found more sunglasses, he wore those as well, mounting them on his forehead. Aaron had no time for sentiment; he wanted his father to take him home to play.

Before closing the last box, Paul O'Neill removed the nameplate from above his locker and placed it on top, along with his glove, and the O'Neills walked out of Yankee Stadium.

At the mouth of the parking lot, father and son bumped into Joe Torre and Tino Martinez and stopped to talk.

Torre told O'Neill how wonderful it was the fans had recognized him as the team was losing in the ninth inning of Game 5, and O'Neill nodded.

Standing outside Yankee Stadium, they shook hands. Then Torre sensed O'Neill wanted more, and the two men hugged and said goodbye.

Epilogue

THE VICTORY PARADE that would have taken the Yankees up New York City's Canyon of Heroes for the fifth time in six years was canceled, so Enrique Wilson, the team's utility infielder, decided to change his flight home. He was supposed to return to the Dominican Republic on November 12, eight days after the end of the World Series, but moved up his departure a few days. He was at home when he heard that American Airlines Flight 587—the plane he was supposed to be on—had crashed in Belle Harbor, a neighborhood in Queens. Two hundred and sixty-five people were killed in an accident that shook a city still reeling from the September 11 terrorist attacks.

When Wilson saw Mariano Rivera in spring training the next year, the reliever expressed great relief that Wilson was still alive. If Rivera had held the lead against Arizona, Wilson would likely have been on Flight 587. "I am glad we lost the World Series," Rivera told Wilson, "because it means that I still have a friend." For Rivera, this was further confirmation that they were all subject to God's will.

• • •

SEPTEMBER 11 would have a lasting effect on baseball. When players and owners held labor talks late in the summer of 2002, they negotiated in the shadow of the sobering international circumstances. The U.S. was engaged in one war and preparing for another, its own economy in decline. Meanwhile, the average salary in major league baseball exceeded $2 million. Player strikes had scrapped two months of the 1981 season and led to the cancellation of the 1994 World Series, but after those disputes were settled, most fans got over their anger and drifted back to the game. During the 2002 negotiations, though, both sides seemed to understand that there was little room for bickering and a senseless standoff.

Veteran players clearly remembered the fans' angry reaction to the 1994–95 strike, and they realized they would become public pariahs if they walked out; they desperately wanted their leaders to make a deal. With the first anniversary of September 11 looming, the players agreed to a form of luxury tax, the union's first major retreat in 30 years of labor wars. Any team that was over the payroll threshold of $117 million in the first year of the deal would be initially taxed at a rate of 17.5 percent, with escalating rates for repeat offenders.

The players association had always fought this kind of tax, believing it would effectively create a drag on salaries. The union and baseball's most aggressive capitalist were in full accord in opposing the tax: Steinbrenner believed it was squarely aimed at the Yankees, and when the owners voted to ratify the new labor agreement, the contract was approved 29–1, with the Yankees giving the only nay.

THERE WERE signs in 2002–2003 that baseball had begun making progress with the problem of payroll disparity, which had stifled the hopes of fans and players in the smaller markets. Ironically, the Yankee excess that had helped create the problem probably helped to diminish it. For years, they had been the financial rabbit that all other teams chased, but in 2002, when their payroll climbed to $150 million, teams like the Cleveland Indians and the Seattle Mariners could not try to pretend they could compete with the Yankees' financial power, and began cutting payroll or holding the line. As many teams demonstrated greater fiscal discipline, the group of middle-class and lower-middle-class teams grew, creating a de facto parity: in 2003, 23 of 30 teams had payrolls less than $85 million, and more teams planned to make cuts. The franchises with lower budgets had an improved chance of competing, particularly in the leagues' Central Divisions, which were filled with low and moderate payrolls.

The Anaheim Angels won the 2002 World Series with a payroll of $58 million, just weeks after the luxury tax was negotiated; there was growing incentive for owners to believe they could compete with a modest budget. In 2003, the Florida Marlins, who had opened the season with a $49 million payroll, aggressively augmented their roster during the season, adding pitcher Ugueth Urbina and outfielder Jeff Conine, and made the playoffs before contending deep into October. Teams were winning more while spending less.

Not the Yankees, however, whose payroll would grow from $150 million to about $180 million in 2003; they were the only team to pay a luxury tax in the first year of the system, and the team's total bill for revenue sharing and luxury tax was $61 million, more than the entire payrolls of 14 teams.

Despite the progress in parity, other issues gnawed at the game. It was evident in the bodies of some players—from ballooning biceps to broadening foreheads—that the sport had a growing steroid problem. Many players began to resemble professional wrestlers, and anecdotal evidence of steroid abuse dripped out. Ken Caminiti, the National League Most Valuable Player in 1996, told *Sports Illustrated* he had used steroids and speculated that perhaps half of the other players took them, as well. As Mark McGwire pursued Roger Maris's home run record in 1998, he admitted he used androstenedione, an over-the-counter supplement. Once the euphoria of his chase faded, he became something of a punch line, an ode to modern-day chemistry rather than talent or work ethic. Baseball began a drug-testing program in 2003, a system that many health officials viewed as pathetically weak because the players generally knew when they were going to be checked and faced no consequences if they tested positive. More than 5 percent of the players failed, triggering a more stringent system that began in 2004.

The games themselves were often tedious—played too slowly to keep up with a society dramatically accelerating its pace. Americans wanted faster computers, faster Internet service, cell phones for instant communication. But the time required to play major league baseball games had increased markedly, partly because of increased commercial time between innings, and partly because the participants competed more deliberately. Between 1969 and 2002, the average World Series game mushroomed from two hours and 20 minutes to 3:37. The average time of regular season games hovered near three hours.

Late in the 1990s, Major League Baseball officials asked Frank Robinson, the Hall of Fame outfielder, to evaluate the slowing pace. Robinson came to believe that if the players, managers, and umpires applied themselves to shortening the games, at least 20 minutes could be cut—"for starters," he said. About 12 to 15 minutes were wasted each game, Robinson determined, because hitters were in the habit of waiting for their theme music to end on the public address systems before stepping into the box. "It is taking longer and longer, and to younger people, baseball is boring," he said. "That's a danger."

Major League Baseball changed course very slowly, Boston executive Larry Lucchino said, "like a dreadnought." And by 2004, the game's administrators had only begun to address these serious problems.

AFTER THE Yankees lost to Arizona, Paul O'Neill retired, as expected, and after Scott Brosius did not receive strong overtures from the Yankees or the Seattle Mariners, he retired, as well. Luis Sojo began working as a coach and manager in the Yankees' minor league system, briefly making a comeback as a player in 2003. Tino Martinez signed a three-year contract with the St. Louis Cardinals; he was traded to Tampa Bay before the 2004 season. As expected, he was replaced by Jason Giambi, who signed a seven-year, $120 million deal.

Chuck Knoblauch would sign with Kansas City in 2002, still possessing an air of promise that he might be a great player again; only a few years before, he had been the game's best leadoff hitter. But he batted

.210 in 300 at-bats for the Royals, and at age 34, still physically healthy, his career was over.

David Cone would sit out 2002 and make a brief comeback for the Mets in 2003 before retiring. Darryl Strawberry served 11 months of an 18-month sentence before being released on April 8, 2003. Seven months later, Steinbrenner gave him a job as a minor league instructor. "My life now is so focused," said Strawberry. "I thank the Boss for this opportunity to work with young players. I can help the players not only with baseball but with the struggles I've been through, with how to prepare themselves for their lives." He lasted in this position less than four months.

Orlando Hernandez was traded to the Montreal Expos before the 2003 season, and after getting hurt, it appeared his career was all but over. Gene Michael signed a long-term deal, for about $600,000 annually, to serve as a scout and give advice—though Steinbrenner listened less and less.

FOR A decade, George Steinbrenner had grudgingly deferred to some of his high-ranking baseball advisors—Michael, Brian Cashman, Joe Torre, Mark Newman—when major decisions were considered. But some of his executives thought the loss to the Diamondbacks damaged their credibility in the owner's eyes. Steinbrenner took the reins back, veering onto his own erratic course, following his impetuous instincts. "You have no idea, day to day, what he's going to do," said one club official in 2003.

David Wells was a free agent after the 2001 season, and Yankees executives had warned Steinbrenner about the downside of re-signing him—he was high maintenance, he had a bad back, and there was the perpetual question of his conditioning. With his talks with the Yankees halted after cursory conversations, Wells negotiated a handshake deal with the Arizona Diamondbacks; the plan was to finalize the contract once Wells took a physical examination.

But Steinbrenner phoned Wells, met him for lunch, and without consulting his executives a second time, offered him a contract. Wells made the deal and went on to pitch well in 2002, going 19-7—a success that encouraged Steinbrenner to make more of the major decisions alone.

IN THE early months of the 2002 season, the Toronto Blue Jays were desperate to dump outfielder Raul Mondesi and the $24 million that remained on his contract, but could find no takers. Even in a sport generously populated by players who partied extensively and slept very little, Mondesi was considered a wild man, staying out all night; teammates sometimes wondered if he slept at all before playing in day games. Mondesi had some productive seasons early in his career, hitting 33 homers and driving in 99 runs in 1999. But scouts thought his 24-hour schedule and unrestrained lifestyle wore on his body, which thickened noticeably as he neared his 30th birthday. Now, in the summer of 2002, his lack of discipline seemed to have taken its toll.

Mondesi had none of the subtle qualities that the Yankees had valued during the dynasty. He was a free-swinging hitter, rather than a contact hitter, and he seemed utterly incapable of making adjustments from pitch to pitch; opposing pitchers repeatedly threw him sliders low and away, out of the strike zone, and he repeatedly swung aggressively at them, rather than trying to punch the ball to right field.

His batting average was barely .200 for Toronto in June, when a series of injuries hit the Yankees' outfielders. Enrique Wilson, a utility infielder, started in right field against the Mets June 29, on national television, and misplayed a fly ball in the second inning, with Steinbrenner watching from his private suite. The owner raged, summoned his executives, and demanded action.

About four hours after Wilson's gaffe, Toronto general manager J. P. Ricciardi was driving on the Massachusetts Turnpike when his cell phone rang; it was Paul Godfrey, the president of the Blue Jays. "Are you sitting down?" Godfrey asked Ricciardi. "Guess who the Yankees want." Mondesi. Ricciardi almost veered off the road.

Randy Levine, the Yankees' president, had called Godfrey. Cashman argued strongly against a deal for Mondesi, feeling his enormous salary would be prohibitive. He and Michael had kept Steinbrenner from making moves like this in the past, but Steinbrenner could not be dissuaded. He wanted Mondesi. Now.

Within hours, the Yankees agreed to pay the rest of Mondesi's salary for 2002, or about $5.5 million, and $7 million of his $13 million contract for 2003. Twelve and a half million dollars, in large part because Enrique Wilson misplayed a fly ball, and despite the fact that Mondesi was a flawed player.

The Yankees won the American League East for the fifth consecutive season in 2002, but the Anaheim Angels knocked them out in the first round of the playoffs. They played sluggishly, rolling over easily whenever the Angels counterpunched in the games. "It looked that way the whole series," said Jorge Posada, who had advanced from being a part-time catcher to an All-Star, and was one of the few holdovers from the Yankees' old guard. "It looked like they wanted it more than we did." Derek Jeter was reminded by a reporter that the team had accomplished so much in the recent seasons. "Some of us have," he replied, softly drawing a line between the Yankees who had shared in the glory years and the growing number who had not.

Steinbrenner looked to cut costs in strange ways. Two weeks after the Yankees were eliminated, the team fired 25 of its employees, including Leo Astacio, who had helped with the videotape machines in the clubhouse and served as an interpreter for Orlando Hernandez. The dismissals probably saved the team less than $1 million, about the same amount of money Jason Giambi might earn for playing 10 games. The employees who were let go were given a choice: sign a waiver in which they agreed not to discuss their dismissals or forfeit the severance package offered by the team.

Cashman and Newman had once managed to bridge the gap between the executives in the Tampa and New York offices, but in the winter of 2002–2003, the lines were distinct again. The goal had once been to debate hard and then present a unified recommendation to Steinbrenner, but more and more of the opinions coming out of the Tampa office reflected Steinbrenner's desire. Cashman became more isolated, and, friends said, more discouraged.

Cashman's arguments with Steinbrenner became louder, more vocif-
erous. It seemed as though Cashman was trying to get fired, a close
friend said; he had three years remaining on his contract, and his passion
for the only organization he had worked for had waned. It's more like a
job to me than ever before, he said to an acquaintance.

Shortly after the Yankees lost to Anaheim, Gordon Blakeley, the Yankees' director of international scouting, was sent to Nicaragua, under or-
ders from Steinbrenner to sign Jose Contreras. The bidding between the
Yankees, Boston, and the Mariners began in earnest at four years, $24
million, for a pitcher without a single day of major league experience.

But Blakeley told rival executives that he had come to sign Contreras,
no matter the cost; Steinbrenner promised Blakeley that he would be
fired if he failed to land the pitcher. Hearing this, another executive realized his team had no chance to sign Contreras, and so he decided to at
least make the Yankees pay exorbitantly and kept matching the Yankees'
offers, driving up the price. The Yankees signed Contreras to a four-year,
$32 million deal—a contract much larger than that signed by many es-
tablished players in the same off-season.

The deal was stunning to executives with other teams, the clearest indication that Steinbrenner intended to plow ahead, despite the luxury
tax. If the tax was designed to impede the Yankees, as Steinbrenner believed, then the signings of outfielder Hideki Matsui (three years, $21
million) and Contreras were a clear response: fuck you. His team was
making more money than anybody else's, building new revenue streams
as the cash flow for other teams was drying up, and they would not be
stopped—and certainly not by the Red Sox. This was business, and now
it was also personal. "The evil empire extends its tentacles even into
Latin America," Larry Lucchino bitterly told Murray Chass of the *Times*.

Before the 2003 season, the Yankees had accumulated eight starting
pitchers; they were back to treating championship building like a hot-
dog-eating contest. After the 2003 season, Steinbrenner personally negotiated a $39 million contract with Gary Sheffield, a perennial All-Star
with a reputation for complaining, without soliciting an opinion from
Michael or Cashman; the GM had lobbied unsuccessfully to shift Sori-

ano from second base to the outfield, and then sign Kaz Matsui, a Japan-born player, to play second. Pettitte was eligible to become a free agent after the 2003 season, but teammates assumed he would re-sign with the Yankees; Pettitte was a strong thread in the lasting fabric of the team, the one member of the pitching rotation drafted and developed by the organization, the heir to Whitey Ford's legacy. Clemens, headed into re-tirement, had made loose plans to visit Pettitte in New York during the 2004 season, to play golf, and maybe do some television work.

But as Pettitte's negotiations with the Yankees dragged out—partly at the request of Pettitte's agents—the pitcher began questioning how seri-ous the team was about retaining him. Steinbrenner, who had initiated the trade talks for Pettitte in 1999, had never really demonstrated the same affection for Pettitte as he had for many of the other players, and while he personally wined and dined Sheffield in the fall of 2003, Stein-brenner never called Pettitte. The pitcher who would win more games than any other during the dynasty would leave the Yankees, unsure of how Steinbrenner felt about him, to play with his hometown team, the Houston Astros. Within hours after Pettitte signed with the Astros, Clemens—who also lived in the Houston area—was on a local radio show, musing about a comeback. Pettitte listened on his car radio and then phoned his friend and asked, "Are you serious?" "Lefty," Clemens responded, "everything's changed." A month later, Clemens signed with Houston as well. The Yankees traded for pitchers Kevin Brown and Javier Vazquez.

A month before spring training began in 2004, third baseman Aaron Boone blew out his knee in a pickup basketball game, and as the Yan-kees considered replacements, Cashman asked about the availability of Texas shortstop Alex Rodriguez, the game's highest-paid player. Rod-riguez agreed to move to third base, and a deal was struck: Soriano for Rodriguez, with the Rangers agreeing to kick in about $67 million of the $179 million left on Rodriguez's contract. In replacing a No. 8 hitter making about $5 million, the Yankees had added $112 million.

The Yankees now had four players with contracts in excess of $100 million; the left side of their infield, Jeter and Rodriguez, would make more in annual salary than the entire Milwaukee Brewers' roster. The projected Opening Day lineup for the Yankees would earn about $85,000 *per inning*.

"I don't know if it's the luxury tax, or maybe his age, or that they've lost two years in a row," Seattle general manager Pat Gillick said in the winter of 2003. "But something is driving [Steinbrenner] to spend money."

The reason for the manic spending, employees within the organization agreed, was Steinbrenner's single-minded quest for championships. The question was whether he could ever dole out enough to overcome the team's lack of cohesion; the question was whether any disparate collection of stars, no matter how talented, could win the championship while playing under the enormous expectations of Steinbrenner and the team's fans. The only thing that mattered was that the Yankees win the last game in October; otherwise, the season would be deemed a failure.

The Yankees' dynasty of 1996–2001 had been achieved in part because of the players' shared history; Martinez, Sojo, Cone, Brosius, Posada, and the rest were fully invested in one another, propping one another up along the way. This was not something that could be purchased.

Through the Yankees' decade of success, club executives had carefully weighed players' personalities when making decisions, but more and more, the choices were based on statistics, the soulless numbers. The Yankees had once acquired or developed players because of their talents but also because they fit, their character adding a necessary ingredient—Jeter's confidence, O'Neill's intensity, Tim Raines's humor, Girardi's professionalism. They were not all superstar players, but together they were extraordinary at winning games. The patience with which the organization operated in the early '90s was all but gone, and the farm system was close to barren. The dynasty was over, and Steinbrenner was desperate, reverting to old habits.

IN AN interview with the *Daily News* prior to spring training of 2003, Steinbrenner suggested that Derek Jeter spent too much time out at night and questioned the work ethic of the Yankees' coaching staff. In subsequent months, he feuded with Zimmer and angered Stottlemyre by reversing a proposed plan of action on Contreras. For seven years, Torre's refusal to engage Steinbrenner publicly had shielded the team from the manic must-win-today metabolism created by the owner's complaints. But in 2003, Torre took the bait for the first time, complaining publicly about how he was treated, telling George King of the *New York Post* that he wasn't having as much fun. Rather than defusing the Yankee powder keg, Torre had begun feeding it, and friends who visited his office thought he had lost his enthusiasm for the job and was fed up with Steinbrenner. Torre had deep and lasting relationships with many players during the championship run, but those personal ties were fading as the Yankees shuttled players in and out. "I think he feels he's lost the connection to the team, in some way," said one longtime friend. "These are guys he doesn't know very well, and he doesn't know how to reach them." Torre's contract was set to expire after the 2004 season, and for months he did not seem interested in an extension.

The Yankees would win 101 games in 2003, but the Red Sox had become a much more formidable threat. For years, team executives had viewed Boston as a sleeping giant, and after John Henry—a former Yankees limited partner—and Tom Werner and Lucchino arranged to buy the team, they hired 28-year-old Theo Epstein as general manager. Epstein was more aggressive than Dan Duquette but also more personable, and he immediately began taking advantage of Boston's enormous revenues, constructing a deep and dangerous lineup. When Boston needed bullpen help in midseason, he made moves quickly, twice outbidding the Yankees.

The old rivals would meet in the American League Championship Series, in a tough and tense playoff, and when Boston took an early lead in Game 7, it seemed the balance of power between the two teams might finally shift. But the Red Sox blew their lead, and Boone hit an extrainning homer to win the game for the Yankees; Steinbrenner was giddy. On his way out of Yankee Stadium, he paused to watch the Red Sox buses depart. "Go back to Boston, boys," he said, with a reporter from the *Daily News* standing alongside him. "They didn't treat us very well in Boston, but you know, we get the last laugh."

His euphoria lasted hours. The Yankees faced the Marlins in the World Series, as prohibitive favorites, and Steinbrenner's complexion was ashen throughout the games, his face tense.

The Yankees won Game 3 in Florida to take a 2–1 lead in the best-of-seven series, and in the 11th inning of Game 4, they had the bases loaded, one out, the score tied; this was their chance to all but finish off the Marlins. But Boone struck out, failing to put the ball in play, before John Flaherty made an out to end the inning. The Marlins won the game in the 12th inning, and went on to take Game 5.

In the eighth inning of Game 6, with Josh Beckett dominating the Yankees, Steinbrenner was seething. He went to Cashman's box to tell him there would be a meeting in Tampa in 48 hours, to discuss the reconstruction of the team; after all, three seasons had passed since the Yankees' last championship.

"There are going to be big changes," Steinbrenner snapped.

A Note on Sources

Much of the information in the book is gleaned from the four years the author covered the Yankees for the *New York Times*. In addition, the following were interviewed specifically for this book:

Jean Afterman, Peter Angelos, Brad Ausmus, Jay Bell, Bruce Bochy, Bob Brenly, Scott Brosius, Brian Butterfield, Orlando Cabrera, Brian Cashman, Roger Clemens, Casey Close, Jerry Colangelo, David Cone, Lynn Cone, Jim Courier, Bobby Cox, Chad Curtis, David Dellucci, Gary Denbo, Steve Donohue, Steve Finley, John Flaherty, Mike Flanagan, Phil Garner, Pat Gillick, Joe Girardi, Rudy Giuliani, Luis Gonzalez, Rich Gossage, Mark Grace, Tony Gwynn, John Hart, Dr. Stuart Hershon, Reggie Jackson, Derek Jeter, Nick Johnson, Randy Johnson, Jim Kaat, Michael Kay, Tom Kelly, Jimmy Key, Ricky Ledee, Jim Leyritz, Larry Lucchino, Andy MacPhail, Kevin Malone, Tino Martinez, Don Mattingly, Kevin McClatchy, Gene Michael, Damian Miller, Gene Monahan, Tony Muser, Mike Mussina, Jeff Nelson, Beryl Newhouser, Mark Newman, Kim Ng, Paul O'Neill, Andy Pettitte, Mike Piazza, Jorge Posada, Tim Raines, Willie Randolph, J. P. Ricciardi, Steve Rippley, Mariano Rivera, Frank Robinson, Terry Ryan, Rey Sanchez, Curt

Schilling, John Schuerholz, Buck Showalter, Luis Sojo, Alfonso Soriano, Shane Spencer, Mike Stanton, John Sterling, Mel Stottlemyre, Todd Stottlemyre, Kevin Towers, Bobby Valentine, Robin Ventura, Ed Wade, Bob Watson, Chris Widger, Bernie Williams, Enrique Wilson, Tony Womack.

Fifteen others asked not to be identified.

George Steinbrenner and Joe Torre each answered several questions in early preparation for the book, but later declined to be interviewed in depth; Torre indicated, through a club spokesman, that he may work on his own book. Chuck Knoblauch initially responded to an interview request but eventually did not meet with the author. Calls to Darryl Strawberry's lawyer were not returned.

Published sources
Periodicals and Magazines
The New York Times
The Baltimore Sun
Associated Press
New York Daily News
New York Post
Sports Illustrated
The New Yorker
The Boston Globe
Newsday
The Bergen Record
The Journal News (Westchester County)
Newark Star-Ledger
Hartford Courant

Books

Angell, Roger. *A Pitcher's Story: Innings with David Cone*. New York: Warner Books, 2001.

Costas, Bob. *Fair Ball: A Fan's Case for Baseball*. New York: Broadway Books, 1994.

Cramer, Richard Ben. *Joe DiMaggio: The Hero's Life*. New York: Simon & Schuster, 2000.

Fainaru, Steve, and Ray Sanchez. *The Duke of Havana*. New York: Villard, 2001.

Halberstam, David. *October 1964*. New York: Villard, 1994.

Hamill, Pete, ed. *The Subway Series Reader*. New York: Simon & Schuster, 2000.

Helyar, John. *Lords of the Realm*. New York: Villard, 1994.

Jeter, Derek, with Jack Curry. *The Life You Imagine: Life Lessons for Achieving Your Dreams*. New York: Three Rivers Press, 2000.

Johnson, Lloyd, and Miles Wolff, eds. *The Encyclopedia of Minor League Baseball*. Durham, NC: Baseball America, 1993.

Lyle, Sparky, with Peter Golenbock. *The Bronx Zoo*. New York: Dell Publishing, 1979.

Neft, David S., Richard M. Cohen, and Michael L. Neft, eds. *The Sports Encyclopedia: Baseball*. New York: St. Martin's, Griffin, 2002.

Nettles, Graig, with Peter Golenbock. *Balls*. New York: Pocket Books, 1984.

The New York Times. *The New York Yankees Illustrated History*. New York: St. Martin's, 2002.

O'Neill, Paul, with Burton Rocks. *Me and My Dad: A Baseball Memoir*. New York: William Morrow, 2003.

Torre, Joe, with Tom Verducci. *Chasing the Dream: My Lifelong Journey to the World Series*. New York: Bantam Books, 1997.

Vincent, Fay. *The Last Commissioner*. New York: Simon & Schuster, 2002.

Wells, David, with Chris Kreski. *Perfect I'm Not: Boomer on Beer, Brawls, Backaches, and Baseball*. New York: William Morrow, 2003.

Woodward, Bob. *Bush at War*. New York: Simon & Schuster, 2002.

Zimmer, Don, with Bill Madden. *Zim: A Baseball Life*. Kingston, NY: Total Sports Publishing, 2001.

ACKNOWLEDGMENTS

Writers are like starting pitchers—inherently selfish, mostly consumed by their own objective, and often propped up by others who have broader responsibilities. With that in mind, there are many for this writer to thank.

Those who inspired: Mary and Ed Lincoln, my parents. My mother played many roles in this, from patient listener to demanding editor who put in many hours picking over the roughest drafts. When I started to drag, I'd think of Ed pushing around Jerseys on the farm and remember that, comparatively, this is pretty simple stuff.

Those who read: Louise and Dick Schwingel, who have steered me for 25 years and, for this, offered exceptional criticism; Todd Radom, a hard-core Red Sox fan who willingly perused thousands of words about the Yankees; Ken Rosenthal, the best possible teammate in the days at the *Baltimore Sun*; Joan Davis, who took a break from watching Bill O'Reilly to make suggestions liberally; Bill Francis, of the Hall of Fame, who checked and rechecked; and Sue Toll, an old chess foe whose husband would have greatly preferred I write a book about soccer.

Those who nudged: Chris Calhoun, my agent, from Sterling Lord Literistic, who strongly encouraged me to revisit the Yankees and later made a last and lasting suggestion.

Dan Halpern and David Hirshey, the editors for this book at Harper-Collins, who took the lump and shaped it with their ideas and red pens, and put up with an anxious first-timer; thanks for taking a chance. Nick Trautwein of HarperCollins did the heavy lifting on the final edit, creating lines in the narrative where it had strayed.

Rob Grover, Dan's lieutenant, endured many, many e-mails and phone calls. Amy Baker and those at Ecco put the wheels to this. Anne Greenberg made great catches and saved me from embarrassing myself.

David Halberstam would call from time to time and ask, Where the hell are you and what the hell are you doing? No words, from anyone else, could prod more. His is a path that other reporters could only hope to follow.

Those who shared: Fellow writers and producers whose memories and work helped with details—Murray Chass, the Hall of Famer. Peter Gammons, who will soon follow Murray, and for good reason. Roger Angell, Tom Verducci, Allan Simpson, Tyler Kepner, Tony Massarotti, Jayson Stark, Ian O'Connor, Andrew Marchand, Bob Elliott, Drew Olson, Charlie Nobles, Ira Berkow, Steve Jacobson, Ron Blum, Ben Walker, Joe Lavine, Jim Ingraham, Tracy Ringolsby, Gerry Fraley, Jim Bouton, and Mike Lupica, who recounted a crazy night moment by moment.

In six years of working together, Jack Curry shared ideas, quotes, complaints, and friendship, and he laughed uproariously when I always fell for his phony phone calls. Many thanks.

Those who are professionals: Ari Fleischer, Sunny Mindel, Greg Aiello of the National Football League, Mike Swanson and Russ Amaral of the Arizona Diamondbacks, John Blake of the Texas Rangers, Rick Cerrone and his staff with the Yankees, Darryl Davis, Dr. John Fleisig, Lisa Skelton, Jeff Idleson and Claudette Burke of the National Baseball Hall of Fame and Museum, Jay Horwitz, John Maroon, Phyllis Merhige, Arthur Richman, and Bart Swain. Illeana Pena of Fox provided taped broadcasts of Games 6 and 7 that were invaluable.

Those who gave: Edward C. Devine, who provided a baseball encylopedia to an information-starved nerd many years ago; Bill Batty, who overlooked zealous mistakes.

Those who helped along the way: Fred Russell, Daniel and Cindy Bean, Gabriel Tornusciolo, Steve Kaludis, George Kaludis, Sam McSeveney, Mike McGehee, Irby Simpkins, Elise McMillan, Joe Biddle, Mark Basinger, Mary Butler, Calvin Godin, Liz Shanahan, Jim and Barbara Schramm, Carolyn Russell, Barry Lorge, Stan and Nelie McNeal, Tom Cushman, Jess Kearney, Doug Williams, Bill Suda, Brian Wong, Hannah Hui, Steve and Kim Oakey, Steve Brand, Ed Graney, Mike Waters, Jack Gibbons, Molly Dunham, Jason LaCanfora, Andy Knobel, Brad Snyder, Elaine Nichols, Charlie Miller, Greg Boro, Jennifer Power, Lee Seigel, and Keith Davis.

Those at the *Times*: Neil Amdur, who built something great; Bill Brink, Carl Nelson, Jay Schreiber, Tom Jolly, Jill Agostino, Alan Finder, Ray Corio, Susan Adams, Bob Goetz, Joe Sexton, Patty LaDuca, Phil Coffin, Mike Hale, Kathleen McElroy, Fern Turkowitz, Dick Goldstein, Susan Adams, Fred Bierman, Judy Miceli, and Julius Greene, who is always looking for TV time. The folks in the graphic department turned fragments into art while on deadline—Joe Ward, in particular.

Joe Lelyveld and Bill Keller ran the place during almost all of my time on the Yankees' beat, and could not have been more supportive. Bill Schmidt gained approval for me to even attempt this while still at the *Times*.

Those at ESPN who inherited this project and helped by patiently hanging in through its completion: John Walsh, Gary Hoenig, Steve Wulf, Jon Scher, Ed McGregor, Matt Szefc, and Scott Ridge.

Those who pushed: The other beat reporters who covered the team in the seasons I was assigned to the Yankees possessed an exceptional work ethic. Ken Davidoff of the *Bergen Record* and *Newsday* and George King of the *New York Post* were daunting competitors for four full seasons. Dom Amore, Peter Botte, Tim Brown, Howard Bryant, John Delcos, Dan Graziano, David Lennon, Anthony McCarron, Jack O'Connell, and Larry Rocca were beat writers for other papers at the same time, and Suzyn Waldman and Sweeney Murti followed the team for WFAN. Fear of them all was perpetual and a constant source of motivation.

Those at home: Lisa and Sydney. No words would suffice.

—Buster Olney, March 2004

INDEX